Drama, Disability and Education

What can society learn about disability through the way it is portrayed in TV, films and plays?

This insightful and accessible text explores and analyses the way disability is portrayed in drama, and how that portrayal may be interpreted by young audiences. Investigating how disabilities have been represented on stage in the past, this book discusses what may be inferred from plays that feature disabled characters through a variety of critical approaches.

In addition to the theoretical analysis of disability in dramatic literature, the book includes two previously unpublished play scripts, both of which have been performed by secondary school aged students and focus on issues of disability and its effects on others. The contextual notes and discussion that accompany these plays and projects provide insights into how drama can contribute to disability education, and how it can give a voice to students who have special educational needs themselves.

Other features of this wide-ranging text include:

- an annotated chronology that traces the history of plays that have featured disabled characters;
- an analysis of how disability is used as a dramatic metaphor;
- a consideration of the ethics of dramatising a disabled character;
- critical accounts of units of work in mainstream schools seeking to raise disability awareness through engagement with practical drama and dramatic texts;
- a description and evaluation of a drama project in a special school.

In tackling questions and issues that have not, hitherto, been well covered, *Drama, Disability and Education* will be of enormous interest to drama students, teachers, researchers and pedagogues who work with disabled people or are concerned with raising awareness and understanding of disability.

Andy Kempe is a Teaching Fellow of the University of Reading, UK, where he is Professor of Drama Education.

Drama, Disability and Education

Drama, Disability and Education

A critical exploration for students and practitioners

Andy Kempe

Routledge
Taylor & Francis Group
LONDON AND NEW YORK

First published 2013
by Routledge
2 Park Square, Milton Park, Abingdon, Oxon OX14 4RN

Simultaneously published in the USA and Canada
by Routledge
711 Third Avenue, New York, NY 10017

Routledge is an imprint of the Taylor & Francis Group, an informa business

British Library Cataloguing in Publication Data
A catalogue record for this book is available from the British Library

Library of Congress Cataloging in Publication Data
Kempe, Andy.
Drama, disability and education: a critical exploration for students and practitioners/authored by Andy Kempe.
p. cm.
Includes bibliographical references and index.
1. Drama – Study and teaching 2. Children with disabilities – Education. 3. Drama in education. 4. Special education. I. Title.
PN1701.K43 2013
372.66'044—dc23 2012011898

ISBN: 978-0-415-67503-1 (hbk)
ISBN: 978-0-415-67504-8 (pbk)
ISBN: 978-0-203-09649-9 (ebk)

Typeset in Bembo and Gill Sans
by Florence Production Ltd, Stoodleigh, Devon

All proceeds from this book are donated to Mencap

About this charity

Mencap is the voice of learning disability. Everything we do is about valuing and supporting people with a learning disability, and their families and carers. We work with people with a learning disability, and all our services support people to live life as they choose.

Contents

Contributors

Andy Kempe is a Teaching Fellow of the University of Reading, UK, where he is Professor of Drama Education.

Alun Bliss is Head of Arts at Springwood High School, King's Lynn, UK.

Simon Floodgate is Programme Director for the Theatre Arts, Education & Deaf Studies BA (Hons) at the University of Reading, UK. He is currently engaged in a Ph.D. study researching the use of British Sign Language within performance.

Rob John is a playwright for stage and radio, a scriptwriter for BBC Education and a schools drama consultant.

Lionel Warner works on a number of QTS programmes at the University of Reading, UK, and is a school examiner in English Literature.

Introduction

A silly question?

If the only way we came to know anything about disabled people was through the way they are represented in plays, what would we end up knowing?

At first glance, this might well seem to be a question that is too silly to bother asking. After all, there are up to 11.7 million people who may be considered as disabled in the UK (Masefield 2006: 38). Given that is around 20 per cent of the population, the likelihood is that, if you are not disabled yourself, you probably have neighbours or work with people who are. Certainly, it would be difficult to imagine an entire school cohort that did not have children who were disabled in some way or another. Nonetheless, 40 per cent of people who are not disabled claim that they do not know anyone that is (Quarmby 2011: 180). There are a lot of different reasons for this, not least the fact that a great many disabled people are quite capable of getting on with things perfectly well in most circumstances, so their impairment becomes largely invisible to the many with whom they come into contact on a routine basis. In another sense, though, disabled people are all too often made invisible by and to a society that considers itself 'able' or 'normal'. It is by failing to recognise and cater for their particular needs that people are effectively disabled. A social model of disability distinguishes between an impairment resulting from, for example, a physical, sensory or intellectual limitation, and a disability arising from social, cultural or material barriers that effectively exclude some members of society from participating fully in that society. Thus, as disabled artist Paddy Masefield (2006: 8) declares, 'once one has grasped the principle of the social model, it becomes clear why we choose to call ourselves dis-abled people, and not "people with disabilities", "The Disabled" or even more strangely, "somethingly challenged people".' In both cases, it could be argued that invisibility amounts to 'out of sight, out of mind', leaving awareness and knowledge of disability to arise from instances when it is fore-fronted, that is, literally, when it is 'in yer face'. When this happens in real life, reactions can be extreme as, for example, in the case of a German travel agency that was forced to pay damages to a family that was confronted with disabled people in a hotel restaurant.

The court reasoned that, 'The inescapable view of the disabled in a small room during meals caused disgust, and insistently reminded the plaintiffs of the possibility of human misfortune. Such experiences do not belong to a typical vacation' (ibid.: 5).

Being reminded of 'the possibility of human misfortune' sometimes causes outrage as well as disgust, depending on how it is communicated. Two newspaper headlines that appeared on the very morning I first started to draft this chapter illustrate how attitudes towards disabled people may be manipulated and myths surrounding what constitutes disability with its attendant implications are perpetuated. The *Daily Mail* (27 July 11) proclaimed that 'Just one in 14 incapacity claimants is unfit to work under new, tougher tests', while the *Daily Express* front page read, 'Sick benefits: 75% are faking'. There is a slipperiness here that synonymises 'sickness', which may be temporary, with 'incapacity', which may represent a long-term or permanent limitation on undertaking certain kinds of work. Similarly, in the reports headlined here, there was no attempt to distinguish between illness and impairment. While both papers reported that, of the 2.6 million people on incapacity benefit, 1.9 million 'could work', both failed to mention that there were 2.45 million people out of work at that time. Such headlines suddenly make some of the invisible very visible indeed, but only in negative terms and only as some sort of amorphous burdensome body. But why do I say only 'some' of the invisible? The reason is to do with how disability is defined, and the considerable differences that occur between, say, various official definitions that serve different economic and administrative purposes, and those that may be based on self-definition or rest on nebulous social perceptions. The result, I would suggest, is that a great many people are left confused as to who might be considered a disabled person. They thus feel uncomfortable about attaching such a label to anyone who is not, in their eyes, obviously impaired in such a way that their impairment is physically manifest in some way. In contrast, there are those that seem all too prepared to lump sizeable sections of the population together by applying the most spurious definitions, leading to some worrying contradictions in the social conscience. Thus, while the *Daily Mail* and the *Daily Express* call for all right-minded, honest, hard-working folk to stand up against the skivers and shirkers who are only pretending to be disabled when it comes to finding employment, a 2010 survey of 1,000 people revealed that nearly 25 per cent of the population believed disabled people should be kept in institutions, while one third believed they were not able to live independently or work anyway (Quarmby 2011: 219).

Beliefs concerning disabled people's reliance on others may again be fuelled by the media, albeit not in such a pernicious manner as by the tabloid press quoted above. Indeed, the BBC *Panorama* documentary 'Undercover Care: The Abuse Exposed' (BBC 2011) caused considerable public outcry when it showed disabled people in a residential care home being physically and mentally abused by staff. The number of disabled people that are in permanent residential care in the UK stands at around 57,000. This is a fraction of the total number of disabled people. While the exposure of this criminal neglect or abuse is vital, it may nonetheless be seen as reinforcing common perceptions of 'truly' disabled people being totally vulnerable and dependent on others, with the concomitant conclusion that others are not actually disabled at all. If perceptions of disability are primarily formed by media representation, regardless of their altruistic or critical intent, then it is, to some extent, understandable that ignorance and confusion results; and the result of ignorance and confusion is all too often prejudice and discrimination. However, in a report for the British Council of Organisations of Disabled People, Colin Barnes goes further in his analysis of the origins of commonly held attitudes:

> Stereotype assumptions about disabled people are based on superstition, myths and beliefs from earlier less enlightened times. They are inherent to our culture and persist partly because they are constantly reproduced through the communications media. We learn about disability through the media and in the same way that racist or sexist attitudes, whether implicit or explicit, are acquired through the 'normal' learning process, so too are negative assumptions about disabled people.
>
> (Barnes 1992)

In her disturbing study of how disabled people are seen as scapegoats for a whole raft of societal ills and failings, Katherine Quarmby (2011) discusses how 'folk memory' derived from 'less enlightened times' casts disabled people as sinners. She reports on a number of cases where disabled people have been grossly abused and murdered, and where misguided beliefs that link sexuality and depravity have resulted in false accusations of paedophilia and perversion, and consequent 'punishment'. Commonly held beliefs from the past that disabled people are freakish, fair game for amusement and mockery, deserve to be treated as slaves, and perhaps should not even be allowed to exist at all, still abound. For example, Aristotle, in *The Politics* (1974: 241), wrote, 'With regard to the choice between abandoning a child or rearing it, let there be a law that no cripple child be reared.' (For an example of a dramatic rendition of what befalls when such wisdom is ignored, consider what happened when Oedipus was rescued and reared by Polybus and Merope!) Notwithstanding what we now know to have taken place under the Nazis' 'T4' programme in which disabled children were among the first victims of the holocaust, there is still a good deal of faith in eugenics and the concept of 'mercy killings' and, as recently as the mid-1960s, paediatricians still advocated institutionalisation and sterilisation for children with Down's syndrome. In Roman times, Cicero talked enthusiastically about how deformity and disfigurement made for good comic material – an enthusiasm that appears to be shared by some contemporary comedians. Seneca the Elder organised entertainments involving as wide a variety of disabled people as he could find, and Pliny wrote, 'We spit on epileptics in a fit. That is, we throw back contagion. In a similar way we ward off witchcraft and bad luck which follows meeting a person lame in the right leg' (Quarmby 2011: 22–4). I am sad to say that I once personally witnessed someone having an epileptic fit in the street in Portugal and being spat on. Somewhat closer to home, my daughter, whose condition of syncope frequently resulted in her fainting when she was younger, was spat on and kicked in a school corridor when the faint was accompanied by a fit.

It might well be comforting for those of us involved in drama and drama education to think that, while the wicked, manipulative or misguided media is exacerbating and perpetuating long-standing negative images of disabled people with dreadful consequences, our predominantly liberal humanist art form is more enlightened, accepting and understanding. Indeed, Paddy Masefield, a leading commentator and activist for disability arts, has written that 'of all the arts, drama especially can change the way the world acts' (Masefield 2006: 127). Kenneth Jernigan, long-time president of the National Federation of the Blind in the US, posited that, 'the myths and feelings of a people are enshrined in its literature. Literary culture in all its forms constitutes possibly the main transmission of our society's beliefs and values' (Jernigan 1974). So, how much evidence for Masefield's claim would there be if one focused on that aspect of drama that is most readily accessible to scrutiny and study – that is, the literary manifestation of drama, the published play script? Hence, the question that prompted me to write this book: If the only way we came to know anything about disabled people was through the way they are represented in plays, what would we end up knowing?

Images of disability in fiction

I found myself pondering this hypothetical question as a result of a colleague telling me he was reviewing representations of disability in novels popularly studied in school. Inevitably, I found myself wondering what I might find if I focused on like representations in dramatic literature. As a result of a conversation with a colleague who teaches in an 11–19 comprehensive, we decided to give a questionnaire to a group of A level Theatre Studies students in order to audit where they had come across representations of disabled people. We asked them to list the films, television shows, novels and plays that had disabled characters. The 19 students came up with a total 34 films, the most frequently mentioned being *Forrest Gump* (18 mentions), followed by *Twilight* (7 mentions), *Shutter Island* (5 mentions) and *Rain Man* (4 mentions). TV soaps *Waterloo Road* and *Eastenders* were both mentioned 11 times, closely followed by the not uncontroversial comedy sketch show *Little Britain*. Ten novels were mentioned, the most prominent being *Of Mice and Men* with 8 mentions. The other novels listed were all linked in that they featured characters that were modern manifestations of the ancient relationship (reinforced by Martin Luther's proclamation that the Devil resided in disabled children) between disability and evil: Bret

Easton Ellis's 2006 novel about a particularly vicious serial killer, *American Psycho*, Stephen King's *The Shining*, and the immensely popular *Twilight* series (OK, I know they're 'nice' vampires but they're still vampires, aren't they?). When it came to citing plays, the group struggled more and could only think of seven. All bar one of these (*Wait Until Dark*) had been studied as part of either the English or Drama curriculum: *Find Me*, *4.48 Psychosis*, *Hard to Swallow*, *Blue Remembered Hills*, *A Streetcar Named Desire* and the rock opera *Tommy* (which had been staged in the school the previous year). I wondered how my trainee drama teachers' responses to the same questionnaire would compare. They were a group of 15. All had studied GCSE and A level Drama and Theatre Studies and gone on to achieve a good honours degree in the subject. What surprised me was how little they were able to add to the list. They mentioned a total of 31 films, the most commonly mentioned being *Rain Man* (11), *Forrest Gump* (9), *My Left Foot* (7) and *A Beautiful Mind* (4). A number of respondents noted how whole genres, such as spy thrillers and horror films, featured disabled characters as villains. Twenty-three television programmes were mentioned. *Glee*, an American musical comedy drama, which features a guitar-playing paraplegic character called Artie Abrams, was mentioned 10 times. This lead was followed by soaps *Eastenders* (9) and *Hollyoaks* (8). The trainees, whose average age was 25, came up with just 9 novels (*Of Mice and Men* getting 10 mentions and *The Curious Incident of the Dog in the Night-Time* getting 6 mentions) and 9 plays (*Of Mice and Men* getting 4 mentions in this category, followed by *Oedipus Rex* (3), and *Richard III* (2)). There is perhaps not a great deal to be learnt from such a trifling enquiry as this other than that the lists tended to reflect what films and novels were popular at the time, and what plays the respondents had been obliged to study rather than what they had encountered of their own volition. However, the films mentioned certainly related to a major issue in debates surrounding representations of disability on screen in that none of the disabled characters were played by disabled actors. Rather, all the films cited above featured major stars, a number of whom (Daniel Day-Lewis, Russell Crowe, Leonardo DiCaprio) are accredited as having considerable sex appeal.

In addition to asking both the A level students and trainee teachers to list where they had encountered disabled characters in fiction, they were also asked to jot down what they felt such representations conveyed. For the sixth form students, the most commonly held interpretation was that representations of disabled people suggest they are dangerous, struggle socially, look different to everyone else, and are a burden to society as a whole and those on whom they are personally reliant. These findings reflect previous larger-scale surveys such as that reported by Cole (1993), which found that one-third of a sample of 2,000 adults believed mental illness was transparent. Similarly, Kyle and Davies (1991) found that children of secondary school age tended to confuse mental and physical disability. People with mental illness were variously described as 'a person who would want to kill someone and can't stop themselves' and 'someone who has brain trouble so they have a deformed face' (ibid.: 103). The study found that one-third of the 13- to 15-year-olds sampled (53 in total) considered mental impairment and mental illness to be the same thing. The trainee teachers tended to state more explicitly that such media depictions reinforced their personally held belief that disabled people were generally misunderstood and that disability is largely created by the attitudes of others. Nonetheless, they still noted that fictional representations conveyed the image that disabled people were reliant on others, wished they were 'normal', were lonely, bullied and easily manipulated, but had unique talents and were somewhat mysterious and sometimes menacing.

A subsequent question asked respondents to comment on how these fictional representations matched their first-hand experiences. Both groups stated that the fictional representation generally contradicted their personal experience. A number recognised that disabled people did not represent a danger or burden to society, and coped with their impairment. Even so, there was still a tendency among both cohorts to make rather sweeping statements that could be regarded as being more liberal and wishful rather than wholly truthful. For example:

> People suffering with physical disability are much more astute and intelligent than they are given credit for. Just because people have physical disability does not mean they have not developed fully mentally.

> In my experience, people with mental disability are aware that they're 'different' and can get very frustrated that they can't communicate their feelings. However, it is true that they struggle to communicate.

If actual, real-life experiences contradict fictional representations, one might surmise that the influence of fictional imagery is lessened. However, this is not necessarily so. In fact, because for many people first-hand experience of disability and 'hard' knowledge of different disabilities is so limited, the opposite may be the case. Anupama Iyer, writing on the depiction of intellectual disability in fiction, notes that:

> Fictional images are very powerful because they have a coherence and accessibility not often present in random real-life experiences or scientific descriptions . . . However, the primary purpose of fiction is narration not instruction. The narrative is influenced not only by writers' factual information but also by the story they want to tell. To tell this story, authors rely on triggering a shared understanding between themselves and the reader. For intellectual disability, this shared understanding depends on what is culturally accepted about the condition as well as what is medically known. Thus, literary depictions, unlike medical descriptions, do not have to be accurate or theory driven.
>
> (Iyer 2007: 127)

It is also worth noting that, in fictional accounts of disabled people, words and images are used to describe and depict those who may not have access to the medium used to portray them or be readily able to change, contest or confirm how the impairment is being portrayed. This was most certainly an issue, for example, in the 1986 film version of Mark Medoff's 1979 play *Children of a Lesser God*, which, while starring deaf actress Marlee Martin, was criticised by some in the deaf community as being inaccessible to them. A similar controversy has more recently surrounded Nina Raine's play *Tribes* (2010), which also explored aspects of deafness.

Drama, disability and education

In a seminar on disability arts and culture in 1991, the then chairman of the British Council of Organisations of Disabled People (BCODP), Richard Wood, noted that:

> It strikes me not only as a disabled person, but also as a lay person in the area of arts and media, that all the arts and media representation of disabled people has so far been totally negative.
>
> (Conroy 2010: 10)

This seems to me to be a very strong statement and, when set against my hypothetical question, 'If the only way we came to know anything about disabled people was through the way they are represented in plays, what would we end up knowing?', I wonder if it is true. Certainly, until it was replaced by the Equality Act 2010, schools were obligated to the Disability Discrimination Act 1995. This Act has a number of functions, including:

> (a) the need to eliminate discrimination that is unlawful under this Act;
> (b) the need to eliminate harassment of disabled persons that is related to their disabilities;
> (c) the need to promote equality of opportunity between disabled persons and other persons;
>
> . . .
>
> (e) the need to promote positive attitudes towards disabled persons.
>
> (OPSI 2005: Chapter 13)

What this book sets out to do is examine how disability is represented in plays that young people may come across during their school career either as part of the taught curriculum or perhaps as part of an extra-curricular programme involving theatre visits and, indeed, school-based productions. The book also questions the extent to which those experiences might help foster positive images and attitudes rather than reinforcing the wholly negative ones Richard Wood encountered. A number of drama teachers will undoubtedly focus on disability issues and try to raise awareness of disability through their own schemes of work. Indeed, published for the first time within this book are two plays written as a result of such work by teachers/playwrights Alun Bliss and Rob John (Chapters 7 and 8). Two other chapters report on and discuss drama projects involving students in mainstream and special schools. Lionel Warner (Chapter 3) discusses how disability may be examined as an issue in a number of plays commonly studied in schools, while Simon Floodgate's chapter (Chapter 4) explores the ethical issues surrounding the performance of plays in which there are characters that are disabled in some way. There are a number of professional theatre companies, such as Oily Cart and Graeae, that have extensive and highly regarded educational programmes involving touring plays about disability or plays performed by disabled actors to schools. However, I have chosen not to discuss these programmes simply because to do so would be to draw on material that is not readily available to all in the way that published play scripts are.

A final word on the nature of this book. In many respects, this is a messy book. That is not an apology, by the way. In fact, I think it is quite appropriate that this is a messy book. As a drama teacher, I am constantly referring to the relationship between content and form. Well, this book is concerned with people and issues that do not tend to sit neatly into simple categories, and defy unquestionable definitions. There is a received wisdom that says one should never start any sort of presentation, written or verbal, by saying what you are not going to do. But this is a messy book. As such, it does not forward any kind of watertight thesis or skilfully balanced scholarly argument for one thing or another. It does not set out to promote or adhere to any particular philosophy, or work within the constraints of an identifiable critical lens. It does not offer any fail-safe methods for teachers or quick answers for students. It most certainly does not get wrapped up in justifying its own terms of reference beyond the statement that I am making right here! The reason for it not doing any of these things is because this is my book and it reflects the very messy way I have engaged with how drama, disability and education come together. Having said that, I am enormously grateful to my fellow contributors and a host of others that have helped bring it about. Like me, these contributors may not have made a systematic, carefully planned journey with the intention of arriving at any concrete conclusions on what are some extremely complex and emotionally charged issues. But they have certainly, with the best will in the world, wanted to engage with those issues.

Chapter 1

Dramatic encounters with disability

The aims of drama in education

I once read a book aimed at secondary school students that claimed that, 'We can actually put a date to the first real theatrical performance – 534 BC' (Burton 1988: 39). Overall, I thought it was a good book with lots of clear ideas and arguments, but it struck me that this particular statement was questionable. One might well state with confidence that American Airlines Flight 11 struck the North Tower of the World Trade Center at precisely 8.46 a.m. on 11 September 2001, but to claim that something such as a theatrical performance, which could be regarded more as a concept than a concrete entity, sprung into being at a precise moment seems to give the history of mankind a certainty that I find hard to recognise. However, while concepts, cultures and traditions may evolve over time in a way so nebulous as to defy any attempt to pinpoint their origins with any exactitude, any history of ideas and actions has to start somewhere and work within some sort of framework. Thus, while it could be argued that disabled people may always have been represented in dramatic literature one way or another, the appearance of disabled characters prior to the mid twentieth century may be considered primarily in terms of their dramatic functionality and symbolic value rather than representing any explorations of disability itself. Tiresias, for example, is an embodiment of the proverb that there are none so blind as those who will not see, while Richard III's deformity and both Lear's and Hamlet's 'madness' are manifestations of something being rotten in the state as a result of the 'natural order' or 'great chain of being' having been disturbed. Chapter 4 explores the symbolic significance of these classical depictions of disability further, and discusses how that symbolism may be so deeply ingrained in our culture and theatrical traditions that its shadow falls over many contemporary plays. What this chapter sets out to do is consider what young people might learn about disability through the dramatic literature they may encounter in the school curriculum or theatre that is readily available to young audiences. Any such discussion is likely to be controversial not least because the language associated with disability is highly contested. For example, in the world of education, the term 'special needs' is used as an umbrella (some might say euphemism) for physical disability, cognitive impairment and mental illness. It can also be used to refer to people of such intelligence or giftedness that they fall outside of what is perceived as the 'normal range'. Yet, 'normality' is itself a problematic term, and a feature of many successful dramas lies in the way notions of normality are challenged or inverted. Indeed, the arts world tends to embrace the term 'disability' in order to establish an aesthetic that can directly counter ableist agendas that either ignore its existence or simply do not know how to engage with it for fear of seeming patronising, ignorant or offensive. The question is: To what extent does dramatic literature provide young people with insight into the lives of people who are disabled and society's response to them?

The near invisibility of disability in pre twentieth-century dramatic literature (there are, of course, exceptions and these are noted in Chapter 2) is hardly surprising given the way those who are disabled have been treated in the past and continue to be treated in many places. In England, for example, it was not until 1893 that school boards were instructed to provide education for children who were blind or deaf (Barnard 1947: 223). Six years later, the Education (Defective and Epileptic Children) Act 1899 directed that children 'not being imbecile and not being merely dull and backward' should be provided for in special classes (Tansley and Gulliford 1960: 3). In the US, a 'free and appropriate education for all handicapped children' was not mandated until 1975; before then, some 4,000,000 children with disabilities did not receive the necessary support, and another 1 million received no schooling whatsoever (Connor and Ferri 2007: 63). The inclusion of children with special educational needs into mainstream schools continues to be a contentious issue (Ainscow and Booth 1998; Hodkinson and Vickerman 2009) with the result being that what many young people learn about disability from dramatic representations may well go unmoderated by any recognisable first-hand experience. Given such a context, what contribution might drama make in raising awareness of disability in mainstream schools? More specifically, what sort of plays that deal with disability might young people encounter in a drama curriculum?

Gavin Bolton (1990) identified four aims for teaching drama in the curriculum. First, he said drama could be used to teach a given content. Second, it might be aimed at enhancing some aspect of personal development or, third, social development. Finally, the aim might be to teach something of the dramatic art form. These aims need not be mutually exclusive. Indeed, when the relationship between drama and disability is considered, their concordance becomes apparent. Thus, a scheme of work in drama that takes disability as a focus may endeavour to teach students something about disability (content), foster empathy and positive attitudes (personal development), promote an acceptance and understanding of the lives and views of others (social development), and consider the ethics, practicalities and effects of different aspects of dramatic representation (subject-specific learning).

Taken independently, each of these aims become problematic. For example, simply imparting 'facts' about the medical dimensions of disability may result in a sense of alienation and 'otherness'. In terms of personal and social development, there is a fine line between empathy and understanding leading to respect and empowerment, and sympathy and benefaction resulting in patronage and disempowerment. To regard the representation of disability as no more than a technical challenge would be to deny Schechner's observation that what happens on stage has 'emotional and ideological consequences for both performers and spectators' (Schechner 2006: 124). In the context of the school curriculum, choosing to represent disabled characters on the grounds that doing so would be an effective means of parading acting ability could thus be seen as exploitative and irresponsible. Conversely, acknowledging the four aims as a matrix would be to appreciate the complexity of disability as both a condition and a concept, and drama as art form and agent of social change. In this sense, focusing on disability in drama might well be seen as satisfying the demand that 'The curriculum should reflect values in our society that promote personal development, equality of opportunity, economic well-being, a healthy and just democracy, and a sustainable future' (Department for Education 2008) and support the view that 'The role of the teacher is to prepare pupils to become moral agents' (Beasley *et al.* 1990: 6).

There is a plethora of resources upon which the teacher might draw in order to inform and shape an exploration of disability through drama. Charities such as Mencap have comprehensive websites, which are a mine of information, ideas and support, while the BFI offers a powerful resource exploring media representations of disability through history (www.bfi.org.uk/education/teaching/disability). Kathy Saunders' book *Happy Ever Afters: A Storybook Guide to Teaching Children About Disability* (Saunders 2000) is a particularly useful resource for Key Stages 1 and 2 in that it explains how popular and readily available books by well known children's authors can be used to heighten awareness of disability. She offers an acronymical framework for evaluating texts written for children, which she calls the DICSEY Code (ibid.: 31). In short, the code interrogates a number of children's books by questioning:

- what they explicitly say about **D**isability;
- what sort of **I**mages they employ;
- the extent to which characters have **C**ontrol over their own lives;
- how **S**ocietal rules are expressed and challenged;
- the ways in which characters are **E**nabled to do things for themselves; and
- what role **Y**oung carers play in the stories.

When it comes to plays published specifically for use in the secondary school curriculum, which in some way broach the subject of disability, teachers may feel frustrated by the limited range. This is not to say, though, that there are not a number of plays that could be used in the context of the secondary school to inform and stimulate debate on issues surrounding disability using Saunders' framework as a guide.

Some old favourites

In the UK, the most commonly studied piece of literature in which the protagonist has an identifiable disability is undoubtedly *Of Mice and Men*. Steinbeck wrote the story in such a way that it could be read as either a novel or a play. It was first performed on stage in 1937, the same year that it was published as a novel. It is the story of Lennie, a gentle giant with the mind of an innocent child, and his friend George who attempts to protect him from a cruel and unsympathetic world. A common reading of the narrative would be a liberal humanist one in which George's final act of killing Lennie is seen as a compassionate and selfless 'act of kindness'. However, it could equally be argued that the characterisation of Lennie as a victim imparts a negative view of those with learning difficulties in that, ultimately, he becomes a burden that is simply too great for George to bear. Such a reading is cognate with the argument expressed by Snyder and Mitchell (2001) that disability has persistently been used to bolster ableist discourses and ideological frameworks. But the play may be considered in other ways. For example, it may be seen as a metaphor for American society in that Lennie and George live in a land built on the principle that dreams can come true. However, like Willy Loman in Miller's *Death of a Salesman* (1949), it is clear that not all dreams do come true and that the 'best laid plans o' mice and men gang aft agley.' The fact that the play/novel was banned by some state and school libraries for promoting euthanasia and holding an anti-capitalist stance supports the notion that the world of Lennie and George may indeed be a metonymic representation of American society.

Of Mice and Men is a useful touchstone in that its depiction of a disability may be interpreted in different ways, each of which may be employed in discussions of other plays depicting characters with some form of impairment. In the first instance, it is worthy of consideration because it is so commonly studied in schools (albeit most usually in the form of a novel rather than a play) even though it was not written specifically for a young audience. Other plays that have appeared on examination syllabuses in England would include *The Glass Menagerie*; in which Laura is depicted as both emotionally and physically 'crippled'; Peter Nichols' tragicomic exploration of the challenges faced by parents trying to look after their profoundly and multiply disabled daughter in *A Day in the Death of Joe Egg*; and Brian Clark's dramatic moral debate on euthanasia for those left paralysed after an accident in *Whose Life is it Anyway?* In the context of curriculum study, students are likely to be required to focus on the text as a piece of literature, and discuss narrative, structure and character development. Alternatively, they may be required to consider what is involved in moving from page to stage, how to play the characters and how to achieve dramatic impact. What the plays may be saying about disability and responses to it tend to remain largely undiscussed in such a context. Is this, in itself, a manifestation of an ableist agenda that cares only to view disability through the lens of objectified study? Or is it a result of teachers simply not knowing quite how to open up the issues for discussion?

Another groundbreaking play that offers insights into a specific disabling condition and the challenges faced by those with severe impairment and those around them is William Gibson's 1957 play *The Miracle Worker*. Based on Helen Keller's own writings, the play imparts the didactic message that children with disabilities should be treated like any others in terms of having high expectations held of them. The play upholds the belief that, given discipline and structure, they can learn, become independent and behave in a socially acceptable way. In contrast, Arne Skouen's *Ballerina* (1984) tends to sentimentalise the problems that occur when social norms are rejected and a disabling condition is indulged. The central character of the play is an autistic teenage girl, Malin, whose mother has snatched her from an institution and built a communication system for her based on balletic movement. When the mother's circumstances change, she is forced to ask for help, only to find that no one feels able to share the esoteric world she and her daughter have created.

A more commonly studied play that focuses on a specific disabling condition is Peter Shaffer's dramatisation of an apparently true (though actually unverified) story of an emotionally disturbed teenager in *Equus*. Even here, though, it may be argued that the play is more about the psychiatrist's frustration with his own ability to make a positive difference rather than an exploration of his patient's experience:

> I'll heal the rash on his body. I'll erase the welts cut into his mind by flying manes. When that's done, I'll set him on a nice mini-scooter and send him puttering off into the Normal world where animals are treated properly: made extinct, or put into servitude, or tethered all their lives in dim light.

In some cases, humanitarian frustration is replaced by a furious indictment of society's response to the disabled, though this may be expressed more forcibly in the author's introductory notes than in the play script itself; see, for example, Nabil Shaban's play about the Nazis' treatment of the disabled, *The First to Go*, and Haresh Sharma's *Off Centre*. The latter of these became a milestone when it was admitted to the curriculum in Singapore, notwithstanding the Ministry of Health withdrawing funding for its development because its depiction of mental illness was considered too extreme.

A number of plays originating in the late twentieth century explore mental illness (Wald 2007), and some of these have proved popular with drama students perhaps because the protagonists are themselves young people. *Find Me*, *Gum and Goo*, *Adult Child Dead Child*, *The Skriker* and *4.48 Psychosis* have all proved to be popular vehicles through which young performers may demonstrate their acting talents. The question is: Are these plays studied because of the insight they give into mental illness, or because the anger that gives them their dramatic power serves as a vehicle for the teenage angst of those performing them?

Tailor-made for teens

None of the plays mentioned above were written specifically for use in the school curriculum or aimed at a young audience. Indeed, very few plays featuring characters with disabilities or focusing on disability issues are. What follows, however, is a commentary on a number of published plays that are readily available.

Flowers for Algernon by Bert Coules is an adaptation of a novel by Daniel Keyes. Published in Heinemann's Windmill series, it is designed for use at Key Stages 3 and 4, and contains suggestions for follow-up activities. It is the story of Charlie Gordon, who, we are told, has an IQ of 68. Charlie works as a cleaner in a bakery but, wanting to improve himself, he signs up for a class with a view to improving his reading and meets Alice, an attractive young female teacher. Meanwhile, an experiment on a mouse named Algernon has convinced a professor and doctor at the local university that they have discovered a procedure for increasing intelligence. Alice puts Charlie forward as a human guinea pig. The procedure is so successful that Charlie's IQ rises rapidly to 185, and he develops both an encyclopaedic knowledge and depth of understanding that challenges the professor and doctor. It soon becomes apparent, though, that IQ is not the magic key to fulfilment. Workmates who once teased him for his 'slowness' become intimidated by his new-found intelligence and eloquence. While he and Alice become romantically attached, Charlie retains an immature attitude towards love, and their relationship does not develop physically. As it turns out, the IQ enhancing procedure is flawed. Algernon starts to behave erratically and Charlie realises that his own IQ will start to regress. Unable to bear the possibility that people will simply feel sorry for him, he commits himself to a care home after writing a letter asking for flowers to be put on Algernon's grave.

Flowers for Algernon is an engaging and accessible play. It is a good story that exposes how much hurt may be caused by 'normal' people when they behave and use language without thought. Charlie's name, for example, is appropriated by his workmates to become a soubriquet for any stupid action:

> Sometimes somebody will say hey look at Joe or Frank he really done a Charlie Gordon. I don't know why they say that but they always laff.

Charlie's workmates perhaps do not mean to be cruel, but while they may be 'only joking' they fail to see the devastating effect on the butt of their jokes, as when they get Charlie drunk so they can laugh at him:

> I never knew that Joe and Frank and the others like to have me around all the time just to make fun of me. Now I know what it means when they say 'to do a Charlie Gordon'. I'm ashamed.

While the play and appended activities are doubtlessly well intended, this alone is not enough to prevent the possibility of negative outcomes arising without discussion. For example, the play is not based on any real science, yet suggests there are links between intelligence, physical ability, and emotional and sexual maturity that may be seen as reinforcing negative stereotypes rather than challenging them. The experiment on Charlie is precipitated by the idea that his low level of intelligence inevitably implies that his life will be unsatisfying or unfulfilled. If Charlie's life is unsatisfactory, then it is because of the way others treat him. There are rich possibilities here for students to discuss their views on how Charlie is treated and why. For example, neither the play itself, nor the follow up activities in the version published by Heinemann, question the reliability of the concept of IQ and what attitudes and assumptions an acceptance of its infallibility may lead to. Teachers may find that they need to guide their students' consideration of what the play is saying, and I wonder how many teachers would accept this suggested question at face value: 'An average IQ (intelligence quotient) is 100. Now look back at Scene 6. If the operation succeeds do you think Charlie will be like other people?'

A source of vibrant new plays welcomed by many drama teachers has been the National Theatre Connections project. Initiated in 1995, the project annually offers schools and youth theatres the opportunity of working alongside professionals to produce and stage a number of specially commissioned new plays. The subsequent publication of the plays makes them more widely available. This is not to say that all of the plays would universally be considered suitable for study and production in school, but three are worthy of mention in the context of this discussion.

The protagonist of *Shut Up* by Andrew Payne is a teenage boy named Dexter who never speaks, though his mother and father talk incessantly. Both appear to do nothing but watch and commentate on what is on the television. Any comments Dad makes about his son are negative and made as if Dexter was not present. Mum does talk to Dexter, metamorphosing his father's sarcastic and demeaning comments into platitudinous expressions of concern:

> What your dad's trying to say is, please make an effort, will you, Dexter? We'll give you all the support you need, but you've got to think of us as well, haven't you? You've got to think of the stress we're under.

Dexter starts a new school and is introduced to William Blake's *The Little Boy Lost*.

The teacher talks to Dexter in a way that is different from his parents, but nonetheless ineffective, in that his talk is little more than a series of rhetorical questions. Dexter is insulted and taunted by his new classmates:

Richie: Special Needs! Is that it, Dexter? Do you have Special Needs?
Anthony: If he has Special Needs, I'm complaining. I'm writing to the governors, I shouldn't be taught with a Special Needs kid. It could hold me back.

When Richie pushes Dexter, he lashes out. Although he never actually hits anyone, the bullies proclaim that he has attacked them like a psychopath. Only the lonely Tats (another 'outsider') stands up for him and gives a true account of what happened.

Dexter is seen by a number of 'shrinks', one of whom is resentful that even he cannot get Dexter to talk. He is 'adopted' by Jack and Jill, who are intent on making a name for themselves by using Dexter as an example of what they claim to be a newly discovered syndrome. Their plan to make a documentary is foiled, however, when, having asked Mum and Dad if they remember what the last thing Dexter said was, he starts to quote from television advertisements (overtones of *Equus* here!). Dad is furious, taking the view that, for the last year, Dexter has simply been playing with them. He hits Dexter, who responds with: 'I remember now. "Don't hit me." That was the last thing I said.'

Even with speech, Dexter's classmates continue to taunt him, yet their bravado is thin and Dexter has no trouble intimidating them. His presentation in the English class seems menacing to all but Tats and the audience, who will recognise the personal anguish that lies behind his interpretation of the Blake poem:

> The dad doesn't lose the little boy by mistake, the dad loses him on purpose, he's fed up with the little boy, he wants to get shot of him. And the mum isn't crying because the little boy is lost, she's crying 'cos she's feeling sorry for herself.

The presentation turns into a demonstration of the vacuity of language as Dexter once again uses sound bites from TV ads to counter the Teacher's attempt to shut him up and get rid of him. Mirroring Dad's actions, the Teacher goes to physically assault Dexter but comes off the worse for his pains. The play ends with Tats visiting Dexter in an institution. Dexter has been effectively disabled by a society in which adults fail to communicate with each other and their children, and resort to physical and emotional violence when they become frustrated at their own inability to communicate.

In contrast, Philip Ridley's *Sparkleshark* is a play about the redemptive power of live communication. The play is set on the roof of a block of flats, where Jake goes to write stories. A blood-curdling 'AAARGHHNAAAHHH!' is heard. It transpires that this is Finn's response to his television falling off station. Finn's sister Polly goes to the roof to adjust the satellite dish for him and meets the meek Jake, who asks her about Finn:

Polly: That's my baby brother.

Jake: Baby! But . . . he's huge! He grabbed two desks. One in each hand. And lifted them up. Above his head . . . The teachers want him expelled already. All the boys are scared of him. They call him the Monster –

Polly: He's not a monster! Everyone calls him that! Everywhere he goes! But he's not! He's very gentle! Cries easily, if you must know.

Finn later becomes involved in the fairytale that Jake spins out to save himself from being bullied and takes the part of the dragon Sparkleshark. He is eventually surrounded by the others and is subdued in a very physical but playful fight. As they are about to 'kill' the dragon, Polly steps in to rescue him:

Polly: STOP! This is a good Dragon! A kind Dragon . . . Everyone is afraid of him because of what he looks like . . . You must lay your hand on the Dragon and say . . . Oh, tell the Dragon you're his friend.

They do this and vow to meet again to tell another story. *Sparkleshark* illustrates the power that storytelling has to teach us about ourselves and each other. The characters are stereotypes that could be found in any school: the Geek, Little Miss Perfect, the Bully and his Henchmen, the Teen Queen and her Handmaiden, Mr Cool, and Finn, a latter day Lennie who is more sinned against than sinning. Being physically powerful yet intellectually limited has no bearing on Finn's ability to contribute to, and exact pleasure from, the social activity of enacting a story that helps all concerned see beneath superficial appearances.

Though also originating from the Connections project, in terms of positive/negative imagery and message, *Those Legs* by Noel Clarke could not be more different to *Sparkleshark*. The protagonist here is Georgia, who, while described as a tomboy, is constructed as a beautiful model now embittered due to the loss of her legs in a traffic accident. Its use of language and exploration of the sexual tension between Georgia and her boyfriend, Aaron, would limit the use of this play in many schools, though some teachers might applaud the way it tackles the issue of disabled people and sex, which has been such a taboo subject. Having said that, some of the values and attitudes expressed in the play regarding sexual politics per se may obfuscate this potentially rich seam of drama.

In making a link between perceptions of what constitutes a beautiful body and disability, *Those Legs* only barely touches on a major issue. A connection may be made here to Mark Wheeller's *Hard to Swallow*. This play has proved to be immensely popular in secondary schools in the UK and abroad. Part of its popularity is doubtless due to Wheeller's stylistic use of minimalised staging, and the potential this opens up for creative physical interpretation. Where limited budgets may be compensated for by ingenuity, such plays have an obvious appeal. It would surely also be true to say that, in telling the story of Catherine Dunbar, a 22-year-old who died after a seven-year battle against anorexia nervosa, Wheeller is exploring a disability and its effect on others that is very close to the lived experience of many young people. Given the assumption widely held among young people that disability mostly equates to obvious physical impairment, it may be that many of the young people who have worked with or seen this play would not actually consider anorexia in terms of it constituting a disability. This would not be the case in another of Wheeller's plays, *Graham: The World's Fastest Blind Man*. Drawing exclusively on the words of blind athlete Graham Salmon, his friends and family, this play may be deemed a piece of verbatim theatre.

Graham Salmon was a remarkable man. Losing his sight as an infant as a result of cancer, he went on to represent Great Britain at every major athletics competition between 1977 and 1987, breaking records in the 100 m, 400 m and high jump. He skied for Great Britain in the Winter Paralympics and not only played for the British golf team in the British Open, but famously hit a hole-in-one in the competition.

What is abundantly apparent in the play is that Salmon was astonishingly determined, tenacious and focused. There are examples of his humour but equally evidence of a self-centredness that may not have always been easy for others to deal with. In his own words, Salmon had always had an unswerving self-belief:

> From the very beginning, I could sense that I was 'special'. Being 'normal' was never a consideration – I wanted to be the best!

and a doggedness that could be construed as bloody-minded:

> I hate being told that I can't do something . . . I'll set out to prove them wrong, or establish for myself that I can't do it . . . but I will not accept someone else making that decision for me.

The climax of Salmon's story is his world record-breaking victory in the 1983 European Championships 400 m race in Bulgaria, when he achieved an astonishing time of 55.5 seconds. A few years later, he lost a leg to cancer. When his remaining leg began to swell up in 1998, the doctors told him that the cancer had not only spread there, but was also in his lungs and the condition was terminal. *Graham: The World's Fastest Blind Man* may not be one of the greatest works of dramatic literature, but it certainly offers any young actor cast as the protagonist a considerable challenge. Moreover, and perhaps more importantly, the play is unusual in that it finds drama in a man's achievements rather than in his disabilities.

The positivity of Graham Salmon's story contrasts with the bleaker exploration of autonomy versus medical patronage of Clark's *Whose Life is it Anyway?* Originally written for television, the stage version was presented in London in 1978, starring Tom Conti, and later filmed with Richard Dreyfus in the lead part. The story concerns a sculptor, Ken Harrison, who is paralysed from the neck down in an accident. There is some dramatic irony in that Ken has become little more than a statue in his own eyes. The play explores the debate over who has the right to keep Ken alive: the medical profession because it is their duty to do so, or Ken because it is his life and he no longer wants it. It is this core argument that has made the play appealing to many teachers wanting to engage their students in a debate that still has considerable currency. The argument is won, in the end, by a judicial interpretation of habeas corpus but the debate seems quite thin in moral, philosophical and indeed political terms. A down-to-earth orderly points out that, for the money it is costing to keep Ken alive, thousands of African children could be saved from death by simple diseases such as measles. Conversely, Dr Scott defends the huge effort that has gone into saving Ken, yet when Ken starts to argue against the will of the doctor he is sedated again. Dr Emerson postures that keeping him alive is a professional judgement, while his solicitor suggests that even professionals must bow to the laws of the land.

Notwithstanding the play's huge success in its early years, its arguments no longer seem robust or sophisticated enough given the amount of (sometimes controversial) media coverage afforded in recent years to actual cases of euthanasia. In contrast to, for example, the depiction of Dr Anne Turner in the television drama *A Short Stay in Switzerland* (2010), and despite the logic of Ken's thinking, it is less clear how he actually feels and thus difficult to find great empathy for him.

Conclusion

Saunders asserts that, 'at least one in four people experience personal disability at any one time, but few will survive a normal life span without experiencing some degree of disability in themselves, their family, friends or through their work' (Saunders 2000: x). Notwithstanding this, as was noted in the Introduction to this book, there remains a massive amount of misunderstanding and indeed misinformation about disability. Saunders questions why so much teaching about this 'fundamental human experience' seems to be 'relegated to a piecemeal approach, or dependent on individual teachers?' (ibid.). It is a fair question in the light of which drama teachers might justifiably respond that raising awareness of disability certainly is not just up to them. Conversely, they cannot be absolved of the responsibility to consider how their subject might contribute towards educating young people about disability. To relate this back to Bolton's four aims, it is not necessarily about choosing to study plays whose content imparts specific information about disability. Rather, it is ensuring that the potential of plays to promote personal and social development and a critical understanding of the art form of drama is fully exploited.

Chapter 2

A chronology of disabled dramatic characters

The melodramatic cripple

In Chapter 1, I noted the difficulty, and potential absurdity, of fixing a specific point in history as the start of something such as theatre, which is a concept rather than an event to which a time and date may be fixed. Finding a starting point for a chronology of plays that have disabled characters is equally problematic. What follows is an annotated, and by no means definitive, catalogue of plays in which the characters' disabilities seem to me an important aspect of the drama. Certainly, the blindness of Tiresias, Oedipus and Gloucester are all important facets of the dramas in which they feature, as are the disabilities of Richard III, *Peter Pan*'s Captain Hook, the stature of the protagonist in Fielding's *Tom Thumb*, and the madness of Lear, Ophelia and Hamlet (but is he mad, or is his 'madness' representative of something else?). In Chapter 3, Lionel Warner provides an intriguing discussion of how disability may be regarded as metaphor and metonym, while, in Chapter 4, I will consider these characters, along with a number of others, in terms of their dramatic symbolism. So, with these caveats acknowledged, I will start my none-too-strict chronology in nineteenth-century melodrama.

The disabled body was, according to Martha Holmes (2001: 5), 'a prominent and popular feature of the nineteenth-century stage'. The first English play to be billed as a melodrama is generally acknowledged to be Thomas Holcroft's *A Tale of Mystery* (1802). An unauthorised translation of Pixérécourt's *Coelina, or The Child of Mystery*, the play unravels the mysterious past of a character said to have been 'struck dumb' by bandits. Mute and deaf characters may be seen to figure in a number of melodramas, including Holcroft's *Deaf and Dumb* (1801), Rayner's *The Dumb Man of Manchester* (1837) and Pixérécourt's *The Mute Girl of the Forest* (1828). One of the defining characteristics of melodrama is its direct appeal to the senses and evocation of emotion. Signalling disability in the title of such plays may be regarded as a direct strategy to attract an audience ready and willing to have their heartstrings tugged. Thus, to the list of plays above, we might add Kenney's *The Blind Boy* (1807) and Wilkins' *The Blind Wife* (1850).

For the first time in English literature, the inclusion of a disabled character in a story became a recurrent feature. As in fiction, so in other aspects of Victorian life and literature:

> The material realities of disabled people's lives were increasingly made visible through the writings of physicians, social reformers, journalists, and 'special' educational theorists, as well as through the writing, speech, and physical presence of Victorians with disabilities. Victorian culture produced such a profuse and varied discourse of disability that blindness or an injured leg, as represented in literature, gestured not only toward metaphor but also toward the cultural management of a social issue.
>
> (ibid.: 8)

Nineteenth-century Britain was a society of contradictions, though what appear to be opposing forces and characteristics may in fact be closely intertwined. It was an age of extreme poverty and destitution. But it was also an age of philanthropy. 'Victorian values' tend to be regarded as synonymous with strict moral codes and 'upright behaviour', yet it was an age of unfettered prostitution, drunkenness and substance abuse. As the work of Charles Dickens attests, fiction was a powerful means of drawing attention to the plight of the poor and 'the afflicted'. While engaging directly with the issue might have been too distasteful, personally difficult or socially unacceptable for most, apprehending it through fiction was perhaps as purgatory and cathartic as subscribing to grand publicly funded schemes designed to edify and enrich society. For those who produced such fiction, such a focus also proved commercially successful!

The explicit representation of disabled people on stage in the nineteenth century reflected tensions between the growing recognition that we are all part of the same species, social justice is the right of everyone regardless of class or colour, and a rapidly expanding economy demands a concern for health. While being pitiful and charitable towards 'the afflicted' was right and proper, 'the afflicted' nonetheless represented an economic problem. The pervading link between disability and moral degeneration would also doubtless give rise to concerns about the sexuality of this sector of the populace and the possibility of their ranks swelling as they had their own children, leading to a greater threat to both the economy and moral rectitude of the nation. To some extent, melodramas circumnavigated these fears in the way they depicted disabled characters. For example, in James Kenney's *The Blind Boy* (1807), the protagonist, Edmond, is drawn as an 'innocent and incapable child, completely dependent upon others for support' (ibid.: 10). As is so often the case in literature of the time, it transpires that Edmond is of royal stock and, through the actions of his faithful and seemingly asexual wife, all turns out well in the end. Virtue is rewarded, the proper social order is restored and, thank goodness, there is no mention of any children coming along. Nor does the play articulate in any way with the reality that was the experience of most blind people of the time: absence of work, abject poverty and 'the attitudes that catalyzed the first two conditions' (ibid.: 11).

Blindness seems a particularly apposite disability for nineteenth-century Britain to be concerned with. It was not an uncommon condition and, being paradoxically a highly visible impairment, it served as a constant reminder of some of the reasons why this was so. In the first instance, blindness may be linked to poor sanitation, diet and health. In Victorian society, it was also popularly perceived as resulting from the result of sexual degeneracy in the form of venereal disease. Significantly, Ibsen's *Ghosts* (1881), which uses inherited syphilis and the blindness that may result from it as a metonym for society's underlying moral decay, was not performed in England until 1891, and then only avoided the censor because it was staged by the subscription-only Independent Theatre Society. A year earlier, Maurice Maeterlinck's *The Blind* (1890) stepped completely away from disability as a cause for social or moral concern, and used the universal stereotype of the helpless blind man to make a philosophical point. Theatre's recognition of disability as an issue worthy of exploration in its own right seems fleeting as well as ambivalent.

Voices from America

Steinbeck's *Of Mice and Men* (1937) remains one of the most commonly studied novels in English syllabuses, not least because teachers continue to see students discovering new insights in the text. While it is less commonly studied as a play, Steinbeck wrote the stage version simultaneously to the novel. The fact that it is such a mainstay of the curriculum surely also contributes to the regular staging of the play version in regional theatres. Lennie has unspecified learning difficulties. He is portrayed as a gentle giant: exceptionally strong physically, but with the mind of an innocent child. As the outside world closes in on him with all its adult nastiness, he increasingly needs the care and protection of George. It is difficult to regard Lennie as anything other than a victim of both the inhumanity of the social system in which he lives and the attitudes and actions of those around him. George's final act of despatching Lennie from a cruel and uncaring world is generally regarded as an act of kindness in much the same way that Carlson shooting Candy's decrepit old dog is seen as an act of mercy, albeit that the way Carlson carries out the action is entirely functional and without pity. Thus, Lennie becomes a lens through which to examine bigger social issues. The novel was, for a number of years, banned from various American public and school libraries for promoting euthanasia and being anti-business.

Like Lennie, Laura in Tennessee Williams' *The Glass Menagerie* (1944) also has an unspecified impairment, though hers is physical and emotional. She is referred to as being 'crippled' but other references suggest that she has nothing more than a slight 'clump' in her walk. Dramatically, this physical characteristic may be seen as an outer manifestation of the more significant impairment she faces in terms of her inability to cope with her mother's social expectations. Her shy retreat from the outside world is signified by her absorption with her glass animals. Meanwhile, her brother Tom is desperate to either escape or cope with the humdrum of everyday life. What he cannot escape from, though, is the thought of Laura. Laura is a part of life's aesthetic: not physically or mentally perfect, but in a way perfect because her imperfection is the one thing that makes Tom feel. Laura thus also takes on a metaphorical value and, as such, is a distinct contrast to the characters of both Helen Keller and Annie Sullivan in William Gibson's *The Miracle Worker* (1957).

Helen Keller was born to a Confederate family in 1880 (her mother was a cousin of Robert E. Lee). At the age of 19 months, she contracted 'an acute congestion of the stomach and the brain', which may have been scarlet fever or possibly meningitis. This left her deaf and blind. The play tells the story of how Annie Sullivan, a 20-year-old who had herself been blind, but partially re-sighted by an operation, became her governess and set about teaching the 6-year-old Helen to communicate. In the first instance, this involved battling with the Keller family who simply indulged Helen, as a result of which her behaviour became increasingly socially unacceptable. What ensued was a battle of wills with both parents and child, but by acceding to Annie's demands that she be given sole responsibility for Helen for two weeks, the girl began to learn how to finger sign words. At first, the signs Annie made on her hand appeared meaningless, though it was clear that she could learn quickly how to copy them exactly. The dramatic climax of the play comes when Helen realises that the sign on her hand for 'water' corresponds to actual water and the half-remembered verbalisation 'wah-wah'. In terms of what is said about disability, the play comes down firmly on the side of Annie Sullivan, who rejects the Keller's response to their daughter:

> *Annie*: Pity? For this tyrant? The whole house turns on her whims, is there anything she wants she doesn't get? I'll tell you what I pity, that the sun won't rise and set for her all her life, and every day you're telling her it will, what good will your pity do her when you're under the strawberries, Captain Keller?

At the end of the play and having associated the sign for 'teacher' with Annie, Helen symbolically gives her saviour a set of keys, lifts off her smoked glasses and kisses her. The play is perhaps the first popular drama (the 1962 film starring Anne Bancroft won two Oscars) to not only feature a character with multiple impairments, but also rest on such a didactic element.

Frederick Knott's 1966 thriller *Wait Until Dark* offers a distinct contrast of another nature. While the 1967 film starring Audrey Hepburn contains a scene rated 10th in the 100 scariest movie moments ever (www.listsofbests.com/list/2948-100-scariest-movie-moments), the English version of the play script reads rather more like a clunky farce. It is an improbable tale of a blind woman (Susy) who is terrorised by three villains in search of a doll containing heroin that her husband (Sam) has unwittingly brought into the country as a favour to a woman he had never met before. However, Susy has given the doll to the rather obnoxious girl upstairs, Gloria. Notwithstanding Susy's blindness and Gloria's need for spectacles, they manage to outwit the 'baddies'. Indeed, Gloria gets the last line when she tells Sam and a policeman to give Susy some respect: 'Leave her alone! Both of you. She can manage by herself. You see – she can manage – she'll be all right.'

Triumph in the face of adversity is similarly a theme that underscores Paul Zindel's *The Effect of Gamma Rays on Man-in-the Moon Marigolds* (1970) (which, in 1972, also became a successful film directed by Paul Newman and starring Joanna Woodward). The disabled character in this play is Ruth, who has epilepsy. Like Helen Keller, she is indulged by her mother (Beatrice), with the result that she is atrophied in her move towards independence. The protagonist of the play is Tillie, Ruth's younger sister, who is plain looking but quietly determined to make the best of what she has. Beatrice may be likened to Amanda Wingfield in *The Glass Menagerie* given her self-delusion, selfishness and inability to give her daughters the love and support they really need. At the end of the play, Beatrice kills Tillie's rabbit. When Ruth rails at her for this, Beatrice says, 'Ruth, if you don't shut up I'm going to have you put away'. Ruth goes into a fit and the audience is presented with the unsettling sight of Beatrice holding her while Tillie puts a wooden spoon under her tongue. The scene is perhaps all the more disturbing given the routine way that Beatrice and Tillie do this, especially as the episode ends with Tillie asking if she should call a doctor, and Beatrice's flat reply: 'No. She'll be all right.'

Epileptics do not, of course, need to be seen by a doctor every time they fit, but the realisation here is that, if Ruth is not all right, it will not be so much because of her epilepsy as the lack of a solid maternal relationship. Dramatically, Ruth's condition provides a contrast to the quiet, self-effacing Tillie, who stalwartly copes with the disabilities of her mother and sister and evades the disabling effect they might have on her.

A very English affair

The first twentieth-century English play of note to address disability is *A Day in the Death of Joe Egg* (1967) by Peter Nichols. Nichols and his wife were themselves the parents of a severely disabled daughter, and the play has elements of autobiography. One of the things that makes the play feel particularly English is its use of dark humour and blend of pathos and tragedy. Towards the end of the play, which is discussed more fully in Chapter 7, Bri takes the disabled Joe out into the freezing night:

> I don't know what I wanted – just to stop them saving her again.

Joe is saved but Bri comments, ironically, that:

> If there *is* anything heartening about such a disaster, I think it's the wonderful way this great operation of mercy has moved into action. And of course the uniquely British optimism that suddenly in moments of crisis seems to suffuse the whole nauseating atmosphere.

The British optimism Bri sardonically refers to is inspected more closely in David Storey's *Home* (1970). Initially, the audience are presented with two elderly gentlemen engaged in phatic communion. Like *Of Mice and Men*, the play features two men biding their time in the hope of something better. However, rather than having dreams and plans for the future, Harry and Jack dwell on the past. But as they harp back to better days, they do so in elliptical terms, suggesting that their memories of the good old days are not reliable. Indeed, as the play progresses, we realise that the eponymous 'home' is an institution for the mentally ill, which in turn serves as a metonym for Britain at the end of the 1960s. The sun is setting on the lives of Harry and Jack, whose struggle to retain some semblance of dignity in the shadow of mental breakdown is a metaphor for the loss of empire and the evaporation of old-fashioned values that cannot actually be recalled with any certainty. In parallel with their nation, their disability is hidden beneath smart appearance and manners. Dignity is similarly a major theme in Brian Clark's *Whose Life is it Anyway?* (1972), in which the protagonist, paralysed from the neck down in an accident, retains his acerbic wit and intelligence, and uses both to argue for his right to take control of his life and how to end it.

The binary themes of how non-disabled people cope with disability, and how disability symbolises the inability of adults and society generally to cope with itself, is further exposed in *Equus*, Peter Shaffer's 1973 play in which psychiatrist Martin Dysart tries to understand a boy's pathological fascination with and brutalisation of horses. In so doing, he struggles to identify his own beliefs and sense of purpose. While the play presents a case study of psychosis that is chilling, tragic and intangible, it is as much to do with Dysart's inability to deal with, let alone 'cure', his patient, Alan Strang. Verity Taylor, the subject of Olwen Wymark's *Find Me* (1977) is as equally perplexing as Strang. *Equus* came about as a result of Shaffer being told a story about a boy who had blinded six horses. Although he was never able to verify the tale, Wymark's play is the true story a young woman who was disturbed from childhood and was eventually incarcerated in Broadmoor high-security psychiatric hospital after setting fire to a chair in a mental hospital. In some respects, the play could be classified as a docudrama being based on true events, but the playwright is keen to point out that all of the scenes and dialogue are fictional and arose out of collaborating with the group of students with whom Wymark worked at Kingston Polytechnic. It is difficult for an audience to know how to respond to Verity. Clearly, she has intelligence and there are flashes of sensitivity, but her unpredictable and often violent behaviour is unnerving. Like her mother, we can feel pity for her but, at the same time, fear her. Wymark (1983: 127) has noted that audiences, 'receive the play with a kind of crucial attentiveness', when actors play it with 'passionate and affecting conviction'. Whereas other plays have attached some sort of symbolic reasoning to disability, there are no suggestions or explanations offered regarding Verity's condition other than that she experienced epileptic episodes and took medication for this. We are told that, as a child, she tended to play on her own and see that other children were threatened by her and avoided her. She has uncontrollable verbal outbursts. While it is never explicitly suggested that she is schizophrenic, her fragmented personality is represented by five actresses. It is certainly easy to sympathise with Verity's family, who are torn apart by her unrelentingly bizarre behaviour, yet, without suggesting that there may be any easy answers as to how to deal with young people such as Verity, the play criticises the inadequacy of the systems that are in place. For example, when the Taylors try to get Verity admitted to hospital, they have to battle through a repetitive and demeaning bureaucracy. Later, as her father pleads for support through a series of letters, it becomes apparent that there simply are not systems in place to deal with cases such as Verity. Wymark remarks that, 'I think . . . there is something profoundly recognisable for us all in this tragedy' (ibid.). What that is, perhaps, is that, far from being a visitation of sin or result of negligence, the instance of disability is, in many cases, purely arbitrary.

This is not the case in Dennis Potter's *Brimstone and Treacle* (1977). Like Ken in *Whose Life is it Anyway?*, Pattie is the victim of a road traffic accident, but this has left her more in a vegetative state akin to Joe Egg. As in *Whose Life is it Anyway?*, the point is made how awful it would be to have a lively mind trapped in a useless body, though in Pattie's case her parents do not know whether or not this is the case. As it transpires, her father has good cause for hoping it is not, and the dramatic turning point of the play comes at the end when Pattie regains consciousness while being raped and is able to remember the circumstances that caused the accident – apprehending her father in flagrante delicto, fleeing from his office and being run down. Pattie's condition is a living reproof of her father's infidelity, yet it is sex that paradoxically awakens her. Thus, while being distinctly twentieth century in its explicit nature, the play recalls and reinforces ancient links between immorality and disability and the punishment of innocent children for the sins of their fathers, a notion that is also present in Potter's later play *Blue Remembered Hills* (1979), where Donald Duck, a boy whose mother is said to be of dubious moral character, is teased and bullied by the other children because he is slow. Ultimately, they lose control of their 'game' and Donald Duck dies in a fire.

In *Every Good Boy Deserves Favour* (1977), Tom Stoppard references disability in an entirely different way, using mental illness as a very deliberate and obvious metaphor for soviet politics. Set in a mental institution, the play reflects the old adage that there are none so blind as those that will not see, and comments on the absurdity of a state run by people that will not recognise that its opponents are just as 'sane' as they are. Conversely, David Edgar's *Mary Barnes* (1978) is a 'biographical' play about artist Mary Barnes, who joined a community in London's East End set up by R. D. Laing as a humane alternative to mental hospitals. The narrative is a stark illustration of Mary's journey through madness as she regresses to her childhood in order to re-grow as a person. Edgar takes the narrative beyond biography, though, in order to comment angrily on society's attitude to mental illness and the way it is treated. A number of anecdotal stories recount what appear to be abusive practices and cases of doctors exercising power over patients in order to fulfil their own agendas rather than acting in the interests of those in their care:

Hugo: The purpose of most psychiatric practice is to cauterize dissent.

In this, the play becomes a vehicle for attacking capitalism per se, though at times some of the characters' views seem misleadingly romanticised:

Brenda: The very word is *in*valid. In*valid*. You know, in feudal times, there were no mad, or sane, defined as such. Communities supported those who couldn't work, quite automatically. But then, when people started being paid in cash, as individual workers, then the criminal, the ill, the lunatic, were separated off. Defined as 'other'. On the grounds of being unexploitable. Their *functioning* impaired.

While a valid point is being made regarding the wilful disengagement of disabled people from the rest of society, the given etymology of the term 'invalid' being inferred here is inaccurate, and it seems odd to invoke feudal society as being imbibed with community spirit.

Like *Mary Barnes*, *The Elephant Man* (1979) also tells a real-life story. Bernard Pomerance's short 'documentary' is a straightforward narrative that traces the 'discovery' by Frederic Treves, a surgeon at the London Hospital, of Joseph 'John' Merrick, whose condition of neurofibromatosis had led to his appearing in a freak show as a means of existence. Merrick is shown rapidly moving from an uneducated exhibit to a cultured and sensitive man. Merrick's story captures some of the contradictory attitudes Victorian society had towards disability: while the crowd almost kill Merrick when he arrives at Liverpool Street Station, an appeal in *The Times* brings in enough money to look after him for the rest of his life. He is befriended by the rich and famous, leading to his ex-manager, Ross, accusing him of remaining a whore but just to a richer clientele. The same year also saw the television airing of Peter Durrant's *The Brylcreem Boys*, the stage version of which premiered at the Theatre Royal Northampton in 1984. Drawing on an actual experience of the playwright's father, the play tells the story of George, a sentry at a Second World War RAF base who gets frostbite one night. He is sent to a nearby hospital to recover and is placed in a ward full of aircrew who have lost their mental stability as a result of their experience of bombing raids. Bemused and bewildered by what he perceives as the deranged chatter of the other patients, George asks to be moved. His request is turned down by the ward Sister, who sees him as being unsympathetic to what the others have been through. That night, George gains new and terrifying insights when, by the light of the full moon, the hitherto catatonic skipper comes to life and the crew re-enact a bombing raid. As the re-enactment progresses, it becomes ever more apparent that each member of the crew is reliving their own personal nightmare. *The Brylcreem Boys* makes no overt social or political comment, nor is it an obvious protest against war, though it imaginatively and sensitively illustrates how otherwise fit and strong young men may be tipped into insanity by it. *Not About Heroes* by Stephen MacDonald (1986) is in a similar vein in its exploration of the meeting of poets Siegfried Sassoon and Wilfred Owen at Craiglockhart War Hospital for nervous disorders. Owen was admitted in June 1917, suffering from shell shock after four months in the trenches in France. Sassoon was already an acclaimed poet and critic of the war. He was sent to Craiglockhart in July 1917 on the grounds of mental impairment, though this may have been a strategy to discredit him and so invalidate his protest. Owen was unknown at the time, but went on to become one of the greatest poets of the First World War. The importance of their meeting is now recognised as being a significant factor in Owen's development.

It happens with young people too

The 1980s saw the appearance of a number of plays that recognised that young people were not immune from disability, though the depictions of disabled young people were as varied in the messages they seemed to communicate as they were in their apparent purpose.

Children of a Lesser God by Mark Medoff was first performed professionally in 1980. The play traces the tempestuous professional and romantic relationship between Sarah Norman, a young woman deaf from birth, and her teacher, James Leeds. The play was specially written for the actress Phyllis Frelich, who was herself deaf, and is, to some extent, based on her relationship with her husband. Perhaps for the first time, the play politicised the debate by giving a voice to a character with a sensory impairment, and so enabling her to articulate first-hand experience of disability. Roy Kift's *Stronger than Superman*, also from 1980, similarly features a character who is physically disabled, yet in every other way is a 'normal', articulate and playful boy. The play is discussed further in Chapter 8, as is Richard Cameron's 1988 play about the pupils of a special school, *Strugglers*. Both of these plays were written specifically for young audiences, as were *Lives Worth Living* (1983) by Lawrence Evans and Jane Nash (see Chapter 7) and Haresh Sharma's *Off Centre* (1993). What also links the plays mentioned here is their explicit intention of informing their audience about disability. To some extent, this is also true of Arne Skouen's *Ballerina* (1984), though, curiously, while it is clear that the little girl Malin is autistic, the condition is not named, nor can the play be regarded as a particularly accurate depiction of it. Malin's sweetness and innocence seems rather romanticised, not a charge that can be levelled at Clare Dowie's *Adult Child, Dead Child* (1987), in which the apparently schizophrenic narrator delivers a harrowing, humorous, poignant and ultimately uplifting monologue tracing her journey from problem child through uncontrolled teenage angst and psychiatric care to independent adulthood. The play can be linked to Sarah Kane's posthumously produced *4.48 Psychosis* (2000) in form and content, in that it is a monological journey through a mentally disturbed life. Like *Find Me*, the play evokes sympathy from audiences by presenting a realistic rather than sentimentalised insight into the character's unpredictable swings between violence and childlike innocence. This also links it to Valerie Windsor's *Effie's Burning* (1987). Effie Palmer has been incarcerated in a mental institution for over 50 years. As a 'simple' girl, she was raped and repeatedly abused by local men until she became pregnant and taken away from her home:

Dr Kovacs: She'd been categorized under Section 1 Part D of the 1927 amendment . . . they said that she was classed as a moral defective. What on earth is a moral defective? A not-very-bright girl of thirteen classed morally defective? On whose terms?

When Effie is moved from the institution in which she has spent most of her life, she is involved in a fire and suspected of being the cause. Dr Kovacs is assigned to her case. Like Effie, Dr Kovacs is abused by men and oppressed by a patriarchal society. Effie swears that she did not cause the fire deliberately. Rather, the incandescence she feels inside becomes literal and expresses itself in spontaneous combustion:

Effie: Everything in here boiled up and boiled up . . . and the darkness pressed in through the windows. And I could hear the boiling getting louder and louder and I was afraid that if I . . . *(She presses the sheet to her mouth)*
And the pent-up anger explodes. Effie suddenly flings the sheet away and stands there full of power like a column of flame.
And then it poured out of my mouth, out of my arms, great walls of it, streaking up them silly curtains, dancing all round the room – and I burned their house down, Miss, I burned their house down.

Disability and the physical and mental abuse of young people go hand in hand in a number of plays, including Lucy Gannon's *Keeping Tom Nice* (1988) (see Chapter 8), while the now familiar link between disability and infidelity occurs once more in Lee Hall's acclaimed *Spoonface Steinberg* (1997).

First performed on radio, the Royal National Theatre Studio developed a stage version of it in 2000. The play is an 'autobiographical' monologue of a seven-year-old autistic girl dying of cancer. Spoonface is not only a genius with numbers, but a consummate opera buff, factors that may reinforce the common conception of autistic savants that was so notably fostered by Dustin Hoffman in *Rain Man*. The dramatic conceit gives Spoonface the ability to remember conversations and events that a real 7-year-old would be extremely unlikely to remember. Both parents are academic and wrapped in their own world. While Spoonface says that, 'I was never right since I was born', her mother blames her father for her not being 'right' on account of her falling on her head during an argument about him being out with a female student. Spoonface possesses a straightforward honesty that contrasts with adults' use of euphemism and equivocation. Her innocence makes her the repository for adults' woes, and she takes on an almost religious function as confessor: 'I believe that I was supposed to be backward – I believe it was all part of what is supposed to be.'

The child's forgiveness shames adults and perhaps makes them feel guilty but ultimately changes nothing. For example, her mother would 'come home to me and say "My poor sweet angel, my poor sweet angel" – and then drink the vodka', while her father 'said I had suffered the worse out of anyone in the world and it was all his fault – that he didn't know what he was doing – that he was such a young man and he was just a poor philosophy man because he couldn't think of what else to do'. Spoonface's own philosophy is simplistic and fatalistic:

> There is day and night and black and white and all these things but in the very beginning and in the end – everything will not be divided and there will be no me or you – there will be no this or that, no little puppy dogs or anything.

Philip Ridley's *Sparkleshark*, also from 1997, offers a very different message in its evocation of the redemptive and healing powers of children's storytelling and play, while Andrew Payne's *Shut Up* (2006) uses the vacuity of language as a symbol of adults' inability to understand and communicate effectively with the young people they are supposed to care for. David Watson's *Flight Path* (2007), on the other hand, explores the fraught but nonetheless loving and supportive relationship between a young man and his disabled brother. The abiding message here is that the tenacity and resilience of youth will prevail (see Chapter 7), whereas Caryl Churchill's complex and unnerving play *The Skriker* (1994) offers a vision of the future that is, by contrast, apocalyptic. In the centre of the narrative are two young women. Josie is in a mental hospital having murdered her baby and baked it in a pie. She is visited by her pregnant friend, Lily, and both are soon joined by the Skriker, an ancient, shape-shifting, malignant faerie. Post-natal psychosis and environmental catastrophe are intertwined but this is not fatalistic in the way that Spoonface Steinberg's philosophy is. Rather, it uses magic in its darkest manifestations to highlight the realities of how man has broken nature:

> It was always possible to think whatever your personal problem, there's always nature. Spring will return even if it's without me. Nobody loves me but at least it's a sunny day. This has been a comfort to people as long as they've existed. But it's not available any more. Sorry. Nobody loves me and the sun's going to kill me. Spring will return and nothing will grow.

Laughter and darkness

Originally broadcast on Channel 4 in 1989, Peter Barnes' *Nobody Here But Us Chickens* is a trilogy of darkly comic plays about disabled characters who manage to assuage the effects of their disabilities. Barnes has said of the work that:

> No special sympathy is shown for these disabilities, as that would merely emphasise the differences between the disabled and those without such handicaps, whereas the object is to empathize with the similarities. Acceptance is needed, not sympathy . . . The disabled are not a different species but, like the rest of us, absurd and ridiculous; only they have it harder. Cripples are the rest us, dramatized.
>
> (Barnes 1993: 172)

In *Nobody Here But Us Chickens*, two men meet in a cell. Both believe that they are chickens and are set on resisting the idea, being put to them by white-coated doctors, that they are in fact men. Between them, they hatch (excuse the pun) a cunning plan that involves them pretending to actually be men so that they can escape their cage and move about the outside world under cover. In *More Than a Touch of Zen*, two men attend an introductory session on judo run by Carver, an instructor committed to the idea that there are no barriers that cannot be overcome through the spiritual discipline offered by his particular system. However, both of his new pupils have spastic paralysis, which causes their muscles to spasm involuntarily. At first, Carver is sceptical that he can do anything for the men until one of them literally floors him while having a spasm. This leads Carver to remember 'the great Zen principle of turning disadvantages to advantage'. He encourages them to shake with more energy in order to 'throw your opponents off balance and keep 'em guessing.' Perversely, the more adept they become at deliberately shaking with energy, the more they find they can also achieve moments of rest and relaxation. Finally, *Not as Bad as They Seem* appears to be a straightforward farce involving a pair of lovers being disturbed by the woman's husband. What heightens the farce is that all three characters are blind. While some may see the plays as cruelly taking advantage of other people's misfortunes, Barnes' project is to reject such a view as patronising: 'We have to find consolation in order to survive: if the text is lousy admire the binding . . . You see, things are never as bad as they seem.'

Rather than focusing on what abilities disabled people may inherently possess, Burt Coules' 1991 radio play *Flowers for Algernon* (see Chapter 1) looks at what may happen when disability is replaced with ability. Like Lennie in *Of Mice and Men*, Charlie is an adult who has retained his childlike innocence and charm. The Algernon of the title is, in fact, a mouse with whom Charlie empathises, for they are both part of the same experiment to see if it is possible to increase intelligence. Like Lennie, Charlie is teased by workmates. However, after an experimental procedure gives him an IQ of 185, he suffers more from their hostility and suspicion. In this, the main theme seems to be prejudice against anyone who is 'not normal'. The play is not well informed, though, suggesting that it is only when Charlie has a higher intelligence that he can experience sexual feelings. The sub-text is that angst and pain come with intelligence and the ability to know and articulate, reinforcing the notion of ignorance being bliss. Conversely, the intense pain of retaining an awareness of a disabling condition is powerfully explored in Alan Bennett's *The Madness of George III* (1991). It is now believed that the king suffered from porphyria, a condition that can cause hallucinations, anxiety and paranoia. In the course of the play, which may be read as an overt attack on society's inability to understand and accept anyone 'deviant' from the norm because of their mental condition, we witness George being subjected to appalling medical treatment, including being bound and gagged and strapped into a chair for hours while his bodily functions are subjected to the most intense scrutiny. Historically, George eventually regained his 'sanity'. Dramatically, the questions are: who determines what constitutes sanity, what dignity must be afforded to those diagnosed as insane, and how can any of us cope with the idea of a working mind being shut away and rendered incapable of showing itself? In some respects, this enigma is a theme in Tom Stoppard's *Arcadia* (1993). Rated by the *Independent* newspaper as one of the best plays of the twentieth century, the play examines the relationship between order and disorder, madness and genius. In the context of this discussion, it is the character of Gus who is of most interest. Mute since the age of five, Gus appears to have profound understanding and insight. He leads an expert directly to the correct site for an archaeological investigation, is a talented musician, but hates people shouting. While all this may suggest that he is autistic, to categorise his character in such a way would be to miss his dramatic function as a link between the past and the present. At the end of the play, it is Gus who provides the answer to the mystery that has underpinned the narrative of the play in the shape of a drawing: the fact that the answer lies in a picture and that Gus is mute may both suggest that words cannot always provide the answers we are looking for; his 'off-centredness' highlights that a 'special need' may be as much a manifestation of society's inability to understand as it is a condition of a particular individual.

From 1996 come two distinctly different treatments of disability. Nabil Shaban's *The First to Go* tells the story of the Nazis' systematic attempt to purify the Aryan race by exterminating the disabled. The play draws on actual characters such as Claus von Stauffenberg, the one-armed, one-eyed 'terrorist' who tried to assassinate Hitler, while the villain of the piece is Dr Josef Goebbels, who was himself disabled by a club foot. Shaban is disabled himself and a co-founder of the renowned Graeae Theatre. Shaban's introduction to the published version is something of a bitter diatribe in which he expresses his frustration at the amount of coverage that the Jewish Holocaust has at the expense of other groups, notably the disabled. However, many may find it difficult to afford much sympathy with his proclamations that this is largely because the arts and entertainment industry is dominated by Jews, whereas disabled people 'are not film or theatre directors or producers . . . so plays, books, films, television dramas don't get produced about the Disabled Holocaust'. While *The First to Go* deals with a powerful subject worthy of attention and full of dramatic potential, it has been criticised as being over-long, over-written and poorly structured, with characters that are seemingly either two dimensional or little more than thin parodies:

> There is no real dramatic tension to be felt and, as such, when things end up as they do, it's difficult to truly feel sympathetic or regretful. To put this very simply, the play is just too long and doesn't 'do' enough.
>
> (Softely 2008)

On the other hand, Lyn Gardner's four-star review of a 2008 production of *The Cripple of Inishmaan* proclaimed Martin McDonagh's 1996 play as being 'break-your-heart, cruelly funny'. The eponymous protagonist of the play is the orphaned and crippled Billy Claven, who tries to escape poverty and boredom by putting himself forward for a part in a Hollywood film being shot nearby. Billy's character is both a metaphor and metonym, but in the context of the play's unsentimental depiction of life on the west coast of Ireland in the 1930s, he is also three dimensional and so capable of evoking both pathos as well as unsympathetic laughter.

Comedy is certainly a word to employ in connection with Lee Hall's *Cooking With Elvis* (1998), albeit of the dark, Ortonesque variety. Once again, disability is depicted as a punishment. Mam threatens Dad she will leave him, he drives off at speed, crashes, and ends up in a vegetative state, though his erections show that the libido is still functioning. As in *Brimstone and Treacle*, the catalyst for the drama is the introduction of a young man who turns out to have stronger animalistic drives than humanitarian ones. However, unlike the interloper in *Brimstone and Treacle*, Stuart does not seem an evil presence. He 'services' Mam because she needs his body, sleeps with her daughter Jill because he thinks in a childlike way he might be in love with her, and masturbates Dad as an act of charity. Dad, like Spoonface Steinberg, is a sounding board for the thoughts and feelings of the other characters in that he does not talk back to them when they offload on him. However, in a number of surreal sequences, Dad comes to life in the persona of Elvis to issue cod philosophy. Ultimately, his glib message is exactly the same as Spoonface's: 'there are only people, human beings who love and hope and fear.'

The attraction of angst

Catherine Dunbar died at the age of 22 after a 7-year battle with anorexia nervosa. Maureen Dunbar's account of her daughter's illness is interspersed with extracts from Catherine's diary, and reveals the conflict between her body's demands and her mental turmoil. *Hard to Swallow* (2000) is teacher/playwright Mark Wheeller's adaptation of Maureen Dunbar's book, *Catherine*. The subject matter and deliberately minimalist staging requirements no doubt helped the play to rapidly become a popular vehicle for school-aged drama students and youth groups to display their talents. The same may be held true of Wheeller's 2001 biographical play, *Graham: the World's Fastest Blind Man*, though I suspect that, while Graham Salmon's remarkable achievements as an athlete present interesting challenges in terms of performance, they are not as alluring as the angst that underpins Catherine Dunbar's story or Sarah Kane's as depicted in *4.48 Psychosis* (2000), which has also proved hugely popular with drama students. Popularly regarded as Kane's suicide note, *4.48 Psychosis* is an indictment of human cruelty as well as being an explication of mental illness. It is at once dramatically exciting and appalling; an aesthetic experience in that it reminds its audience that they are alive and capable of feeling. Her demand, 'I REFUSE I REFUSE I REFUSE LOOK AWAY FROM ME', is thus paradoxical because we do look and, by doing so, refuse to refuse. However, while Kane's terrifying drowning in what has been described as 'pathological grief' may be revered as an expression of extreme angst by some A level Theatre Studies groups, the play can seem accusatory, though it is not clear exactly what the audience is being accused of. Conversely, like *Find Me*, the play may be seen as giving a public voice to a character whose internal pain is a manifestation of the tragedy, shame and iniquity of humanity. However, such a reading only recognises the irresolvable nature of the problem. Alternatively, and I am not at all sure this would suite Kane's intentions, the play could be interpreted as a call to resist the destruction of depression and seek a more positive path.

Perhaps more positive, in a curious way, is Joe Penhall's *Blue/Orange* (2000). This sardonic play intertwines the issues of race, mental illness, and twenty-first-century British life. At heart, though, the play may not be so much about mental illness as power, ego and racial prejudice. Two psychiatrists, one young and scrupulous, the other older and ruthless in his pursuit of self-aggrandisement, lock horns over the diagnosis and treatment of Christopher, a young black man who appears to be delusional. Christopher, though, is not without power himself, and can use this to control those who are trying to control him.

This leaves the audience questioning how they can trust the verity of his narrative and the authenticity of the doctors' interpretation of it. This links the play, thematically, to Martin McDonagh's *The Pillowman* (2003), a tenebrous comedy that explores, among other things, the relationship between the real and the made-up (see Chapter 4).

While *The Pillowman* links mental health and the health of the state by creating an entirely fictional world, Ron Hutchinson's *Head/Case* (2004) uses a situation that is closer to home and more immediately recognisable to examine the relationship between thought and feeling and the purpose and effect of inter-personal communication. Tracey talks unremittingly as a result of being hit on the head by a brick in a riot in Northern Ireland. Julia experiences no feelings, and so has little to say after a car crash. The contrasts between these women serves as a vehicle by which national stereotypes are explored and the question is asked, 'How do you define yourself when you literally don't know who you are anymore? And how much does nationality, culture and memory shape who you actually are?'

Angst of a different nature permeates Nina Raines' *Tribes* (2010), which delves into the politics of deafness but, by doing so, raises discussions about the way in which attitudes and beliefs are passed on to children, and the devastation that may occur when evolving personalities clash with familial (read, tribal) loyalties. A key character in the play is Billy, who is born deaf to a hearing family. He meets Sylvia, who is born hearing to a deaf family but is going deaf. With Sylvia's help, Billy learns to sign and gets a job as a lip reader for the Crown Prosecution Service. Being born deaf, he has high status in the deaf community, which bores Sylvia, who is frustrated by their hierarchical structure and politics. Billy, however, becomes increasingly politicised and rejects his family. His brother Christopher is deeply hurt by this and has trouble of his own. More and more, he is hearing voices. Taken literally, there is the suggestion of schizophrenia here while, metaphorically, his condition could be interpreted as a manifestation of the destructive tension that arises when one's own sense of personality seems at odds with the expectations of those closest to one.

It seems fitting that the last play in this chronology was written for young people and has young people as its subject. Noel Clarke's *Those Legs* (2011) touches on a number of issues relevant to this book. As noted in Chapter 1, however, other aspects of this play may deflect the audience's focus on disability. The chapters that follow illustrate how this is a common consequence when disability is used as a dramatic device rather than being the actual subject of the drama.

Chapter 3

'Damaging mythology'

Disability and stereotype

Lionel Warner

Questions arising

The question that is central to this book is: How are people with disabilities portrayed in plays? The question immediately raises others, as we try to be clear about what is being asked. In part, it is a question of semiotics: What are the signs, in speech and action, space, properties, and form, and what do they signify? It might be a question of the artist's intention, insofar as that is deemed relevant and can be reliably determined. It is undoubtedly also a question of audiences' interpretations.

I want to raise these questions with two particular focuses in mind. The first is the anxiety of many that representations of disability in popular, and also perhaps high, culture tend to confirm stereotypes and reinforce rather than erode prejudice. The second is a pedagogical focus: How do students studying plays that portray disabled characters interpret them, and how might their responses be influenced by teachers and assessment regimes?

I would like to start my discussion of these questions impressionistically, referring to coincidence of recent experiences. At a meeting, I am told about *Fireworks*, a new play that was first performed at the Etcetera Theatre in north London in November 2010, and which centres on a 15-year-old called Katie who has Prader-Willi syndrome. I am not familiar with this condition, and immediately realise that portrayals of disability can raise awareness. I discover that Katie's condition is characterised by 'an insatiable appetite, learning difficulties and behavioural problems' (playwright's introduction). I begin to research the play's performance and find a review that begins 'A sometimes damagingly mythologised condition, Prader-Willi Syndrome is little known and little understood' (Rampley 2010). The implication of this review comment is not only that a play can beneficially raise awareness, but also that such a process is necessary in the face of negative stereotyping. On the train back from the meeting, I read a review of Kevin Spacey's *Richard III* at the Old Vic, which contains this: 'Wearing his deformity like an extra limb, Spacey revels in Richard's enormous ego as he confides in the audience and has great fun with Richard's mordant nihilism' (Lougher 2011).

The medieval-renaissance 'vice' of interpreting outward deformity as a sign of inner corruption is turned, thanks both to Shakespeare and the actor-director, into a theatrical virtue. I find myself wondering whether my response to Richard's disability differs between reading the play and seeing it in the theatre. I begin to research tickets and times but rapidly discover that it is a sell-out! In the car on the way home, I switch on the radio and hear *Pinball Wizard* by The Who, and register with additional clarity the lyrics, which describe the transformation of the 'deaf, dumb and blind kid' who 'stands like a statue, becomes part of the machine'. I become acutely aware of the 'supercrip' stereotype, and wonder whether a young reader/listener/viewer would tend to read this differently from someone older.

Fireworks

A brief examination of this play and some of its reviews will serve as a further introduction to the discussion. There are four characters in Valerie Jack's play *Fireworks*. Katie suffers from Prader-Willi syndrome, two results of which are that there has to be a combination lock on the fridge, and that she can be disarmingly frank in what she says. As she approaches her sixteenth birthday on 5 November, we become acutely aware of not only the particular symptoms of her syndrome, but also the difficulties all teenagers face in moving from childhood to adulthood. She lives with her parents; mother Clare, who is 34 years old, and bus driver father Danny, who is 8 years older. The fourth character is the Cambridge-educated documentary film-maker Alex, who sets out to be an unobtrusive 'fly on the wall' film-maker, but in fact becomes a participant and causes 'fireworks' in terms of all of their personal relationships. There is a fascinating implication here for the present discussion that the notion of a totally objective portrayal is probably a false grail, an unhelpful and impossible target.

Consider this extract from a contemporary review:

> I can report that *Fireworks* is entirely compelling and the acting absolutely convincing. It manages to be many things at once: an exploration of a particular medical condition (Prader-Willi Syndrome), a critique of 'reality TV' and a sustained meditation both on long term relationships – their stresses and strengths – and on the divisive and redemptive aspects of parenthood. Valerie's ear for dialogue is acute and my colleague Patrick Milton, who has worked in the area of special needs, found the character of Katie absolutely credible. Bethan Knight managed to generate in the audience the see-saw emotional effect she had on her parents, affection and frustration jockeying for position. She avoided all sentimentality in her playing: a major achievement. We slowly realise both that she is the one most in control and that the other three characters have 'special needs' too, only some of which will be satisfied.
>
> (Martin 2010)

Notice that the play is praised both for an authentic 'absolutely credible' portrayal of a particular medical condition and also for its sense that all the characters 'have "special needs" too'. Perhaps this is what much art attempts to do: to convey a recognisable texture of the world as well as a wider, more general significance. More specifically in this case, it seems that the portrayal of the syndrome is sympathetic both in the particularities of the case and also in locating the girl in a social context in which she is, in some sense, no more disabled than anyone else. The reviewer also emphasises that the play passes comment on the impact of 'reality TV'. This reminds us that all representations, especially perhaps those that lay claim to aspects of realism, merit analysis based on their language and conventions. To judge from the above accounts of the play, it would seem that *Fireworks* can bear different readings and avoids mere stereotyping of the medical condition. The play does not contribute to damaging mythology, but erodes and subverts it.

Metaphor and metonymy

In a previous discussion of this issue (Warner 2011), I invoked the basic semiotic concepts of metaphor and metonymy in order to examine a small number of plays. I was concerned to explore the different readings that plays, like other literature, may bear. It is often remarked that language, like other sign systems, operates on a spectrum between metaphor, which is the perception of similarity, and metonymy, which is the perception of a part representing a larger part or whole. Both metaphor and metonymy are, in a sense, the detection of something wider or deeper beneath, as it were, the sign. But metaphor implies a link being made with something other, a figurative likeness, a sense of symbolism, whereas metonymy entails wider linkage with the same or a similar field.

Chandler (2001) quotes Jakobson in asserting that these linked concepts are fundamental to meaning-making, and points out that David Lodge's novel *Nice Work* is a source of entertaining and clear illustration in the celebrated Silk Cut episode of the difference between them: 'In metaphor you substitute something *like* the thing you mean for the thing itself, whereas in metonymy you substitute some attribute or cause or effect of the thing for the thing itself' (Lodge 1989: 222).

To use a familiar example, 'I wandered lonely' could be taken to be metonymic of a bigger picture of a person's behaviour and mental state; 'I wandered lonely as a cloud' adds to this by making an explicit metaphorical, figurative reference. The distinction may not be absolute. Discussions of the moving image make the point that whatever is in shot in a film or television programme relies for its meaning on the viewer's sense of the bigger world beyond and around, and is, in this sense, metonymic. Nevertheless, it can also be argued that film may more likely tend towards the metaphoric or symbolic. An example often given for metonymy is 'the Crown' as a metonym of the Queen or royalty.

Yet, it seems to make perfect sense to say that 'crown' is a symbol of royalty. It is perhaps a matter of emphasis rather than binary opposition. The character of Katie in *Fireworks* can, according to the review, which found the portrayal 'credible', be seen as a metonym of the condition from which she suffers. She is perhaps more metaphorical when considered as indicating the 'special needs' of the others.

Two set texts

It is possible to see these different emphases in commentaries on plays that have been studied in schools. The questions arise, then: how do and should school students respond to them? What are the breadth and nature of interpretation that we might expect?

William Gibson's *The Miracle Worker* (1960) concerns Helen Keller, who is known for overcoming extreme disability. Illness in early childhood rendered her deaf and bereft of verbal language. She first appears in the play as troubled and violent. The play goes on to portray the patience of her teacher, Annie Sullivan, in gradually finding ways to overcome the challenges she faced. Having learnt how to communicate, in adulthood Keller became an internationally famous activist. The play on the page is often a mass of stage directions, in which touch and movement constitute the only language that is viable. It is likely that, in the theatre, the audience will imaginatively partake in the particularities of this acute case. It is something of a surprise to note that Gibson himself argued that, in a sense, the play is not really about Helen's impairments but, 'an epic story of the young against the old; a metaphor of growing up and learning what the reality of life is'.[1] Similarly, 'Everyone, however, has challenges', says a study guide to the play.[2] Is this a helpful pedagogical invitation to broaden interpretation, or an unhelpful reinforcement of a stereotypical view of disability? Might it be argued that the metonymic interpretation, a case study of impairment and its treatment, is somehow inferior to the metaphoric, human-condition view? These and other questions of interpretation indicate that classroom study of the play is unlikely to consist merely in reinforcing stereotypes.

In Pinter's *The Caretaker* (1960), a play that has been studied in a variety of syllabuses in the UK over the last four decades, the psychology and motivation of all three characters remain enigmatic, but it does seem as though Aston is different from the other two and suffers from a particular yet unspecified condition. One sign of this is the disengaged, inconsequential way in which he speaks; another, his reiterated and apparently ineffective tinkering with plug and toaster. But most memorable of all is his extraordinary long speech that concludes the second act; a speech that is virtually a soliloquy since the lights are gradually dimmed; a speech that is delivered with many false starts and hesitations, and that relives a cruel episode of electric shock treatment forced upon him against his will: 'pincers on my skull'. Martin Esslin sees *The Caretaker* as operating both metaphorically and metonymically, arguing that there is a 'complete synthesis' (Esslin 2000: 100) between realism and metaphor in this play, and considers the possibility that Aston's quasi-medical treatment may be seen, in keeping with Pinter's avowed politics, as symbolic of the way the state treats the artist.

It is important to reflect on whether different media, or we could say different circumstances of consumption, might affect our interpretations. There is probably in the theatre a tendency to respond as it were literally, that is to say metonymically, to scenes of cruelty. One thinks of the blinding of Gloucester in *King Lear*, and the notoriety of scenes in Edward Bond's *Saved* and Sarah Kane's *Blasted*. It needs reflection outside the auditorium, or a substantial amount of Brechtian distancing, to consider what the cruelty might symbolise. For Lockett, the understanding of metaphor is more likely to accompany the kind of close reading associated with poetry and prose. In his view, plays have 'extra semiotic channels' (Lockett 2010: 403) that make metaphorical reading less likely. This may be true of the experience of a play in the theatre. Whether this is equally true of the experience of the play in classroom discussion is an interesting matter for further research. Alexander claims that 'apprehension of metaphor may be more a matter of intuition and imagination than of rational thought' (Alexander 2011: 266), but the reverse may be true where plays are concerned. Perhaps, when a play is read on the page, and discussed in the classroom, symbolic interpretations, such as Esslin's reading of *The Caretaker* above, come to the fore. Intuition and imagination help us to read the performance, in a play as in a film or a television drama, but it is rational reflection that opens out other readings.

In a broad and illuminating investigation of different kinds of audiences, Kennedy offers helpful insights to support the present discussion. He draws a comparison between audiences and tourists: both are willing strangers who are encouraged to look closely and see below surface features, to see 'not the authenticity but the metonym' (Kennedy 2009: 96). Thus, he argues that 'everything to do with spectators in the theatre . . . can be related to a problem in semiotics' (ibid.: 12) and recognises that, 'in standard semiotic analysis the meaning of a performance occurs in the mind of (a) spectator' (ibid.: 95). He goes on to develop a notion of mind in which the individual and psychological is not entirely to be accounted for in socially constructed terms. While it is true that interpretation is a mental activity and minds are shaped by societal attitudes, human individuality and the richness of the theatrical sign also play their parts. Kennedy's idea is important for educators since it holds out the possibility of different readings of a text, and of teaching and learning. This brings us back to our two important focuses, outlined at the start: In what ways can the field of disability studies alert us about portrayals of people with disability, and what are the implications for teachers of the kinds of meaning-making we are discussing?

Disability studies

The social constructionist view of disability has shown us that 'disability' is a reflection on society rather than the individual; social arrangements rather than individual impairments are what disable people. A key part of society in this respect is those portrayals of people with disability. Patterns of misrepresentation of people with disability lead to patterns of discrimination and oppression. One such pattern of misrepresentation is the implication that categories of impairment are somehow natural or essential, rather than located in and generated by particular historical and social circumstances. This is a point made, for example, by Abberley in discussing 'historically specific categories of "disabled people"' (Abberley 1987: 19), and by Holmes (2001) in discussing the portrayals of physical impairment in Victorian melodrama.

Another, perhaps more pervasive, pattern is that of stereotyping. Iyer (2007), for example, points out the tendency in fiction to portray characters with mental impairments as animal-like. Three categories of disability stereotype in the moving image are identified by Cumberbatch and Negrine (1992): the criminal, the subhuman, and the powerless or pathetic character. Barnes (1992) finds 11 such stereotypes. The influential work of Biklen and Bogdan (1977) suggests 10 common media stereotypes of people with disabilities and sets out to give examples of each category. These examples are variably convincing: *Ironside* (the wheelchair-using TV detective) would seem to be a good example of the 'supercrip' stereotype, but it is less convincing to suggest that Lennie in Steinbeck's novel *Of Mice and Men* is simply an example of a 'Person with a disability as the object of violence' (ibid.: 60–1). Similarly, Rubin and Watson (1987) make tantalising reference to Clark's *Whose Life is it Anyway?* (1978) when they say that this play 'clearly analyzes' the 'issue' of a 'Person with a disability as incapable of fully participating in everyday life' (ibid.: 61). While it is clear that Ken feels that he is incapable of participating in life, the play's analysis is arguably of the legal, medical and ethical issues around the right to die.

A particular charge is that metaphor in portrayals of impairment is destructive. Sandahl (1999) argues that there are parallels between metaphors of femaleness and freakishness in some cultural products, which may also have a negative impact on spectators. This echoes a broader concern that metaphorical use of disabled terms such as 'blind rage', 'deaf to . . .' and 'train strike cripples . . .' may reinforce negative public and personal views of people with disabilities (Power 2007). Roper (2003) argues that such portrayals tend to create a metaphorical reading of disability by trading on a sense of both voyeurism and unease in the audience. Iyer similarly suggests that, 'symbolic qualities assume centre stage and displace the human figures' (Iyer 2007: 131), while Hartnett claims that, 'Disabled characters . . . are over-simplified and used not for their complexity as people but for their easily identifiable impairment which is exploited by scriptwriters for dramatic effect, for emotional appeal or for blatant symbolism' (Hartnett 2000: 21). I wonder about 'blatant symbolism'. Would it be somehow better if the symbolism were covert to the point of invisibility? Presumably, playwrights, like other creative artists, aim for symbolism that is subtle rather than blatant. Perhaps symbolism is inevitable; all language, like all signs, moves back and forth along a spectrum of metonymy and metaphor.

Literature teaching

Literature teachers do not set out to reinforce stereotypes, nor are they likely to believe that the texts they teach set out to. In their classroom work, teachers, in encouraging a polysemic view of works of art, tend to militate against the very notion of stereotyping. This is a key pedagogical issue. English teachers will tell you that they are concerned with extending their students' range of interpretations of texts and promoting personal response, and that this aim is consonant with the kinds of assessment their students face at the end of the course. For example, the first of four GCSE English Literature Assessment Objectives is: 'Respond to texts critically and imaginatively; select and evaluate relevant textual detail to illustrate and support interpretations.'[3]

The pedagogical aspiration to help students towards personal response to texts is not without its critics. The apparent consonance of open classroom discussion and friendly-sounding examination questions is challenged by Nightingale, who examines what he calls 'the ideology of personal response' (Nightingale 2011: 147) and wonders whether there might be a tension for older students between genuinely personal and taught critical responses when the actual assessments arrive. The research of Hennessy and McNamara similarly suggests that students find studying literature for an exam is a 'divergent learning' experience (Hennessy and McNamara 2011: 214) from other literature work that they do. Yandell expresses concern about the unequal power relationships at work, especially in examinations, and suggests that personal response 'is a concept that . . . has tended to promise more liberality . . . than it has delivered' (Yandell 2008: 73). Taylor (2011) demonstrates that students' responses to texts are, or ought to be, dialogic in both an interpersonal and an intrapersonal sense for meaning-making to take place; a teacher (or an exam paper) asking an apparently open question may only be half the battle.

Teachers nevertheless aim high, and their students mostly do respond thoughtfully and deeply to the literature they study. Although, according to Goodwyn, teachers feel that the responses of students to literature have been shifted by the assessment regime away from the 'personal' and towards the 'analytical' and 'formal' (Goodwyn 2011: 129), he nevertheless offers hope: 'The findings of . . . two large-scale surveys are clear that English teachers are seeking to offer their students an authentic engagement in literature where assessment promotes and enables a personal response' (ibid.: 133).

And such authentic engagement may be able to counteract the stereotypical. For example, Hatton argues that 'fictional role-taking can counteract mental health stereotypes' (Hatton 2009: 92). It seems that an enlightened and far from negatively stereotyped representation of disability is being achieved in children's literature (Rushby-Smith 2009). It is possible that combating stereotyped attitudes may transfer from one field to another (Kawakami *et al.* 2000). There is thus a pedagogical imperative for teacher trainers: 'Training English teachers with the tools to interrupt normative discourses might include guidance in how to frame questions that lead to self, text and world connections that are truly critical' (Shieble 2010: 383).

Whose Life is it Anyway?

So what do school students actually say about a play they have studied? When they have undergone a course of study on a set text, and have thought about the play from all angles, what are the characteristics of their considered responses? In order to attempt an answer, I will focus on Brian Clark's play *Whose Life is it Anyway?* This was first written for television but became a successful stage play in 1978, with Tom Conti in the central role. It was famously revived in 2005 starring Kim Cattrall, of *Sex and the City* fame. The play has often been studied in schools; it has been an examination set text in the UK, and is currently a set text for the International GCSE. There may be a number of reasons why this play has been selected for study: length and number of characters are manageable, it foregrounds an issue (about the right to die) worthy of debate, and its scenes generate a range of emotional response, including amusement, anger and pathos. The Introduction to a popular school edition tells us: 'The play centres around Ken Harrison's determination to exercise a choice over his own life or death. Opposing him are the forces of medical bureaucracy' (Speakman 1989: vii).

The protagonist has been paralysed from the neck down after an accident. He is, or was, a sculptor. School students are undoubtedly engaged by the strong characterisation and the pointed 'issue' in the play. Ken himself berates the 'so-called professionalism' of those treating and dealing with him. There is a striking tension between his immobility and his vivacious wit. It is to be expected that audiences, whether or not school students, will see the play as a criticism of some aspects of the caring professions; that is to say, they are likely to see the play metonymically. But the extraordinary physical fact of the suspended body, fixed and isolated on stage, might evoke comparison with a number of Beckett's plays and suggests some sort of portrayal of the human condition. The two perspectives or emphases can be seen in comments from reviewers of the Cattrall production: first, 'Clark's script is stronger on debate than deep feeling' (Spencer 2005), in which 'debate' implies the play's critique of the healthcare and other professionals; and, second, 'Imagine the horror of a universe where an opt-out clause was absolutely impossible' (Taylor 2005), which takes a broader, metaphorical, human-condition view.

In an earlier discussion (Warner 2011), I analysed a very small sample of examination scripts to try to obtain some sense of what school students who had studied the play were saying about it when given the impetus to consider it seriously and at some length. I found that student responses to Ken could be broadly placed in three categories, which I called *hero*, *pathos* and *critique*. That is to say, some responses were centred on admiration for Ken, others on sympathy and pity for him, and yet others on a sense that the play might be expressing some criticisms of the medical and perhaps legal professions via their dealings with him.

An account of a much larger sample of students' work in examinations can be gained from reports on examination boards' websites. For example, the reports on OCR's GCSE paper 2441 from 2007–11, both January and June sessions, include detailed reference to answers on *Whose Life is it Anyway?*[4] For this examination, students study just one play. Exactly how many students studied this play is not made explicit, but it is often said in the reports to have been a popular choice, and the total annual candidature in this period ran into the tens of thousands. These reports are intended to be helpful to teachers, but may also offer an indication of what students think and feel about Ken, albeit filtered through the lessons they had and the exam questions that were set, and indeed the session-on-session insistencies of the principal examiner who wrote the reports. I have not subjected these reports to rigorous analysis but a cursory reading reveals that the hero/pathos/critique pattern is evident. For example, the examiner includes the following common responses which read Ken as a 'hero', describing him as 'such an intelligent, witty, and articulate character', noting his 'fascinating and memorable qualities', and identifying a point at which Ken is 'beginning to take control of his destiny'. Pathetic readings focus on 'the tragedy of Ken's predicament', 'Ken's frustration and sense of despair', and his 'angry death-wish'. And students offer 'critiques' that center on 'the irony of a Consultant Psychiatrist destroying Ken's mind' and 'Mrs Boyle's unwitting exacerbation of Ken's suffering' and that express 'reservations about the Valium prescription'.

It must be remembered that these remarks are not by the students themselves, but are summaries composed by an adult assessor. They nevertheless indicate that all three perspectives on this character have been articulately expressed.

Another indication of possible student responses and of ways in which those responses might be channelled or inflected comes from the exam board's support material. For example, this is from a sample response that models an answer to an empathic question, asking the candidate to imagine that he/she is Dr Scott, one of the medical professionals treating Ken:

> Ken is truly a fantastic man with a brilliant mind, it would be such a shame to put all that skill to a rest. But when I come to see him day in and day out, and I see him just lying there, I can't help but feel for him. When he isn't talking, joking or completely overstepping the mark, he looks dead anyway. He's motionless, unable to move and stripped of his

> dignity for the fact of he can't even clean himself. He's lost everything, his arms, legs, whole body in fact. He's even lost out on love. I stand there and think how brave he is and question how he can even manage to smile. I would like to sometimes praise him but dare not for the chance of offending him.[5]

The marking notes given for this answer do not suggest very high marks, but the answer nevertheless embodies a good deal of knowledge plus a sensitive response. In particular, the condensation and amalgamation of ideas in the answer is noteworthy, the blending of 'hero' ('a fantastic man with a brilliant mind') and 'pathos' ('stripped of his dignity') in a coherent voice. Another inflection of student responses might be syllabus support material. That provided by Cooper suggests an encouragement to consider different views of Ken: 'There is a great deal of scope for personal response here' (Cooper 2005: Activity 8). Cooper's suggestion of three key themes in the play (dignity of choice, professionalism and desire) might be taken to be constraining. But, equally, it promotes a teaching agenda that at once focuses on the individual and also raises wider human dilemmas and issues. The impression of students' work on this play derived from what they are taught and what they say in exams is that stereotyping is being challenged rather than reinforced.

Conclusion

Some evidence of what students actually say in class about plays they are studying that involve characters with disabilities would undoubtedly be illuminating, as would a more rigorous analysis of their writing; further research may lead to firmer conclusions. Nevertheless, Kennedy suggests that investigating audience response is venturing on to 'intellectual quicksand' (Kennedy 2009: 3). For that reason, a judicious conclusion to my discussion consists of questions. Is 'deaf to the cries of . . .' a damaging metaphor? Is the idea that Katie symbolises the 'special needs' of the others also damaging? Damaging to whom? Can young people respond to what they see and hear on different planes, and hold in their minds both metonymic and metaphorical interpretations? Perhaps the view that portrayals of characters with disabilities reinforce prejudice is a damaging myth in itself.

Notes

1 Quoted in Bloomsburg Theater Ensemble study guide to the play, available at www.bte.org/uploads/pdfs/MW_StudyGuide.pdf (accessed 10 October 2011).
2 Available at www.teachervision.fen.com/biography/resource/9357.html (accessed 10 October 2011).
3 See, for example, www.ocr.org.uk/download/kd/ocr_31049_kd_gcse_2010_spec.pdf (accessed 30 April 2012).

4 Available at www.ocr.org.uk/qualifications/type/gcse_emi/english/english_lit/documents/index.html (accessed 20 October 2011).
5 'Exemplar Response 6', available at http://community.ocr.org.uk/core/community/public/download_file?rid=1045 (accessed 20 October 2011).

Chapter 4

The dramatic symbolism of disability

Finding a voice

Bertolt Brecht's masterpiece of epic theatre *Mother Courage and Her Children* (1939) could be discussed at length in terms of what it symbolises. Written in rapid response to Germany's invasion of Poland at the start of the Second World War, Brecht creates a distance from the immediate situation by setting his play in the Thirty Years War. Using time as an alienating device in this way at once gives the play a metaphorical value, suggesting that the two wars share a number of characteristics, and a metonymic value in that the protagonist's story is representative of the experience of many. In the context of this discussion, though, the character of most interest is Mother Courage's daughter Kattrin. We are told that a soldier stuck something in Kattrin's mouth when she was young and that she has been mute ever since. Whether she is medically unable to speak because of some kind of physical damage, or her silence is the result of psychological trauma, is irrelevant in the context of the play. The point is that she initially appears to be an innocent victim and helpless witness of war. As the play develops, Kattrin's kindness and maternal instincts may be seen as something of a counter to her mother's seemingly ruthless exploitation of the war for capital gain. The war is Mother Courage's livelihood and, as such, she has no yearning for its end. Conversely, for Kattrin, the war is an unassailable barrier to her fulfilment: her mother has assured her that only after it is over will she find a husband and have children of her own. In scene 6, the Chaplain is asked his views on peace. He proclaims that even in war there are islands of peace, and that war, like love, will always find a way. His words encourage Mother Courage to get more supplies in and she sends Kattrin, now distraught at the thought of the war continuing, to buy them. When Kattrin returns at the end of the scene, she has been attacked and will now be disfigured for life, the implication being that even after the war she will not find a husband and will therefore remain a victim. At the end of the play, however, Kattrin finds a voice of sorts when she climbs on to a roof and beats a drum in order to alert the people of Halle to an impending attack so that they may save their children. Her actions speak louder than any words, and she pays the ultimate price for becoming actively involved in the war.

Abbs (1994) has argued that the creation of symbols lies at the heart of artistic endeavour, while an understanding of the semiotics of theatre leads us to appreciate that a symbol does not simply represent something other than itself but *means* more than what it is (Esslin 1987). That the meaning is embodied in the work refutes attempts to divorce the meaning from the work (Reid 2004). Thus, to reduce Kattrin's symbolic meaning to the aphoristic would be a gross disservice to Brecht's artistic creation. Nonetheless, the character of Kattrin may serve as a useful touchstone for a discussion regarding the symbolic value of disabled characters in plays and what we learn from their presence. If we read Kattrin as a metaphor, we may conclude that she stands for kindness and hope in a world of cruelty and desperation; generosity and chastity in a world where everything may be sold or stolen; care and innocence in a world that is cynical and corrupt. As a metonym, she substitutes for all those disabled, disfigured and dispossessed by war; those who have lost their childhood to abusive adults; those who speak out when it would be safer for them to stay silent. What is apparent in this analysis is that metaphor can be seen as sliding into metonymy on a kind of continuum.

Figuratively, Kattrin's loss of voice may also be considered a trope; that is, a recurrent theme that acquires a significance as a result of the frequency of its appearance. For example, in Andrew Payne's *Shut Up* (2006) the protagonist, Dexter, stops speaking because the adults in his world either have nothing sincere to communicate to him (for example, his mother and the media) or, in the case of his father and teacher, seem to see violence as the only effective medium of communication. Similarly, in *Ballerina* (1984), Malin best expresses herself through dance as did her mother, Edith, an ex-ballerina. Malin's silence and relationships with various inanimate objects such as an old tree called Mr Carl and a rock named Mrs Ludovica reflect Edith's inability to cope in the real world and accept her daughter's life as something other than a fairy tale:

Edith: An alert little girl said to her mother: 'I'm out of tune too, Mummy.'
(Pause)
So intelligent. So deliberate. The Sleeping Beauty was awake. It only lasted four seconds. She looked at me. She saw herself. And her eyes were full of sorrow . . . She'll come again, I know, and I'll be prepared.

Even in plays that seek to explore disability in a non-figurative way, one might still arrive at an interpretation that ascribes a symbolic value where none may have been intended by the playwright. Thus, in *The Miracle Worker*, Helen Keller's disability, while in actuality a result of childhood illness, could be seen as being exacerbated by her parents' social situation. A comfortable white family living in the Southern States, they could afford to indulge their daughter, though doing so was not seen as being in her best interest by her teacher, the visually impaired daughter of poor Irish immigrants, Annie Sullivan. The key to a better, independent life in Annie's philosophy was language:

Annie: . . . she has to learn that everything has its name! That words can be her eyes, to everything in the world outside her, and inside too, what is she without words? With them she can think, have ideas, be reached, there's not a thought or fact in the world that can't be hers.

Sullivan's refusal to kowtow to her employers or their wilful child in favour of taking up the gauntlet of instilling in the child a sense of self-worth and self-reliance through learning how to communicate may be considered to symbolise the ability to use language as an antidote to disability, dependence and social inequality.

Sex, sight and insight

Perhaps the oldest and cruellest trope in the archives of fiction is the use of blindness as a punishment for sin. Oedipus is blinded as a punishment for incest, Shakespeare's Gloucester for adultery. The representation of the disability often goes hand in hand, with the act of blinding being regarded as a kind of purification rite, an act that wipes the slate clean and transforms human failing into purity and goodness. In *Oedipus Rex* and *King Lear*, the act of blinding is explicit and violent and mirrors other references to blindness in the plays. Tieresias, while blind in actuality, sees the past, present and future as Oedipus cannot. Gloucester, like Lear, is blind to the real nature of his offspring.

Maurice Maeterlinck's *The Blind* employs blindness as a stereotypical symbol of helplessness that latter day audiences may find unacceptable. The play is about a group of blind people who have been taken out of the institution in which they live for the day by a priest who they obviously trust, but who inexplicably abandons them. Peter White (2008), a journalist who is himself blind, recounts how actor Gerard McDermott advised people not to go and watch a 2008 production of the play with their disability-activist hats on: 'You're likely to take offence – hopefully.' White, though, was a little more sympathetic, noting that, at the time of writing, seeing blindness as symbolic of the human condition would not have been conceived of as offensive: 'the bulk of us (are) led astray, deceived, puzzled and abandoned by powerful political establishments. He's not talking about blind people, really: he's talking about the disempowered.'

Nonetheless, in his paper 'Blindness: is literature against us?', Kenneth Jernigan (1974) objects to the characters being portrayed as sightless purely in order to make a philosophical point, not least because what emerges on the stage is 'a ridiculous tableau of groping, groaning, and grasping at the air'.

In her critical review of representations of disability in Victorian melodrama, Holmes (2001) notes how blindness was popularly conceived of as being linked to sex, most especially of the illicit variety. Medically, blindness could occur as a direct result of inherited venereal disease, or indirectly as babies were born through infected birth canals. The connection between blindness and sex in this manifestation of the sins of the Father being visited upon the child was not just confined to melodrama, as witness Ibsen's *Ghosts*. Indeed, it would seem that the ghost of Victorian sanctimony has continued to haunt the stage through the twentieth century to the present day in the guise of the symbolism of disability. *Ballerina*, for example, has certain similarities to *A Day in the Death of Joe Egg* in that Malin's condition is both the cause of tension between her parents and a lens through which the inadequacies of adult relationships may be examined. In fact, the reflection of adults' foibles and failures in children's disabilities appears to be quite a common feature, with disability serving as a trope for adults' emotional or moral instability. Joe's mother Sheila, for example, blames herself for her daughter's condition because she was promiscuous. In *Spoonface Steinberg*, the father is blamed for his daughter's condition because she fell off a chair and banged her head while her parents were arguing about his infidelity, while in Dennis Potter's *Brimstone and Treacle*, Pattie's vegetative state is the result of her being knocked down by a truck while running off after catching her father in flagrante delicto. Another Potter play commonly studied in English schools is *Blue Remembered Hills* in which the slow-witted Donald Duck is noted to have a mother of loose morals. While all of these plays offer quite sympathetic portrayals of disabled characters, what may be surmised from them is that disability is a punitive manifestation of some fundamental code of normality being broken. In a sort of human embodiment of pathetic fallacy, the protagonist is effectively de-humanised, or as Iyer (2007) suggests, displaced, by being reduced to a dramatic device, exactly the objection Jernigan pitted against *The Blind*.

Lee Hall's *Cooking With Elvis* links sex and disability in a rather different way. The 'Elvis' of the title is an Elvis impersonator who has been left brain damaged in a car accident following an argument with his wife in which she threatened to leave him. His wife, still quite young and missing a close relationship, has embarked on a number of brief sexual encounters notwithstanding the ever-present reminder of faithlessness:

> *Mam*: I'm still a young woman, Davey. I still want to laugh till it hurts and drink till I'm stupid and fuck till I'm numb and cry till I'm happy again, Davey, and be alive, I want to be alive. *(Pause)* But it's the silence. The silence.

Her latest affair is with a young baker called Stuart, who satisfies her sexual appetite but is nowhere near her intellectual level. Meanwhile, her daughter Jill is trying to cope with the situation by cooking for her father and herself, and consequently piling on weight. Although Jill is still only 14, this does not stop the apparently amoral and hedonistic Stuart having sex with her, with the encounter meeting some kind of need she has (at one point, she gets him to rub marmalade over his naked body). The one part of Dad that still apparently works is his sex drive. Noticing that he has an erection, Stuart starts to masturbate him. Is this charity? Altruism? Or self-concern masquerading as such?

Stuart: I know you must be thinking who's this bastard coming here seeing wor lass and the young un as well. But I never did it out of spite or nowt. I mean, I know I shouldn't have fucked the bairn. But she doesn't seem like a kid to me. I mean, in a way I thought I might be falling in love, you know. Sorry, me hand's getting a bit sore. And I just want you to know like, I don't usually mess about with blokes, like. I'm only doing this because you're a cripple. And I just want you to know. I mean, even though I've been fucking your wife and everything. I want you to know you have my utmost respect. I mean, I wouldn't be doing this if I didn't respect you. And they love you. And they're both yours, you know that. I've fucked it now. I've got nobody, me.

The association between Dad and Elvis may be read as symbolising exploitation in a number of ways. Before his accident, Dad was exploiting the image of Elvis, himself a damaged and dysfunctional soul, for, we assume, both personal gratification and financial reward. In his post-accident state, Dad's inability to respond is exploited by Mam, who can now openly conduct her extra-marital affairs without him intervening. He is exploited by Jill, who uses him as an uncomplaining partner in her culinary excesses. And he is exploited by Stuart, who, while masturbating him, is in effect masturbating his own conscience. Dad's disability becomes, in effect, a metaphor for the other characters' dysfunctionality.

The naturalism of what is, in one part, a domestic farce and, in another, quite a sordid take on a soap opera is disrupted by Dad/Elvis intermittently coming to life to sing or make increasingly paranoid speeches on drugs, philosophy, politics and sodomy. The dark epilogue leads us to believe that Jill has disposed of the problem of what to do with Stuart by cooking him, and the play ends with a parody of Puck's speech at the end of *A Midsummer Night's Dream*:

Dad: Remember that all the world's a stage and all of you good people in it are merely players and this vast and shimmering world of ours is all love and all light. And there are no crippled Elvises, no sad mams or Burger Kings, no fat girls or cake-makers, there are only people, human beings who love and hope and fear.

The truth is, of course, that there are sad mums and fat girls and people who experience more hope and fear than love. That it takes the perverse logic of a crippled Elvis to tell us this reinforces the notion that we are all disabled in some way or another. The value of such an insight is questionable, not least because it shifts the focus away from the disabled characters themselves and so away from the issue of disability. The number of plays that appear to have the specific intention of exploring disability is limited. *The Miracle Worker* and *Graham, the World's Fastest Blind Man* have an element of the documentary to them, being concerned with real people and, as such, largely resist interpretation of symbolic value. Plays written for young people such as *Stronger than Superman*, *Strugglers* and *Lives Worth Living* similarly focus specifically on disability as an issue in ways that do not present disability as a symbol. Conversely, plays such as *The Elephant Man*, *Whose Life is it Anyway?*, *Flowers for Algernon*, *Effie's Burning*, *Find Me*, *Tribes* and indeed *Of Mice and Men* may all be read as comments on the failure of others to accept or deal effectively with disability, thus implying once more that we are all in some way disabled. Hence, when an audience encounters the line in *4.48 Psychosis* that reads:

> We are anathema
> The pariahs of reason

they might ask who are the 'we' that is being referred to here: People such as Sarah Kane who remind the rest of us of our brutality? Or all of us?

The objection to the conclusion that 'we' are all somehow disabled is that it equates degree with type. The inference is that inability and disability are synonymous. Thus, someone who has some emotional, intellectual, social or political difficulty with accepting the disability of others is placed on the same scale as those who are physically or mentally disabled. This is not to say that these are 'bad' plays. By many other criteria, they are excellent pieces of writing that can be realised as powerful pieces of theatre. By way of an example of how a character can be portrayed as disabled in order to serve the drama through symbolism, one might consider Tennessee Williams' *The Glass Menagerie*.

Amanda Wingfield is something of an archetypal Williams' female character in that she is a faded Southern belle whose existence is more reliant on memories and fanciful hopes for her daughter than any capacity to deal with everyday realities. Within the context of a study of plays with disabled characters, she has links with Edith in *Ballerina* and Beatrice in *The Effect of Gamma Rays on Man in the Moon Marigolds*, both of whom similarly struggle to cope effectively with their disabled daughters. Amanda's daughter Laura is portrayed as being physically and emotionally 'crippled'; a more tangible manifestation perhaps of her own vulnerability and ineptitude. Laura's physical condition is certainly not grossly severe, however:

Amanda: Why, you're not crippled, you just have a slight defect – hardly noticeable, even!

Jim: You dropped out of school, you gave up an education because of a clump, which as far as I know was practically non-existent! A little physical defect is what you have. Hardly noticeable even.

Similarly, her 'mental' condition is more one of sensitivity and reclusivity than anything medical. Her brother Tom says that she is different from other girls as she is 'terribly shy and lives in a world of her own and those things make her seem a little peculiar to people outside the house', yet he himself variously escapes humdrum reality by burying himself in the world of literature or cheap movies. Like his father, he eventually runs away by fleeing, symbolically, down the fire escape as 'The bastard son of a bastard!' who 'fell in love with long distances'. The play is rich in symbolism. Tom and Amanda are unable to accept or cope with aspects of their lives. Their inability is symbolised through and reflected in the lens of Laura's disability. Indeed, Tom is both a character in the play and its narrator who says that his friend Jim, a potential suitor for Laura, is the most realistic character in the drama:

Tom: But since I have a poet's weakness for symbols, I am using this character also as a symbol; he is the long delayed but always expected something that we live for.

In this, Jim is the antithesis of Laura, whose minor disabilities may be seen as the ever-present and ultimately accepted reality of life. One of the overt symbolic devices employed is that of pathetic fallacy. For example, Jim's arrival is accompanied by an oncoming summer storm that finally erupts into thunder at the very moment Laura physically stumbles, accentuating her disability and pre-empting Jim's revelation that he is already engaged.

What is being argued here is that, while plays such as *The Glass Menagerie* may justifiably be held to be great plays, when they are evaluated in terms of the symbolic inference they attach to disability, their message may be considered negative or trite.

Disability as a social critique

The use of disability as a metaphor for dysfunctionality is not, of course, limited to inter-personal relationships. As previously noted, *Of Mice and Men* can be interpreted as a critical comment on American capitalist society, while David Storey's *Home* reflects the demise of the British Empire and questions the validity of the 'traditional values' it held so dear. Tom Stoppard's *Every Good Boy Deserves Favour* makes a more overt use of disability as a means of symbolising that something is rotten in the state. In this case, mental illness is employed as a means of reflecting the lunacy of a totalitarian regime. In his introduction to the published version, Stoppard relates how he met Victor Fainberg in 1976. Fainberg had been arrested in Prague in 1968 during a peaceful demonstration against the soviet occupation and had been pronounced insane. Stoppard's idea for the play (which he had been asked to write by André Previn so that a full orchestra could be used as an integral part of the drama) concerned a lunatic triangle player, Ivanov, who thought he had an orchestra, sharing a cell with a political prisoner, Alexander. The play strongly makes the point that sanity is as much a matter of perspective as the rationality underlying a political system:

Doctor: We cannot make progress until we agree that there is no orchestra.
Ivanov: Or until we agree that there is.

Alexander: I have no symptoms, I have opinions.
Doctor: Your opinions are your symptoms. Your disease is dissent.

At the end of the play, the two prisoners are inspected by a colonel who asks the lunatic Ivanov, 'Would a Soviet doctor put a sane man into a lunatic asylum, in your opinion?' Ivanov, baffled, answers, 'I shouldn't think so'. The Colonel goes on to ask the dissident Alexander if he hears music, which of course he does not. Satisfied that the system has effectively cured the men of their conditions, the colonel, who obviously believes that when the wind is southerly he knows a hawk from a handsaw, orders them to be released. Although the target for Stoppard's satire was the soviet regime, to consider the relationship between sanity and insanity as a matter of perspective could be regarded as another manifestation of the dichotomy between the medical and social model of disability.

Like *Every Good Boy Deserves Favour*, Martin McDonagh's *The Pillowman* (2003) is also set in what appears to be a police state. In this instance, though, the play not only questions the morality of extreme state control, but links this to the effect of parental oppression and abuse, and the implications of this for freedom of expression. It is a dark comedy about a writer of short stories called Katurian. The stories Katurian writes are grisly and frequently rest on incidents of violence towards children. In this, they may be seen as lying in a tradition that includes works such as those by Heinrich Hoffman, for example *Der Stuwwelpeter* (*Shockheaded Peter*). Katurian is arrested because a number of child murders in the area seem to closely resemble his stories. Katurian has an older brother, Michal, who we are told has learning difficulties. We also learn through one of Katurian's stories called 'The writer and the writer's brother' that Katurian's disturbed imagination has derived from listening to his brother being abused by his parents when they were children. As a result of this, Katurian has killed the parents. However, there are ambiguities in the story and what Katurian says about it, suggesting that the line between fact and fiction is blurred and not to be trusted. Indeed, this is a theme for the whole play, as Katurian argues that what happens in stories cannot be held responsible for what happens in real life. Just as he writes stories, so the two detectives questioning him cannot be relied on to always tell the truth and the confessions they extract are not necessarily reliable.

While the play has overtones of Kafka's *The Trial* in its comments on the power of the state to curb freedom of expression, it also questions the moral integrity of the artist in his use and depiction of violence. Michal admits to having killed the children, claiming that his brother had told him to do it through his stories. However, Michal's own testimony cannot necessarily be trusted: 'the man said he was going to torture me, but I thought, "No way, boy, that'd hurt", so I just told him whatever he wanted to hear, and he was fine then.'

Katurian asks him to swear that he did not kill the children, but he later gives details about how he killed two of them and suggests that he has also murdered a third. In a Cimmerian parody of *Of Mice and Men*, Katurian suffocates Michal in order to protect him from the pain of execution. However, Michal could not be more different to Lennie. He is certainly not gentle or completely dependent on his brother. He has snooped around Katurian's room and read his stories for himself, then, if we believe him, committed what must be seen as pre-meditated murders: 'I was just testing out how far-fetched they were. 'Cos I always thought some of 'em were a bit far-fetched. *(Pause)* D'you know what? They ain't all that far-fetched.' Michal is a monstrous character:

> And I *didn't* enjoy killing those kids. It was irritating. It took ages. And I didn't *set out* to kill those kids. I just set out to chop the toes off one of them and to put razors down the throat of one of them.

Taken at face value, the depiction of Michal could be seen as perpetuating the Platonic notion that inner beauty is reflected in appearances. Such a myth underpins the depiction of a great many characters in literature and popular culture. In turn, it permeates popular thought and has been seen as the reason why some parents pull children away from disabled people or those with learning difficulties because of some perceived danger. Or is it the other way round? Do such figures in art derive from and continue to feed off bigotry and prejudice? Consider, for example, the way the Nazis portrayed children and adults with learning difficulties as an imminent danger and threat to humanity. On the other hand, Katurian's story regarding listening to his brother being abused as a part of an experiment designed to make him a writer could make us regard Michal as a victim of his actual upbringing or, in a more metaphorical sense, a victim of a political regime that favours some at the palpable expense of others.

It must be remembered, however, that *The Pillowman* is a story about stories and utilises literary and drama devices to create symbols in the same way that *The Glass Menagerie* does. Plays have an internal logic that need not relate to the world in a psychologically realistic way. Katurian and Michal are no more 'real' than Ashputel and her sisters, and Michal's sadism is no more real than the self-mutilation Ashputel's stepmother demands of her daughters, or indeed Ashputel herself commands at the end of that story. Rather, the play is about the oppressive abuse of power, whether by the individual or the state, and the cruelty that is invariably linked to that. What links Michal to Lennie is not his character per se, but that someone who apparently cares for him takes it upon himself to save him from what he perceives to be greater cruelty. Nonetheless, the net result of such a representation is that contemporary young audiences (and *The Pillowman* is very popular in schools) experience disability as symbolising something else, be it through metaphor or metonymy, in much the same way as Greek or Shakespearean audiences would have done. In this light, the argument that 'theatre reconnects perception and experience, thus perhaps healing wounds which are both personal (psychological) and social (political)' by 'placing actors and spectators in the same space as each other and permitting both to understand that the production of images in theatre is something in which they are collaborating' (Rideout 2009: 57–8) raises questions about how disability is actually portrayed on stage, by whom, and the extent to which audiences actually do collaborate in the production of such images. It is these questions that Simon Floodgate discusses in Chapter 5.

Chapter 5

Performing disability

Simon Floodgate

What do we wish to learn by 'performing disability'?

I could probably research factual information concerning specific impairments in a much more fruitful manner than portraying a disabled character. I would gain more actual information from books and the Internet. But by physically embodying a character, it is hoped that I will understand their experience to a greater extent. The premise is founded on the old axiom of the benefits of learning through doing. It conforms to the term adopted by the actor Harriet Walter articulated in the title of her book *Other People's Shoes*. I learn about the character and the experience of people such as the character by, literally, inhabiting their shoes and experiencing their situation by 'walking in their footsteps'.

This is the job of the actor. The actor assumes the mantle of another. They embody a character, a person other than themselves. In many cases (such as most mainstream Hollywood cinema), the audience is encouraged to 'buy into' the illusion created by the narrative and within this illusion the protagonist represents the spectator. The actor stands in for the spectator and lives through experiences on their behalf. Identification is such that it is an emotional imperative for the spectator that the character succeeds – they beat the 'baddie', or at least achieve a new and satisfactory state of equilibrium. The audience has been told a good story and they have had a cathartic experience

The actor's portrayal of a disabled character is encountered differently by the audience. While identification can still promote the spectator's desire for the protagonist to succeed, the portrayal promotes something else. The spectator is encouraged to become more understanding of the character's life experience, and hence more compassionate largely through sympathy than empathy.

I would argue that such a line of thought needs challenging. In the first instance, what is meant by a 'portrayal' of character? Does assuming the mantle of another require the actor to become the character or demonstrate it? The notion of disability requires analysis and, in so doing, exactly who is disabled becomes challenged. Subsequently, there is a need to appraise how playwrights have tended to represent disabled characters in dramatic literature.

As programme director for the Theatre Arts, Education & Deaf Studies BA at the University of Reading, I am, of necessity, conversant with the issues surrounding the portrayal of deaf characters and accessibility to these portrayals for a deaf-hearing integrated audience. Deafness can, of course, largely be an invisible impairment, though hearing aids and the increasing occurrence of cochlear implants can prove highly visible.

I would like to encompass the debate by referring to three plays in which deaf characters are represented – Mark Medford's *Children of a Lesser God* (1979), Kaite O'Reilly's *peeling* (2002) and *Tribes*, written by Nina Raine and premiered at the Royal Court Theatre in 2010. Each provide vastly differing representations of deaf characters and also alternative methods of accessibility for deaf-hearing integrated audiences – an issue that cannot, I believe, be ignored when considering the effectiveness of the actor's portrayal of a character. In the professional theatre, this raises ethical questions regarding casting and opportunities for disabled actors to access actor training and be auditioned on an equal basis.

The actor's job

> Suit the action to the word, the word to the action, with this special observance, that you o'erstep not the modesty of nature: for anything so o'erdone is from the purpose of playing, whose end, both at the first and now, was and is, to hold as 'twere the mirror up to nature: to show virtue her feature, scorn her own image, and the very age and body of the time his form and pressure.
>
> *Hamlet, Prince of Denmark*

What is the intention for an actor when attempting to achieve an accurate portrayal of a character in a play? Hamlet's advice to the players suggests achieving verisimilitude – reflecting no more or less than that which exists in reality. Yet, this is not as straightforward as it seems. Verisimilitude applies to something that *appears* to be true; it provides no more than a seeming truth.

Plato and Aristotle both analysed *mimesis*, discussing the notion that the actor imitated or *impersonated* reality. The Elizabethans believed the actor's job to be one of, what they called, personation. This described the way that the actor behaved as the imagined person come to life. The gestures, movement, look and sound of the actor needed to match that of the character exactly. The theories of Darwin and Freud impacted upon theatre makers of the later nineteenth century such that inner truth – psychologically motivated – determined authentication of character as well as an exact visual match.

Verisimilitude immediately presents the actor with a problem when attempting to depict a disabled character, the challenge being how to create an exact visual and/or aural match of a character's impairment when the actor has no such impairment. With the additional prop of a wheelchair, is the depiction of a wheelchair-using character achievable? Are the portrayals ruled out those that involve a missing limb or some physical impairment that is simply impossible to recreate even after the actor has attempted to act on his/her knees or tie an arm behind his/her back? Perhaps any character that does not involve the removal or alteration of a body part is achievable. Physical impairment is ruled out but hidden or invisible impairments, such as mental illness or deafness, are attainable?

The problem is one of ethics, not the skill or ambition of the actor.

The ethical problem lies in neither the actor nor the audience being encouraged to learn anything of real meaning about the disabled character. Such an attempt at verisimilitude is unlikely to lead to anything more than a completely superficial and possibly demeaning portrayal of character, not to mention the likelihood of accompanying physical discomfort for the actor.

A different methodology is required in order to re-focus the encounter between the disabled character and the actor. Let us reflect upon Hamlet's mirror. The argument for verisimilitude is related to the understanding of acting as creating an *imitation* of the character; in other words, as exact a physical and aural copy as possible. This is something that the actor can never achieve for the portrayal of any character. The spectator might marvel at the mimetic skills of the actor in many plays and films, but they never create a perfect copy. For example, there have been many representations in film, television and the theatre of Adolf Hitler. His physicality created an iconography that is instantly recognisable. However, with any visual representation of the character, it is impossible to state with any certainty which is the most accurate, as none of them can be an exact copy of the original, not least because the actor is always present – physically, mentally and emotionally – within the portrayal.

Approaches to playing a character

The method acting approach to playing a character calls for the portrayal to evolve from the actor being able to think and feel as the character. The actor's preparation for this depends upon recreating the character's life circumstances in order to 'lose' himself/herself and 'become' the character. This apparent transformation, however, can only ever provide clues to a character's portrayal. Daniel Day-Lewis was never fully going to be able to become Hawkeye in *Last of the Mohicans* by camping out in the woods for a couple of weeks nor grasp Gerry Conlon's torment for *In the Name of the Father* by submitting himself to interrogation in a prison cell. I suspect that Day-Lewis would claim that this was merely research to supplement the necessary use of imagination to portray the characters. By contrast, Robert De Niro attempted to create physical accuracy by putting on a huge amount of weight to play the post-boxing version of Jake La Motta in *Raging Bull*. These examples are from mainstream film, however, in which the relationship between actor and audience relies upon the actor's physical imitation of character. A more recent example involved

Dominic Cooper's portrayal of Uday Hussein in *The Devil's Double*. As *The Independent* noted: 'Thankfully, advances in make-up and Cooper's naturally swarthy looks meant that he did not have to get out the boot polish in order to play an Iraqi' (Aftah 2011).

In theatre, the audience is more conversant with a different set of conventions frequently employed to enable the suspension of their disbelief concerning what is visually presented to them. Demonstration of character is accepted more easily by the theatre spectator than the film-goer. Nonetheless, the desire for verisimilitude predominates even in the live auditorium.

The actor is always required to draw upon his/her imagination to create the character. The fully lived experience will never be possible nor, I suggest, desirable. Reappraising the role of the actor requires a different approach to character within theatre.

The word 'character' derives from the Greek *Kharakter*, meaning 'engraved mark' or 'symbol or imprint on the soul' (Harper 2001–12). This could be understood to mean the 'defining quality'. Within the argument of portrayal of character – becoming or demonstrating – it is the defining quality that the spectator needs to relate to. This quality is not, therefore, necessarily physical and indeed a 'truthful' representation of character might well address the psychological or emotional make-up of the character. As actress Harriet Walter has noted, 'It is more important for an actor to communicate a person's spirit than to laboriously mimic them' (Walter 2000: 210). Hence, the audience member is not required to resonate with the verisimilitude of the actor's portrayal, but something else – something beneath the surface. The defining quality of the character could be recognised via empathy, and the portrayal depends upon the actor's ability to empathise with the character. In achieving this, the actor, like a conduit, conveys the defining quality of the character to the audience, an idea reflected by the character of Beth in Nina Raine's *Tribes*: 'And the thing I'm finding, it's all about empathy.'

The challenge of empathy

Empathy, literally 'in-feeling', means the actor attempts to create for the audience a strong feeling of affinity with the character. The character is someone with whom they can form a link and who will 'stand in for them' as quests, trials and tribulations are undergone – a three-dimensional, live avatar as it were.

Character portrayal based upon verisimilitude creates a problem for many disabled audience members, as they are denied this empathy by rarely recognising the characters presented to them. The lack of disabled actors for disabled audience members to relate to is a matter for concern that I will discuss later in this chapter.

The experience portrayed is usually 'abled', and 'abled' is equated with normal. When disabled characters are represented, they conform to a range of 'stereotype assumptions', according to Colin Barnes (1992); for example, the pitiable or pathetic (Joseph 'John' Merrick in *The Elephant Man*), the sinister and/or evil (*Richard III*) or the super cripple (Christy Brown in *My Left Foot* or David Helfgott in *Shine*). These are just a few of the stereotypes that rely upon a medical model for understanding disability. This is one in which disability is about illness and suffering; about loss and abnormality that has to be, often courageously, endured. Feelings of fear, hatred and particularly sympathy are frequently evoked within the audience.

If the majority of representations of disabled people within plays is negative, then being able to achieve the dramatist's intentions and portray the character in any way accurately is counter-productive. Stereotypical assumptions are merely reinforced. The task of performing disability would be made simpler if there were more disabled characters written and if the ones that were did not conform to these stereotypical assumptions attributed to disabled people. The methodology required in order to re-focus the encounter between disabled character and non-disabled actor would also be dependent upon an alternative model to comprehend disability. The representation of disabled characters through the lens of the medical model of disability amounts to the character's defining quality always likely to be their impairment(s). This is surely what occurs in our everyday world on a habitual basis, and is precisely what needs to be challenged. If the intention of depicting disabled characters is to be able to empathise with someone who lives with a specific disability, then the project is doomed to failure because:

1. The full, lived experience can never be encapsulated.
2. The experience of the character will not be the same as anyone else living with the impairment. Everyone is subject to a range of varying sensory, cultural, social and political circumstances.

Can we ever truly understand the experience of any particular impairment when (surprise, surprise!) everyone, disabled or non-disabled, is an individual who lives a unique existence? Thus, the encounter between the disabled character and the actor needs to be a critical one. Such an enterprise is aided by drawing upon the social model of disability. Through this model, disability is regarded as the loss or limitation of opportunities to take part in normal life on an equal level due to physical and/or social barriers. Within this model society is where any problem lies not in the physical, sensory, intellectual or hidden functional limitation of the individual. It becomes desirable, indeed it becomes an imperative, for the actor to address the portrayal of a disabled character within this context.

If the search for clues within the play for the 'engraved mark' of the character is not purely aligned with the character's impairment, then new opportunities present themselves. The actor is not looking to 'become' the character but will more likely draw upon Brecht's *verfremdungseffekt*. Within this methodology, the actor looks to 'demonstrate' the character in order to address the social implications of loss or limitation of opportunity. This approach, depending upon the perceived intentions of the play, focuses the actor upon the intentions of the character as of greater concern than the mimicry referred to by Walter.

Relating representation to intention

With this last point, I am addressing the difference between plays that are written with the intention of specifically addressing disability, for example *Children of a Lesser God*, and those in which disabled characters appear but in which the disability is not the focus. In theatre, the latter is more likely when the terms of reference never even appear, for example *Richard III*, though this, as previously mentioned, creates a negative stereotype around disability. In many cases, one might not even be aware that disability is being represented, as may be the case with Caliban in *The Tempest* or of Büchner's Woyzeck. Indeed, this is where the restrictions of the contextual frame become contested, as will be seen later in an analysis of Nina Raine's play *Tribes*.

Under the terms of the social model of disability in which society is the one with the 'problem', then, the question of quite who is disabled becomes relevant. However, using the methodology of epic theatre, an expectation might be that the actor is able to represent any character on stage simply by placing a placard around their neck proclaiming who they are at any particular moment in the production. This is clearly a flippant and superficial approach to the ideas of Brecht, whose advocacy of the visibility of the actor within the character's decision-making is more sophisticated.

Brecht is famously remembered for the contradiction of his theory of epic theatre acting, with the immense portrayals of central characters such as Helene Weigel's Mother Courage and Charles Laughton's Galileo; performances lauded for the ability of the actors to create huge sympathy for the characters and their plight. The argument comes back to the non-disabled actor's definitive inability to portray a disabled character with a physical impairment that cannot be achieved without surgery. A play such as Kaite O'Reilly's *peeling* would simply be unplayable for most actors, as it specifically requires three female actors – one wheelchair user, one four feet tall and one deaf who uses sign language. At a stretch, the wheelchair user could be portrayed (bring in that prop). At another stretch, the deaf character could be portrayed though some British Sign Language (BSL) and Sign Supported English (SSE) would need to be learnt (but it is an invisible impairment). But, the four-foot actor? However, this is to miss the salient point. O'Reilly wrote this play with the distinct intention of providing opportunities for disabled professional actors – opportunities regrettably all too often lacking. The commission by Graeae Theatre Company falls firmly within their remit of creating opportunity for people with physical and sensory impairment. In relation to the discussion of empathy, then, work such as this is vital. It is vital that audiences are presented with disabled characters with whom they can empathise via positive representations of disabled people. In my own context of creating work for deaf-hearing integrated reception, I actually prefer the term, *spect-audience*, drawn from the definitions of 'audience' (Latin *audire*, meaning 'to hear') and 'spectator' (Latin *spectare*, meaning 'to behold').

Disabled actors performing disability

Doors have historically been closed for disabled actors. Disabled characters have either simply not been written or, as discussed, have conformed to negative stereotype assumptions. Disabled actors have been relegated to minor roles depicting the mad, bad or sad. Indeed, the lack of opportunity for disabled actors has extended to a lack of provision, or flexibility of provision, within schools for actor training. In 2006, Arts Council England attempted to address this by establishing the Into the Scene project to investigate inclusive performance training. The project highlighted issues concerned with assessment and curriculum within actor training organizations. In addition, notions of 'process' and 'excellence' were also problematic, as Alex Bulmer, the project co-ordinator, noted:

> I do not believe we should be talking about an excellent voice type or an excellent body type – in an educational environment we should not simply be looking for what are deemed to be current acceptable types within the profession.
>
> (Dacre and Bulmer 2009: 137)

Opportunities for disabled actors do exist, but they continue to be marginalised from central roles. The three plays I have mentioned with parts for deaf characters are obvious exceptions, though they approach issues of disability in completely different ways. *Children of a Lesser God* is well known, not least because it became an Oscar-winning film for the lead actress Marlee Matlin. Written in 1979, its licensing contract demanded that the three central deaf characters be portrayed by deaf actors. The three characters embodied different models of deafness on the continuum of hearing loss. Because the National Theatre of the Deaf in the US was well established and had created its own professional training programme, the production was served by a pool of trained deaf professional actors.

The play itself attempts to locate the protagonists' dilemmas within hearing societal attitudes as opposed to specifically linked to their impairment. However, it was written by a hearing playwright from a distinctly hearing perspective. It was clumsily communicated to a non-signing hearing mainstream audience via the oral repetition of signed lines. Because the central hearing character, James Leeds, was essentially the protagonist, the oral English became dominant and prioritised, thus disempowering the signing characters and consigning them to the negative stereotype of the angry or frustrated misunderstood others deserving of our pity. Though it could be argued that Medford intended to challenge the hearing perspective through the content of the play, its form certainly did not. This was further exacerbated in the film version. The way in which it was shot made much of the signing inaccessible to sign language users, making the film only fully accessible to a hearing audience.

Kate O'Reilly's *peeling* took an alternative approach. Addressing form as well as content, the play was written specifically for disabled female actors with specific physical and sensory impairments including a deaf character whose first language is BSL. It is impossible to sign BSL and voice at the same time, as BSL, a visual/spatial language, has a chronological syntax and does not conform to the syntax of its oral partner, English. The writer's intention in *peeling* was clearly to create positive opportunities for disabled actors within the professional theatre; a professional theatre that might usually rely upon the verisimilitude I referred to earlier. The intention was to focus upon the specific experience of particular impairments and for the articulation of the experience to come from the disabled characters themselves as opposed to a 'normal' co-protagonist or helper figure. Indeed, the fictional characters are members of a Greek chorus that would normally be the marginalised support to the protagonist. The play focuses upon their discussions backstage, foregrounding them in a similar way to Tom Stoppard's *Rosencrantz and Guildenstern are Dead*, in which the two minor characters in *Hamlet* become the central characters. Since the original Graeae production of *peeling*, it has rarely been re-staged because of the embedded requirements for actors with specific impairments to portray the characters.

The issues of verisimilitude persist. In the case of both *Children of a Lesser God* and *peeling*, the need for disabled actors to portray the characters has been enshrined either within the writing of the play or the legal licensing of it. The attempt to write positive representations of deaf and disabled characters has worked with the very same tenets that the 'normal' theatre has done to bar disabled actors from assuming central roles. More recently, there have been attempts to create deaf characters within dramas that have not made the impairment the central or sole issue. In the BBC thriller *The Silence* (July 2010), for example, the central character is Amelia. She is deaf but is coming to terms with a recent cochlear implant. In the drama, it is clearly her hearing mother who has been unable to accept her deafness and has taken every opportunity to 'heal' her. Amelia's struggle to come to terms with the degree of hearing now afforded by the implant and her mother's pressure is significant but not central to the plot, as Amelia is also the only witness to a murder. These two narrative strands are interwoven.

While *The Silence* should be lauded for providing a central deaf role and for incorporating some of the issues surrounding deafness within a classic murder mystery plot, there are some problematic concerns around both the writing of the character and of the casting of the actor who played Amelia, Genevieve Barr.

The process of adapting to change following a cochlear implant will be different depending upon the individual. However, the drama gave the impression that Amelia would now be able to 'hear' when wearing the implant and 'not hear' when taking it out. Thus, the impression is given that a cochlear implant can 'cure' deafness. This is far from the truth. While the drama did problematise Amelia's use of the implant in terms of her cultural identity, it also gave the impression that it would go a long way to 'fixing' the impairment of her deafness. Perhaps even more interesting in this debate about positive deaf characters and progressive casting of disabled actors in the context of verisimilitude is the fact that Genevieve Barr, who is indeed herself deaf, could not sign. She had to learn the signing for the part. In addition, she had to take her own hearing aid out to create verisimilitude for the character. This raises the question of whether a deaf actor was actually required for the role, as Genevieve's own experience of deafness was clearly very different to that of the character, Amelia. Was there a sense of cultural identity, perhaps feelings of isolation within a mainstream hearing world, that was significant to Genevieve's ability to truthfully portray the character? Could this have been achieved by a hearing actor undertaking the imaginative work of the actor?

This debate was further fuelled in the casting of Nina Raine's *Tribes*.

Tribes: a case study

Tribes encapsulates many of the debates engaged with in this chapter. Premiered at the Royal Court in 2010, it was nominated for several awards mostly as a result of the portrayal of the supporting deaf characters. Like *Children of a Lesser God*, it presented different models of deafness, and perhaps its most positive outcome was in its ability to convey to a mainstream theatre audience that deafness exists on a continuum and that the deaf community is not one homogenous whole. The two deaf characters portrayed are Billy, born deaf and raised to lip speak within a hearing family,

Christopher: . . . Billy's not deaf –
Ruth and Beth (in unison): Billy *is* deaf –
Christopher: He is not, he's been brought up in a hearing family, he's been protected from all that shit!

and Sylvia, his girlfriend, born hearing but progressively losing it, and who has learnt BSL. Billy learns sign language as a result of their relationship.

Raine draws clearly upon the social model of disability and questions who really has the impairment and the problem among the play's characters. The opening scene sets up Billy's isolation within his hearing family as the 'chaotic and noisy conversations' between them during a family dinner completely isolate Billy, who sits in silence. However, nobody is really listening to anybody else;

everyone is fighting their own corner. Metaphorically, they are all 'deaf'. The frenetic conversation is punctuated by an apparently deaf aware silence from the family when Billy speaks, though there is an air of condescension about it. They treat Billy with kid gloves to a large extent, even though he has recently returned to the family home after completing his degree. This is a challenge to a negative stereotype of a disabled character in that it is Billy who has managed on his own, away from the family abode, while his brother and sister, Daniel and Ruth, have struggled to be autonomous. He has taken an opportunity and they are struggling to do so.

Roles are further reversed in that it is Billy who is portrayed as the better 'listener' within the family, as evidenced in the scene with his brother, Daniel, when he returns home from a night out. He does not compete to be heard and is, and clearly has been, his brother's confidante and shoulder to lean on.

The play explores the notion of isolation. Billy is the least isolated character in the play. Not only has he been away at university, but he forms a relationship with Sylvia that means that he can again move out of the family home and nurture himself. He meets other deaf people via Sylvia and begins to learn BSL. His parents' marriage is one that has endured more through convenience than love, and they have little in common. His father, Christopher, goes into self-isolation – wearing headphones while learning Chinese. His brother and sister are also unable to successfully form relationships, and both feel incredibly isolated within the family set-up. Billy is the glue for them all.

The play asks the question: Who is disabled? Billy has the sensory impairment but has taken up every opportunity afforded him, while his hearing family appear more damaged and isolated, even though they are highly educated and extremely articulate. They are not apparently impaired, but their inability to listen and their verbal diarrhoea creates barriers that limit their ability to take part in normal life.

Deaf characters are not the only disabled characters Raine presents us with in the play. Billy's brother, Daniel, is hearing voices, suggesting that he is mentally disturbed, though has yet to be stigmatized with any label. Indeed, within his family, his problems have barely been noticed and certainly not identified as any form of impairment. The collective portrayal of the dysfunctional family as well as of Sylvia, progressively struggling with the increasing separation from her hearing family caused by her failing hearing, blurs the lines concerning impairment and disability. Raine does not allow us to make any easy assumptions. Even the somewhat vile father, Christopher, is attractive in his clever and cynical humour:

Christopher: No, it's about *them* feeling persecuted.
Beth: *Who?*
Christopher: The deaf! The fucking Muslims of the handicapped world.

It is in this aspect that the play is, perhaps, most successful, and would question any assumptions about what might be learnt through focusing upon the performance of disability.

In terms of casting and spectatorship, the play is perhaps more problematic. Billy was portrayed by a deaf actor who was a graduate with a BA in Theatre Arts, Education and Deaf Studies. The actor was born deaf and could both sign and voice. His casting served a purpose as a positive role model. It was clearly challenging to some hearing members of the audience, as his obviously 'deaf voice' was interpreted as meaning that he was also intellectually impaired by one member of a student group that was in the auditorium for the performance that I saw. With some gratification, I noted that this student's aping of the character's/actor's voice was pounced upon by both his teacher and some of his cohort. It was clear whom they thought was intellectually challenged!

The actor was nominated for an award for his role as Billy, as was the actor who played Sylvia. This was controversial. The actor was herself hearing and had to learn to sign for the part. She had been successful in audition as opposed to some professional deaf actors who also auditioned. In order to truthfully portray the character, the deaf actors had matching credentials (as the male deaf actor had for his portrayal of Billy), yet the hearing actor was regarded as the more appropriate choice to step into the shoes of Sylvia. Clearly, the casting team felt that the actor was using her imagination more effectively to play the part than the actors who had actually lived a similar experience.

What conclusions can be drawn from this? Does it raise questions about the positive casting of professionally trained disabled actors? Was the casting of Billy determined by the fact that the character required a 'deaf voice' that the deaf actor was easily able to employ? Was the hearing actor able to portray Sylvia because she was not pre-lingually deaf and therefore did not?

I would suggest that Kate O'Reilly wrote *peeling* precisely to confront such controversy. Despite the fact that *Tribes* was a skilfully written and provocative play that addressed issues around deafness and disability, its very form proved problematic for deaf audience members. It was not accessible. In order to be able to follow the majority of the dialogue, the first scene being a prime example, the spectator really needed to be hearing. In a captioned performance, the sheer speed of dialogue that was overlapping was difficult to follow. For first-language BSL users who could only attempt to gain access via a sign-interpreted performance, this was negated in a number of ways. Again, the solo BSL interpreter had little hope of keeping pace with the rapid opening dialogue of four speaking cast members. When the characters of Billy and Sylvia foregrounded BSL in their communication in Act Two, this was also inaccessible because the way that the scene was staged meant that the characters could see each other signing clearly but being side on to the audience inhibited the ability of deaf spectators to follow the dialogue.

In conclusion

In conclusion, I would like to crystallise the different approaches of the three plays I have referred to. *Children of a Lesser God*, in both form and in terms of accessibility, prioritised a mainstream hearing audience. *peeling*, both in form and the specific detail of its characters' impairments, embedded opportunity for disabled actors and provided positive role models for disabled spect-audience members. *Tribes*, drawing upon the social model for understanding disability, questioned the concepts of ability and disability yet remained inaccessible for its spect-audiences.

In order to usefully consider performing disabled characters from dramatic literature, certain priorities need to be foregrounded – spect-audience accessibility, equal opportunities for all actors and an inclusivity that does not present disabled characters within negative 'stereotype assumptions'.

Verisimilitude is clearly not the solution to performing disability, within the conventions of the theatre at any rate. The demands of the text can be met in positive and creative ways that respect the skill of the actor and challenge the audience's perception of disability.

I leave the final word to Graeae's artistic director, Jenny Sealey:

> I was talking to a casting director and he couldn't find the right disability for this particular role and I said, 'I tell you what, why don't you cast that role as a non-disabled actor but cast the others as disabled, there's equality, that's great' – actor is actor, they can play disabled they can play non-disabled.
>
> (Machon 2011: 166)

Chapter 6

The body beautiful, the beautiful mind

Starting from where they are

'Starting from where they are' is a received wisdom in drama teaching. In the introduction to this book I reported on a simple investigation into how both sixth-form Theatre Studies students and trainee teachers related their personal experiences and attitudes towards disability to dramatic and literary representations of it. The point was made there, I hope not in a critical way, that, for most of the respondents, the scope of their knowledge about and understanding of disability was quite limited. For two trainees on the University of Reading's Post Graduate Certificate of Education (PGCE) course, Liz Owen and Rachel Broadhead, this suggested a good reason to investigate further just how all four of Bolton's aims for drama in the curriculum could be addressed by taking aspects of disability as the content of a short scheme of work in drama.

Liz Owen's interest in this area of research developed from experiences of working with Key Stage 3 students in her first school placement. During a PSHE lesson exploring diversity, she discovered that the class consensus was that 95 per cent of people with disabilities were wheelchair users. What became clear from the comments the students were making was the inability of some of the students to identify disability as being anything other than a physical condition. It was also apparent that the students knew neither how to respond when faced with a disabled person nor how to interpret their behaviour:

> Disability is ugly isn't it? No one really wants to see it because you end up staring.
>
> I don't think I treat people with disabilities differently if I can see what is wrong with them, but I know that there are some of the kids at this school that have things wrong with them that you can't see. Then it can be hard because you don't know if they are just being idiots.

This lack of awareness of what might constitute a disability and the concomitant uncertainty about how to respond can be attributed to a number of contributory factors, including the influence parents, teachers and the media have on the formation of the students' knowledge and attitudes. The question for the two trainee teachers whose work is discussed below was whether drama could be an effective way of raising students' knowledge and understanding of disability and enabling them to discuss and respond to issues relating to it more confidently.

Drawing on Saunders' observation that, 'To most people teaching children about disability appears to be artificial political correctness' (Saunders 2000: 1), Rachel set out to avoid imparting a simplistic 'don't discriminate' message. Rather, she wanted to explore how people's responses to disability could be shaped by working with a variety of printed and media texts, then allowing the students to form and discuss judgements and attitudes they felt were emerging from the knowledge they were gaining. Drama's potential as a dialectical teaching tool largely rests in the way it provides students with a means of distancing themselves from a given attitude by adopting a role. Essentially, they may play devil's advocate in order to try out for themselves how holding a particular viewpoint feels while observing the responses of others to it. Thus, they are given license to say things that are not necessarily perceived as socially acceptable or express strong views, both positive and negative. However, it is naive to suggest that, because an opinion is expressed from within a role, this has an anodyne effect on both the role taker and the audience. What Rachel wanted to explore was how the power of being in role and the freedom that gives compared to and affected students' behaviour and attitudes out of role. She recognised a danger here in that using role to provide a distance could lead to escapism where the students failed to connect the drama with reality. To avoid this, she ensured that discussions about the drama became just as important as the drama itself.

Turning on and tuning in

During initial discussions about representations of disability, Rachel's Year 10 students were hesitant in talking about television programmes such as *Little Britain*, *South Park* and *Family Guy*, the inference being that, because the depictions of disabled characters in these shows could be construed as comedic and negative, it would not be considered OK to openly admit to liking them in a classroom setting. However, as the students became more comfortable in the discussion, references to the shows increasingly provoked laughter and impersonations. While such mockery would be socially unacceptable when targeted at real people, the fact that the characters being laughed at and impersonated only existed on television somehow seemed to make it acceptable. Starting from where they were, in this way, allowed Rachel to make the students feel safe and freed them in the way they used language to express what they found funny without guilt. This was an essential precursor to the drama that was initiated by Rachel adopting the role of a controversial director who wanted to break new ground by making a reality TV show. By using the TV reality show as a framework, the students were being given a familiar basis from which to explore the unfamiliar territory of disability. While trusting that, by modelling language and attitude, most students would follow her into the fiction, she also chose to invite a popular and talented student to be her co-director, briefing him to play a thoroughly insensitive and grossly prejudiced character. Although initially nervous and not entirely comfortable with this request, he completed the task by enthusiastically addressing his classmates, who were in role as a potential production team: 'Cripple Island! We're going to get a load of thick, useless, disabled people, stick them on an island and see how long they last. Cook, clean and take care of themselves. They won't last long.'

As with the antecedent discussion on depictions of disability, initial reticence quickly developed into a lively role play in which most of the students created exaggerated characters to express extreme opinions within the safety of these emphasised stereotypes. However, as this extract from Rachel's research diary illustrates, some of the other students found it difficult to adopt such a role, being appalled by the concept for the show:

> *Sarah (quizzical)*: Are they going to have help?
> *John (confident)*: No that's what the show's about. It'll be a right laugh.
> *Sarah (confident)*: But it'll be dangerous for them.
> *Me (over confident)*: Right, let's think Paralympics. What is the message? Disabled people can do it for themselves. *(Threatening)* I think you're prejudiced by thinking that they need help.
> *Sarah (shy and unsure)*: Well they may do, everyone needs help sometimes.
> *John (mocking)*: Give them some freedom.
>
> I challenge other people to argue with me but they don't.
>
> I ask, 'Does everyone love the idea?' Most say yes, but Sarah only says 'yes' once I stare at her. She remains angry throughout the lesson by shaking her head and huffing at me.

Breaking from the role play, Rachel showed the class extracts from *Body Shock* and the darkly satiric comedy *Cast Offs* in order to stimulate discussion regarding the decisions that may lie behind the production and transmission of such television shows.

Leicester argues that disability awareness should 'move away from negative perspectives which see disability as "illness" or "tragedy" and generate pity rather than genuine recognition of rights and equality' (Leicester 2007: 9). The role-played creation of the television show took the group away from pity and began to make them consider the implications of equality. However, this was generated negatively. For some, it reinforced the idea that disability could be 'funny'. This is what Rachel expected and accepted as an expression of where most of the students were; the project was to move both them and students such as Sarah, who were starting from a more sympathetic place, on to a more considered viewpoint. This meant addressing the use of discriminatory language at the start of the next lesson by presenting a PowerPoint containing the different words and phrases that had been regularly used during the previous lesson. Many students felt bad about using such language but were initially unable to explain why. This seemed to reflect the pointlessness of insisting on political correctness without examining its *raison d'être*. Beasley, Morrison and Quicke believe the key to disability education is that 'We need to ascertain not whether it is "negative" or "positive" in a superficial sense but whether it is rationally based. Pupils should be asked to provide reasons for their responses, and it is this reasoning which has to be evaluated' (Beasley *et al.* 1990: 106). The next task within the drama was to select prospective contestants for the show. Having discussed the use and effect of language through careful questioning, Rachel helped the students articulate something of what is unacceptable and why, the students began to use it more carefully, and discriminate between what they said in role and out of role.

A strategy intended to enhance understanding of what it feels like to be disabled is to simulate some kind of impairment. Though Parrish asserts that, 'Jumping in a wheelchair for a few minutes, wearing a blindfold, and stuffing cotton in one's ears does not make a person understand life with a disability' (Johnson 2006: 1), Rachel believed that this might be a good way of altering the tone of the lesson by considering disability from a different perspective. With this intention, she introduced exercises in which the students had their fingers taped together and tried to escape, or were blindfolded while concentrating on listening to a story. Johnson's reservation about such exercises is that, 'They focus on what people with disabilities cannot do rather than on what they could do with appropriate access, technology, or skill' (ibid.: 17). Rachel's questions to the students focused on what could have helped them manage the task, which, she argued, allowed them to consider how disability could be mitigated. This led to the introduction of a new character from the Disability Discrimination Act committee who had been appointed to ensure that the TV company's schedule was fair and balanced by creating *SeeHear*, a programme designed for disability education. Students were tasked to research different types of disability and prepare a section of this new show. Through this work, the students came to recognise that the media has a motive, and this influences how shows are created and how perceptions of disability are contingent upon conceptions of it. From this point, the class went on explore extracts from Joe Penhall's *Blue/Orange* and Lucy Gannon's *Keeping Tom Nice*, both of which gave opportunities to consider broader definitions of disability, how disabled characters might be played on stage, and to what effect.

In *Blue/Orange*, Christopher has a psychological condition that has physical side effects such as twitching and hyperactivity. Rachel wanted to see how the students would set about playing this character without her guidance. Their performances ranged from extreme overacting to overly simplistic representations. Choosing interpretations at either end of the spectrum, she questioned the class whether they were realistic. The answer was that neither led to experimentation of how to suggest elements of a given disability that was more truthful, though not necessarily mimetic. This informed the students' approach to playing the eponymous Tom of Gannon's play. Here, instead of trying to show the physical elements of Tom's disability, the students played the emotions. Rachel noted how this was a significant step in the students' development in drama, as well as in their heightened sensitivity towards disability as an issue: 'They were more comfortable when they felt they could promote awareness through character portrayals without fearing causing offence.'

From prejudice to respect

Like Rachel, Liz was also keen to discover the extent to which Horitz's claim that, through drama, 'children [can] confront their innate prejudices and, in some cases at least, are enabled to form new understandings of disability based on respect rather than pity or fear' (Horitz 2001: 82) could be verified. Her project was with a Year 8 class and her aims were to:

- use forum theatre and image theatre techniques to deconstruct social issues around disability;
- explore the portrayal of people with disability in the media; and
- explore and inform the attitudes of students towards disability.

In order to ensure the preservation of the drama studio and drama lesson as a space in which students could express and explore their own thoughts, opinions and attitudes while being mindful and considerate of the thoughts and feelings of other members of the group, a class contract was drawn up:

- If you're thinking of using a word to describe disability that you think will get you told off, don't use it, because it will probably upset someone in the group.
- Be respectful. Everyone is entitled to his/her own opinions, and they might be different to yours, but you should still listen to them.
- If you are creating a character with a disability, think about how they would act, don't play for laughs.
- If you have any questions, then ask them. Don't be afraid to ask questions or say what you think!

The first lesson considered the character of Joseph 'John' Merrick, whose condition of neurofibromatosis type I led to him being referred to as 'the

Elephant Man', a soubriquet that later became the title of a play by Bernard Pomerance and David Lynch's Oscar-winning film. Having studied visual images of Merrick and heard his story, the group used the role-on-the-wall device to capture their ideas regarding how he might have felt about his disability, and how others would have reacted to him. While the students were eager to express how they believed the character would have felt, the behaviour of some indicated they found it hard to deal with seeing some of the images (noticeably the authentic, historical images rather than those taken from the film) without laughter and inappropriate comments. In addressing this, one of the students responded that:

> It is hard to know what to do, isn't it Miss? Because it makes you feel uncomfortable, and then you laugh; when really, you feel like crying for them because they must have a horrible life.

As homework and preparation for the second lesson, Liz set the class the task of investigating depictions of disability in the media. The results from this exercise gave an interesting insight into their exposure to disability. One student commented on how he really struggled to finish it because:

> At the end of the day, most people don't think disability is pretty, so the bosses who want viewers aren't going to put people on the TV who aren't pretty, are they, or no one would watch.

The main focus of this lesson in terms of subject-specific learning was to consider verbatim theatre by using scripts from the *Creature Discomforts* adverts for the charity Leonard Cheshire Disability. These adverts, animated by Nick Park, aimed to promote inclusion and disability awareness by using the voices of disabled people to tell their own stories. By discussing the concept of verbatim theatre, students were able to give reasons as to why the genre could be an effective medium for drawing attention to issues. One of the students commented that:

> Using the words of people with disabilities makes it real. We can only guess how they feel and we would probably get it wrong, because we are not in their position.

The students were given an opportunity to perform some of the scripts. Liz noted how well they took to their roles, endeavouring as they did so to create a sense of honesty. On this, a student noted that it was:

> Well hard to make it convincing without looking like you're taking the mickey out of it.

The lesson was rounded off by showing the students some of the animated advertisements. They were surprised at the way in which they were presented, with one commenting that:

> It makes it easier, you know, to look at and deal with, because they are clay things. You're listening to what they are saying about the things that they have, rather than staring at them.

While some may contend that this is an anodyne approach to raising disability awareness, a counter argument would be that it offered these young students an introduction to reflecting on where they were in terms of their knowledge and understanding, and a way of moving on without feeling threatened or ashamed.

The penultimate lesson in this short unit of work used David Watson's *Flight Path* (2007) as a stimulus. One element of this play concerns how a family deals with the return home of Daniel, who has Down's syndrome, following his lengthy stay at a residential school for young people with special educational needs. At the start of the lesson, six members of the group volunteered to act out the core narrative of the play using what it is popularly known as the 'whoosh' technique. Although this strategy (which involves the teacher giving a sort of bullet point synopsis of the play while students spontaneously improvise actions to illustrate the narration) can often appear to be quite silly, the students that had volunteered in this instance showed the utmost respect, particularly when in reference to the main character's disability. The lesson continued with an exploration of the characters and their relationships through a group examination of monologues from each character. Groups then rehearsed an extract from the play, and some of these were shared and discussed at the end of the lesson. All of the groups that performed displayed a level of maturity that had been absent from their previous work, with none of the students corpsing or falling out of character. Their commitment to creating a piece of drama that justified the play was evident. Feeding back to one of the performing groups, one student told her peers that their work had been:

> different to your normal work. You kept character and I genuinely believed that Daniel was really someone with a disability, not because you acted stupid or anything, but because you used your facial expressions and gestures and stuff to show how your character was feeling.

The students had clearly found the selected extracts accessible. Referring to the work undertaken in the previous lesson, one remarked that:

> The way that the character of Daniel is written to speak is really real. But what if you don't have an actor that's got Down's syndrome to play him? What happens then? It might look like we are making fun of him.

This comment underlines how, when using drama as a vehicle to develop awareness and positive attitudes, an onus is placed on the art form. Within popular media, television and cinema in modern years, the debate around actors without disabilities portraying characters with disabilities has been a contentious topic, and is the subject of Simon Floodgate's chapter 'Performing disability'. O'Reilly compares the casting of non-disabled actors to play disabled characters to the popular entertainment traditions of the nineteenth and early twentieth centuries: 'cripping up is the 21st century answer to blacking up' (O'Reilly 2009: 35).

For Liz, the comment demonstrated a development in the consciousness and sensitivity of this particular student. Her research diary records that:

> In the first lesson of the unit, I had to redress his language after he made some disparaging remarks in reference to a female member of his year group and her own specific educational needs. After this lesson, as he was about to leave, I asked the student what he thought of the lessons so far, and he responded that, 'At first, I thought the lessons were going to be really preachy, like they are when we do PD [personal development]. But they're not, it's like we learn about the people isn't it? I need to think about how I act.'

As enrichment work for this lesson, the students were asked to write a diary entry for the character of Daniel, describing his feelings when he decided to run away.

The final lesson used forum theatre techniques and whole-class role play to explore the subtext and context of the play, and the emotions of the characters involved. The lesson began with students creating a short scene to show the emotional impact felt by Daniel's family when he ran away, and they discovered the diary entry that students had asked to complete as homework. Through their own improvisations and exploration of the text, the students were able to draw out different themes within the scene. This led to several different threads that could be explored during the whole class in role activity. This involved them working in role as police officers, hot-seating characters from the play and additional characters of their own creation that they believed would be able to further develop the narrative regarding the whereabouts and reasoning behind Daniel's disappearance. In role, one student speculated that he had run away:

> because of how people treated him, like a freak and a pain and something that took up too much of their time. If someone was treating me like that, I think I would leave too.

In the plenary session, a number of comments highlighted the students' recognition of a need for more to be done to help them extend their knowledge of disability and learn how to respond when encountering disabled people. For example, one student observed that:

> Although we see X and Y [students with Down's syndrome] around school, we don't ever get to talk about it. I think that might stop them getting bullied . . . they [teachers] expect you to just accept it.

What is being indicated here is that there is an appetite among young people to heighten their awareness and understanding of disability. Lionel Warner has suggested it may be a damaging mythology to assume that young people simply reproduce negative stereotypes when they encounter disabled characters in literature or on stage. However, if teachers do no more than expect them to just accept disability without providing opportunities to talk about it, then the consequences are likely to be that they are not as equipped to know how to respond to it as they might wish themselves to be.

Chapter 7

Who cares?

For Ever and Ever

For Ever and Ever by Rob John was first performed in March 1991 by Far East Youth Theatre Company at Paston Sixth Form College, Norfolk. Later that year, the production extensively toured schools in Leeds, Cambridge, Norfolk and Suffolk, and was performed at the Cockpit Theatre, London. Since then, *For Ever and Ever* has been regularly performed by schools and youth theatre companies across the UK but is published here for the first time. The author explains the play's inception thus:

> The idea for this play leapt at me one night when watching a television news item on the annual 'Children of Courage Awards'. Amongst the amazing children being applauded for rescuing dogs or stoically enduring horrible hospital treatment was a teenage girl who for years had more or less single-handedly cared for a younger brother with severe learning difficulties. The news item described the daily grind of this girl's life and a speaker at the ceremony invited the audience to celebrate her extraordinary achievement. I think it was the word 'celebrate' which got me angry. I couldn't see anything here to celebrate. This girl didn't need an award; she needed someone to come and rescue her and give her back her life. The applauding audience at the award ceremony didn't seem to see it this way so in a way the play was addressed to them. My story is completely fictional but it's trying to speak up for the real Megs struggling out there in the real world.

Meg lives with her father and brother Billy. It is not specified exactly what disability Billy has but Meg says of him, vaguely, 'He's . . . got learning difficulties'. The initial stage direction reads: '*Billy is present throughout the play. Although he never speaks, he watches everything.*'

Rob John suggests that, 'he observes the action but doesn't understand it. He is responsive to tone of voice but doesn't grasp language. We must be constantly aware of him but never distracted by him.'

Dad is a church-going, God-fearing and, indeed, God-trusting man. Meg attends church with him and joins in with his prayers. However, rather than facing up to his family's challenges, he resorts to the ritual of praying in order to avoid actually discussing any practical matters to do with either Billy's or Meg's well-being. Religion, rather like the awards Rob John refers to, may effectively be disabling agents in that the celebration of life and achievement does not, in itself, make life easier.

Meg's friend and ally is a young girl called Terri. We never find out much about Terri, though she is a habitual truant, suggesting she has issues of her own. To some extent, her role is functionary in that she takes Billy as he is, being neither embarrassed by him nor abashed by talking about him. She is sympathetic to Meg's situation and even condones her plan to run away in order to get on with her own life.

Meg has constructed a vision of her mother as a successful businesswoman in the fashion world who had no choice but to leave the family in order to pursue her career and reach her personal potential. Meg dreams of leaving, finding her mother and going on to fulfil her potential. The reality, though, is that Mum left because, as Dad puts it, 'She was full of dreams Meg. Full of dreams, just like you. She never quite seemed to be able to . . . pin things down. She never quite got to grips with the situation.' As it turns out, Mum is in the fashion business, but as an assistant in Marks & Spencer. Meg nonetheless attempts to leave home in the middle of the night in order to find her, but returns immediately to witness her father helplessly wondering what to do with Billy. As Meg quietly begins to take charge again, dad suggests they join in the Lord's Prayer. Meg kneels, sensing that for her this will be life 'forever and ever . . . amen'.

Ostensibly, *Forever and Ever* is about Meg and the pressures and constraints she experiences as a primary carer. However, while society often effectively makes disabled people invisible, Billy's presence on stage at all times does not allow the audience to similarly dismiss his existence, and perhaps also suggests that, while he may not have a physical voice, he is cognizant of what is happening around him. This highlights the inappropriateness of what might be referred to as the 'does he take sugar' syndrome in which it is assumed that disabled people always need someone to answer for them. When Meg runs away after leaving her father a letter explaining why, Billy is left alone on stage: '*He goes to the exit through which Meg has left and stares after her puzzled. He slowly returns to the table and looks at the letter. Then he waits patiently for something to happen.*'

Such a depiction of Billy may be seen as subtly positive. In fact, his permanent positioning on the stage and the few actions given to him suggest that the character has a considerable symbolic function. For example, when Dad and his young friend Colin are playing chess, 'Billy leans forward and watches the game with his nose just above the board. Although he doesn't understand the game he watches the pieces move with fascination.' In a later scene, Colin calls on Meg and, at the suggestion of her father, asks her if she might like to go out. The scene has comic potential in that Meg misunderstands his intention and thinks that Colin, who comes across as a bit of a nerd, is offering to look after Billy while she goes out. Thus confronted, Colin is left squirming in the face of his misguided attempt at charity. Billy's presence throughout the scene cannot but help to add an irony to the tragic-comic episode for the audience who, like Billy, can only watch the unfolding events. In another scene depicting one of Meg's nightmares, Billy's passivity is the cause of painful dramatic tension as he is teased by a group of girls who encourage him to walk on a thinly iced pond. Here again, the sequence casts the audience as helpless observers of an act of cruelty; like Billy, they are relieved and grateful when Meg arrives to prevent a tragedy.

Confronting the audience

Positioning a disabled character on stage in order to remind the audience of their continued existence and centrality to the narrative is a dramatic device used in a number of other plays. In *A Day in the Death of Joe Egg*, for example, Sheila and Brian recount the details of their young daughter Josephine's life so far in a series of comic impersonations of the doctors, specialists and various good-hearted souls that have been involved with her. For Brian at least, the knockabout comedy routine serves as a means for him to cope with the strain he feels Joe's needs have placed on him. Sheila's complicity in these 'games' is largely for his sake, although she also recognises the heavy toll that looking after Joe has on their marriage. From an audience's point of view, the juxtaposition of the comedy routine with Joe's presence on stage adds to the sense of tragedy. Concerns were expressed when the play first appeared that it could be considered offensive because of its irreverent use of comedy, though others argued that the comedy underscored its tenderness and supported the belief that shared laughter can be an effective tool in coping with sorrow. By way of stretching the boundaries of what may be considered 'good taste' even further, Act 1 is brought to a close by the actor playing Joe skipping on chanting 'Mrs D, Mrs I, Mrs FFI, Mrs C, Mrs U, Mrs LTY', then announcing the interval.

In the second act, Brian's overt political incorrectness (recent productions have felt obliged to edit a number of his lines) is set against the earnest goodwill of their friend Freddie, who we learn does what he can to support charities for disabled children. However, while his genial optimism serves as a balm for Sheila's unerring belief that she has, in the past, seen a flicker of responsiveness in Joe, he is also a foil to Brian's conviction that the best thing for all concerned would be to have Joe institutionalised.

Another dimension to the moral debate that underpins the difficulties Brian and Sheila face comes from Brian's mother, Grace. This rather vile, chain-smoking, self-centred stereotype of a mother-in-law whose apron strings still firmly cuff her son is openly antagonistic to her daughter-in-law, whose pre-marital promiscuity is held to blame for Joe's condition. Brian counters this belief by suggesting that Sheila blames herself for Joe's condition on account that she held back during the birth because of the guilt she feels about her past. Nonetheless, the link between disability and sexual wantonness is reinforced, for example, in the way Brian quotes back to Sheila details of her youthful 'sexploits'. The idea that disabled children are a burden in that they represent a living manifestation of their parents' guilt finds a more recent expression in Lee Hall's *Spoonface Steinberg* (1997). The eponymous protagonist recounts how her autism has been attributed to her father's infidelity resulting in an argument in which neither parents were paying sufficient attention to their infant daughter: 'Mam says to Dad that maybe it is his fault that I am not right – on the fact that on the day Dad came back when he was out with the floozie, I did fall off the chair.'

That autism might be caused by a bump on the head is nonsense in medical terms, suggesting that Hall is drawing on deep-seated cultural myths in order to give another layer of meaning to the drama, and in so doing is reinforcing a damaging apologue.

In some ways, Nichols' play uses Joe as a lens through which to examine Brian and Sheila's relationship. Joe's inability to look after herself or even articulate who or what she is may be seen as a metaphor for the adults' inability to hold a firm grasp on their own identity and relationship. There is thus an irony in the way they talk about Joe's absent future:

> Joe could have grown older and developed into a real person before it happened. Or she could have been a very intelligent spastic without the use of her limb. Which is worse, I think, than being a kind of living parsnip.

This failure of adults to recognise that children such as Joe are, in fact, the same species is also demonstrated by good-intentioned Freddie, who urges Brian and Sheila to put Joe in a home and adopt another child: 'at least you'll have a proper working child.'

Freddie's good nature is not, however, shared by his wife Pam, whose reactions to the child are harsh but honest. For example, when it is suggested that Joe is brought downstairs to hear the carol singers, Pam panics and states that they really must be getting on their way. In a piece of direct address, she delivers her logical solution to children such as Joe who do not fit into her vision of a perfect world: 'if I say gas-chamber that makes it sound horrid – but I do mean put to sleep.'

Pam is constructed as a character that it would be difficult to warm to and, as a result, her views might be easily rejected in the safe darkness of the auditorium. But Nichols does not let the audience off that lightly, and a question she poses to her husband is as much addressed to them as to him: 'If one of our kids was dying and they had a cure and you knew it had been discovered in the Nazi laboratories, would you refuse to let them use it?'

What she is doing here, of course, is twisting logic in exactly the same way as the Nazis and other eugenicists did by suggesting that ends can always justify the means. In contrast to Pam's revulsion of Joe, Grace appears to accept her unconditionally. She chats away to her and treats her as many a grandmother would treat their granddaughter. However, her talk is fatuous and more a comment on her own loneliness and childish resentment of Sheila than a conscious recognition of Joe as a fellow human being.

At the end of the play, Brian leaves with his case. Sheila obliviously tidies up ready for bed, proclaiming how lucky Joe and all the pets are to have such a lovely daddy. Will Brian really go? Probably not, for, like Joe, he cannot survive on his own. Ultimately, the vulnerability and incapacity of the disabled Joe serves to accentuate the vulnerability and incapacity of those who care for her. The play is more about their inabilities than her disabilities.

The drama for the carer

This same conclusion could be drawn from a number of other plays. In Arne Skouen's *Ballerina* (1984), for example, a retired ballerina has devoted her life to her daughter, who appears to be autistic and synaesthetic (though neither of these conditions are actually named in the script). Malin, the daughter, best expresses herself through dance and relates to a number of inanimate objects that she has personified into the cast of a private world. The intensely naturalistic writing of the play is highly elliptical, leaving the audience to work hard to surmise that Edith, the mother, has herself had some kind of breakdown resulting in her and Malin being treated separately. Edith has consequently resolved to kidnap her own daughter and set off on a new life. However, within the timescale of the play, she calls on her husband and son to offer financial support so that she and Malin can return to their family farm with Rutta, a girl who seems to be able to manage and understand Malin well.

Malin is depicted as existing almost entirely within her own world. She has bad thoughts that must be flushed down the toilet and recognises the colour of people's voices – nice, kind voices are blue, but angry and frightening ones are black. What drives Edith on in her quest to stay with Malin is the memory of an incident when she was a little girl and, having broken her father's mandolin, proclaims, 'I'm out of tune too, Mummy.' The incident is reminiscent of Sheila's memory of Joe repeatedly knocking down a tower of building bricks before another grand mal robbed her of the capacity to do even that. Malin's father, like Bri, has found himself unable to cope with the domestic situation and left Edith. What he has particular difficulty facing is the horror of the specialist's diagnosis that, for short periods of time, Malin may be able to 'function adequately', with the result that, 'for four seconds, she was able to see her own fate.'

Once again, the play is not so much an investigation of Malin's condition, but a drama built on the effect that coping with such a condition may have on those who face choices and dilemmas when faced with a duty of care.

Another dramatic trope apparent in *Ballerina* is the question of why it is always down to women to look after emotional needs while the men only deal with money and logistics. In a similar vein, Evans and Nash's *Lives Worth Living* (1983), a theatre-in-education play, aimed to help its young audiences 'examine the stereotypical role of women as carers within our society and, most importantly . . . show that mentally handicapped people are people first'. The authors, who performed in the original production, considered that the project successfully raised questions but ultimately failed to change attitudes. It is not wholly clear, however, what questions the play actually raises, and imagining that a piece of theatre could radically change deeply embedded attitudes might be regarded as unrealistically optimistic. In fact, given the 'deliberate' use of stereotype employed in the play, it could be argued that it would be just as likely to reinforce a number of negative attitudes.

The action of *Lives Worth Living* takes place on 'a beach in Southend' (though later stage directions such as '*Julie steps out of the sea and crosses to the rocks*' suggest that neither author had ever actually been to Southend!). Julie is a qualified yet out-of-work nursery nurse. She is ferociously defensive of her younger brother Mark who is 'mentally handicapped' (stereotypically signified by involuntary arm spasms and a 'slightly spastic gait, a lolling tongue and loud voice'). The opening of the play is designed to shock as we hear Mark being taunted as a 'spazzy mong' but this image is quickly inverted when he skilfully manages to erect a deckchair after Julie has failed to manage the task. As the play develops, we learn that their mother has died of an illness. Dad left sometime before, unable to cope with the fact that his firstborn was a girl and his son was defective and never likely to be a boxer or famous footballer. In this, the play may be seen to be obfuscating the central issue with feminist sentiments. As in so many other plays, there is a hint that mental disability is some sort of punishment on the parents; in this case, Mark's mother is concerned that she had the children too close together. The character notes state that Mum was pregnant with Julie before she married, but this is not explicitly stated in the text of the play itself, though may have come out in the workshop part of the TIE programme.

The ethical and moral dilemma touched on in the play and further explored in the subsequent workshop (which is published along with the play text) regards Julie's responsibilities: should she 'force' Mark to go and live in a residential centre, or should she give in and allow him to live with her and her boyfriend Trevor? Julie recounts how she fought to defend Mark from anyone who said or did anything to harm him. In *Ballerina*, Malin's brother Audun admits to betraying his sister by laughing at her along with the other children, though Rutta, the servant girl, defended and fought for her. However, while Julie is faced with the dilemma of what decision to take regarding her brother's future, Audun consequently feels huge guilt for not having defended Malin and recognises that 'Malin is my inheritance. Nobody else will have her.' In both plays, the audience are being positioned to feel sympathy for the carer at having to make the choice of abandonment or accepting full responsibility. While this may be dramatically effective, the consequence is that the voice of the disabled character is either overridden or not acknowledged at all. Nor are the audience invited to think about what mechanisms might be put in place to support both the disabled person and those who care for them, or why such mechanisms do not exist. Thus, the idea of disability as a burden on society and a curse on the families of disabled people is preserved.

The nature of the burden

A critical review of dramatic manifestations of disability reveals a sort of moral conundrum: Is disability a punishment resulting from moral laxity and sexual indecency? Or is the inability of individuals charged with caring for disabled people a symptom of their moral laxity or pusillanimity?

In her study of physical disabilities in Victorian melodrama, Martha Stoddard Holmes (2001: 9) notes the existence of two recurrent threads of cultural anxiety evoked by plays at the time: fears about 'the afflicted' as an economic burden, and fears about them being sexually active. There was a widely held belief in the nineteenth century that certain disabilities, notably blindness, were connected to sexual misdemeanour; in infants due to being born through an infected birth canal, and in young males as a result of masturbation. Similarly, there was a widely held belief that mental illness and 'idiocy' were the results of debauchery. As the physician George Man Burrows wrote in *Commentaries on the Causes, Forms, Symptoms and Treatment, Moral and Medical, of Insanity*, published in 1828, 'Insanity is the scourge brought down on sinful men by the wrath of the almighty'. Such beliefs no doubt fuelled policy. For example, in 1907, the state of Indiana acceded to permit the sterilisation of the 'feeble minded and unfit' in order to prevent further harm to 'helpless, unfortunate children of the degenerate and criminally depraved who are brought into the world handicapped at birth, cursed before they see the light of day, stunted mentally, morally and physically'. In all, 37 states followed Indiana's example, and it became standard practice in the 1920s and 1930s to sterilise women born deaf along with anyone with an IQ registered at below 70 (Quarmby 2011: 61). Meanwhile, it is believed that some 63,000 people were sterilised in Sweden between 1935 and 1975 (Evans 2005: 514). In 1942, an article in the *American Journal of Psychiatry* called for the 'mercy killing' of all 'retarded' children over five using the same principles of eugenics that underpinned the Nazis' T4 programme (named after Tiergarten 4, the address in Berlin from which the programme was led). It is worth noting here that the Nazis played on fears that disabled people were the result of sexual degeneracy and, like Jews, had a propensity towards degeneracy themselves. Nazi posters and films such as *Heredity* (1930) portrayed disabled people in a degrading and dehumanising way and bore captions informing the populace just how much such abominations would cost 'the People's community' over a lifetime. Given that the idea of disability arising as some form of punishment for immorality while also constituting a threat to decency has long been manifest in both scientific paradigm and the popular imagination, it is hardly surprising that it has been, and remains, reflected in dramatic literature.

With regard to the second question of the inability of individuals to cope with disability being a symptom of their moral deficiency, one might consider how the characters in *Cooking With Elvis* (discussed in Chapter 4) are all, in different ways, disabled by their own dysfunctionality. Certainly, none of them appear to have any particularly redeeming features, but while this results in a dark farce, Dennis Potter's *Brimstone and Treacle* (1977) is anything but a comedy. Like Edith in *Ballerina*, Amy Bates clings to the hope that her daughter Pattie still holds some understanding of the world around her and will one day return to it. Her husband Tom, however, has given up any such hope. Ironically, in the film version, Tom is shown to be a publisher of hymns and writer of memorial verses, yet has no belief in God as anything other than callous and vindictive or, as Dennis Potter himself put it, 'apparently deaf, dumb and blind'. Tom perhaps has every reason for fearing Pattie's return to consciousness and abhors the idea that she has any capacity for thought, for he knows that what led to her accident was her witnessing his infidelity. From the audience's point of view, it certainly seems that Pattie understands what is going on, as the stage directions indicate that she makes noises and spasmodic movements at significant moments. This gives the character a chilling aspect not unlike the archetypally disturbing ventriloquist's dummy.

Tom makes a number of comments that suggest that he is aware of his daughter as a physically attractive young woman. On the surface, it may be read as fatherly concern that she stay protected, but the inference is that he personally experiences sexual drives that make him aware of the danger that other men represent: 'How can we allow other people – strangers – to come into the house and hear such noises. What if she pulls down her clothes and – and exposes her – her . . .'

Into the Bates' stressed and apparently loveless (certainly sexless) world comes Martin. At a superficial level, Martin is simply a conman preying on the Bates' vulnerability. He soon discovers and plays on Tom's sense of guilt. It is inferred that something once happened between Tom and one of Pattie's college friends. Martin picks up on the suggestion that she was a beautiful girl. Although Tom says she was a slut, it is clear that he went to visit her in her flat and that Pattie also visited on the night of her accident. Martin also spots Amy's need for kind words and actions, which have overtones of flattery that are at once slightly sexual but also play on her motherliness. Martin quickly wins the Bates' trust but at the first opportunity rapes Pattie while Amy is out having her hair done (at his suggestion) and Tom is at work. Later that night, Martin rapes Pattie again but her screams awaken her parents. They discover Martin gone, but their daughter is recovered though confused by what has happened to her.

Martin has something of the Devil incarnate about him. Amy says that she can even smell sulphur when he is around and when he starts to pray with her there is a massive crack of thunder. He is also, though, in some ways, representative of the vitality of life and all its pleasures and pains, hence the title *Brimstone and Treacle*. His immorality is all too apparent to the audience, who may read it as a mockery of Amy's childlike belief in a kind and forgiving God and Tom's hypocrisy. Conversely, Pattie does not so much exist as a character at all. The accident has left her helpless, mute and, as far as anyone can see, non-*compos mentis*. This allows Amy to exercise all her motherly instincts and simple faith in God-bestowed redemption. For Tom, though, Pattie is an embodiment and constant reminder of his guilt, while for Martin she is the means through which the true animalistic nature of the human being is revealed. The voice that continues to be absent, even at the end of the play, is Pattie's.

Colin Barnes, Professor of Disability Studies at the University of Leeds, argues that portrayals of disabled people as a burden effectively dehumanises them in much the same way that the Third Reich cast them as 'existence without life' (Barnes 1992). Such portrayals clearly still exist, and Barnes is particularly critical of Lucy Gannon's *Keeping Tom Nice* (1988). The play, which was televised in 1990, depicts a family driven to breaking point as a result of 'caring' for their disabled son Tom, a 24-year-old described as 'totally immobile, spastic, epileptic and incontinent'. In another exhibition of the link between sex and disability, Tom's sister Charlotte has incestuous desires for him, while his father refers to him as 'sexless and bloody useless' and physically abuses him. Feeling shame for his actions and fearing they will be discovered by Tom's patronising social worker, the father commits suicide. Barnes suggests that the play 'can only have increased viewers' sympathy for families with a similar "burden"', though adds that 'there was nothing in it to evoke empathy with disabled people whatsoever'. He goes on to argue that such portrayals of disabled people as a 'burden' have been used extensively in advertising campaigns by the carers' lobby, and the success of these campaigns has led to the term 'carers' becoming synonymous with self-sacrifice, while the concept of disabled people 'conjures up images of suffering and unhappiness for those around them'. This brings us back to Rob John's play and Meg's plaintive last line, which sums up her lot, 'For ever and ever . . .'. It is not simply that Billy is a burden to Meg, but that Meg is also, effectively, being disabled from living her life not because of Billy, but because she has to compensate for her father's ineptitude and society's inadequacy in supporting her.

The problem would not arise if disabled people were not forced to rely on unpaid informal carers – usually women relatives or friends – for essential services. Due to inadequate community-based provision, disabled people are rarely able to select or employ their own personal assistants. The exploitation of this particular stereotype by carers' organisations is a direct outcome of this unsatisfactory situation.

Towards positive imagery

Rob John is insistent that Meg is not depicted as a saint who has willingly sacrificed her life to serve her brother. Rather, he suggests she is shown as awkward and resentful:

> It's not self-pity but anger that drives Meg. She's angry with her father for his hopeless hypocrisy and angry with a wider world that applauds her selfless achievement but offers her no tangible practical support. Towards the end of the play we also realise that she harbours anger towards Billy.

It is perhaps in this portrait of fraternity that *For Ever and Ever* manages to impart its message without either preaching or sentimentalising, and in this it could be likened to David Watson's *Flight Path* (2007), which attracted extremely positive reviews when it was first produced by Out of Joint. The narrative centres on Jonathan, who, while facing his A levels and supplementing his funds by burgling houses, must also cope with his older brother Daniel. Daniel, who has Downs' syndrome, has returned from a residential care home where he was unhappy. Although Daniel may be seen as something of a burden on Jonathan with his constant temper tantrums and exuberant but uncontrolled use of foul language, the play is successful in painting a believable and warming love/hate relationship between the brothers. To compound the odds that seem to be stacked up against Jonathan leading a run-of-the-mill life of a teenager, his father, a university lecturer, has left the family home. It would seem that fathers of disabled children abandoning ship is de rigueur in plays! Susan, the boys' mother, is ironically so wrapped up with her professional life as a social worker that she appears to be missing everything that is going on at home. The play is fast-moving, witty and positive in that the young characters are so robust that we are reassured that their character and tenacity will see them through, if nothing else does. Charles Spencer, reviewing the Out of Joint production, commended the ending, 'with its beautiful mixture of love, hope and residual sadness' (*Daily Telegraph*, 19 September 2007), but also noted that he 'found it hard to believe that the middle-class parents would be quite so neglectful of their needy children'. Now, how is that for a stereotype that needs challenging?

Play script

For Ever and Ever

Rob John

Characters in order of appearance

Church Congregation (entire cast apart from Billy, Meg and Dad)
Billy
Meg (his sister)
Dad (Billy's father)
Mother (Billy's mother)
Mrs A
Mrs B
Mrs C
Terri
Colin
Miss Lovejoy
Mandy
Debbie
Tracey
Girls in the Park

STAGING

This play requires an open performance space with a table and three chairs centre stage. Upstage of the table, stage right and left, are two benches or pews (four in all). Apart from Meg and Billy, the whole cast are dressed for church. They represent solid respectability – hats, handbags, overcoats and hymnbooks. Underneath their overcoats they wear the costumes of the other characters in the play. Throughout the play they sit on the benches upstage of the action, curiously observing what takes place. The transformations into other characters therefore are seen by the audience and become part of the action. As a scene finishes we see the actors return to the congregation and resume their positions in church.

Billy is present throughout the play. Although he never speaks, he watches everything.

SCENE 1 *As the lights go up we hear a solo voice sing 'Lay Me Low' – traditional folk song – and see the whole cast enter.*

'Lay Me Low, Lay Me Low
Where no one can see me
Where no one can touch me
Where no one can hurt me.'

BILLY sits on a chair in front of the table facing the audience. MEG stands behind him and behind her stands the congregation. As the song finishes a church organ takes up the tune and MEG goes into action. She helps BILLY on with his jumper and he helps her by shooting his arms up in the air like a little child. She fetches a mimed toothbrush, cleans his teeth and he spits into a mimed cup. The congregation stare at MEG and BILLY, fascinated. They bend forward to get a better view, rudely leaning across the table, bringing their faces right up to the back of BILLY's head. MEG brushes BILLY's hair then slowly looks up at the audience. The congregation moves to the upstage benches and watches. MEG speaks directly to the audience. She addresses the audience with an air of weary irritation. She's tetchy, not particularly pleased to see us. We need to feel that if we said the wrong thing she might turn on us.

MEG: Sunday morning. Half past eight. Any second my Dad will come down and he'll say, 'Morning, Meg. Sleep well?' and I'll say, 'Yes thanks,' and he'll say, 'How's the boy?' and I'll say, 'He's fine Dad,' and Dad will say, 'Lovely job,' and then I'll give them their Weetabix. Dad'll say grace and then we'll have our breakfast. That's how it will be won't it Billy? That's how it's always been and that's how it always will be. For ever and ever.
(DAD enters)

DAD: Morning Meg. Sleep well?

MEG: Yes thanks.

DAD: How's the boy?

MEG: He's fine Dad.

DAD: Lovely job.

MEG: Told you so didn't I. Word perfect. Weetabix Dad?

DAD: Lovely.
(MEG serves the Weetabix)

DAD: Dear Lord we thank thee for these thy blessings. We pray we may be worthy to receive them. *(Pause)* Come on then. Chocks away. Tuck in Billy.

MEG has to feed BILLY like a child. She talks to us while she feeds him.

MEG: This is the low point of my week. I can put up with almost anything, come on let's be honest, I do put up with almost anything. I can cope with getting up in the night when Billy gets frightened, giving him his bath in the morning, oh yes I have to do all that, wiping his nose for him every three minutes, taking him to the Day Centre, taking him to the toilet, I can cope with all that, but having to listen to my Dad, showered, clean shaven and smelling of Eau de Cologne thanking God for his Weetabix is sometimes too much to bear. *(BILLY has been waiting mouth open for a spoonful which hasn't arrived. MEG notices . . .)* Sorry Billy. *(. . . and feeds it to him.)* I'd happily do him a couple of eggs, a sausage maybe, a rasher or two of bacon but on Sundays he says,

DAD: Let's keep it nice and simple on the Lord's day, Meg. If the Lord was amongst us this morning I'm sure he'd be quite content to settle for a bowl of Weetabix.

MEG: You can't argue with that can you? You might be tempted to point out that the Lord might have a more varied taste in breakfast cereals. He might appreciate a bowl of Crunchy Nut Cornflakes, for example, the occasional Shreddie perhaps . . . but when you know the Lord as intimately as my Dad does, it's a waste of time.

DAD: I see it was 76 in Torquay yesterday.

MEG: And that's depressing too. He's got over two quid's worth of state-of-the-art Sunday journalism there . . . top quality stuff . . . magazine supplement, sports supplement, arts focus and review section, the week in parliament, scandals, revolutions and three pages of diagrams explaining the impact of deforestation on global warming and he makes straight for the weather reports for the South West coast.

DAD: And 80 in Paignton.

MEG: He's obsessed with the South West coast. He loves it. His reading of the scripture has convinced him that Heaven has been closely modelled on parts of Devon and Cornwall. Illfracombe with angels. He was going to take us there once. Once when I was about 13. On a Sunday morning he suddenly said . . .

DAD: I tell you what we'll do Meg, we'll motor down through Wiltshire, show Billy Stonehenge, then make straight for Exeter, then somewhere down there we'll turn off the A380 and slip down to the coast.

MEG: I think he took Mum down there once. When they were happy.

DAD: Then we'll find a quiet little campsite, Meg. Not one of those ones with caravans and shower blocks and amenities. Take my word for it Meg, you go in for amenities and you can wave goodbye to peace and quiet. No, what we'll do is find a quiet little place on a farm and we'll get our milk from the farmer in the mornings and maybe a few eggs . . . and we'll walk in the woods . . . get ourselves right off the beaten track . . . and the beaches Meg. You wait till you see the beaches. Miles of golden sand and not a soul on them. Billy can have the run of the place . . . charge about, let off steam and not get in anyone's way. Marvellous. How's that sound Meg? God's own country.

MEG: Marvellous.

DAD: Yeah. Lovely old job. That's the place for us Meg. Out of everyone's way.

MEG: Keeping Billy out of everyone else's way was what he was really on about. He never took us, we never went. Something came up. Something always comes up. I've never been anywhere, that's why I'm going now . . . soon . . . in a couple of days . . . week at the most. This time next week I'll be gone. No more Sunday mornings.

On Sundays after breakfast I clean Billy up, put his best shoes on, make sure he's been to the toilet and then we go to church.

We hear an organ playing the intro to a hymn, 'The Churches One Foundation'. DAD puts on his jacket, straightens his tie as the congregation come away from the benches and spread out around the stage facing the audience as if ready for the church service. MRS A, B and C are closest to MEG, DAD and BILLY. The rest of the congregation watch these exchanges smiling benignly.

MEG: And they're all ever so nice. They come up and say . . .

MRS A: Hello Billy. Has he been a good boy this week?

DAD: Top form Mrs A.

MEG: How would he know?

MRS B: And is he still going to his what-does-he-call-it?

DAD: His Day Centre, Mrs B. Oh yes. Happy as a sand boy he is down there. Wouldn't miss his Day Centre would you Billy? It's a marvellous place, Mrs B. They're marvellous people, they really are.

MEG: He's never been there. He doesn't know what he's talking about. He won't go in. Says it upsets him.

MRS C: And are you going to sing this morning Billy? Are you going to sing all those lovely hymns?

DAD: Oh yes, Mrs C. He loves a good sing don't you Billy?

MRS A: Yes.

MEG: And she turns to me and whispers . . .

MRS A: Not too loud today I hope Meg. The choir practice so hard to make a lovely sound, don't they?

MEG: And I say, don't worry Mrs A. I'll make him keep it down this week. And they all turn to Dad and say . . .

MRS A: She's a credit to you, your Meg.

MRS B: A truly remarkable girl.

MEG: And he says to them in that shiny aftershave voice he saves for the church . . .

DAD: I know ladies. The Lord has truly blessed me with Meg.

MEG: And I shut my eyes and we sing *(hymn starts and MEG shouts above the singing)* and as the church fills with sound I'm willing Billy to start. I'm saying, 'Come on Billy, go for it, it doesn't matter, Jesus doesn't mind, sing Billy, sing,' and then he shuts his eyes too . . . and he sings.

BILLY opens his mouth to sing – freeze – silence for a couple of seconds. The organ quietly plays the hymn tune as the congregation return to their benches.

SCENE 2 *MEG addresses the audience as if we'd just criticised her mother for leaving. She's not happy with us.*

MEG: She had to. She had to go away. It wasn't her fault. She had a business to run didn't she. She runs this business see . . . in London. She's really successful. Employs all these people. She's in the clothing industry . . . fashion mainly. She's a designer of some sort. She writes me letters. I've got them all. I'll be staying with her when I leave here. When I get away . . . She's going to get me a job. It's all fixed up more or less . . . I don't blame her for going. She had to. She had no choice. She couldn't have done it if she'd stayed here. Course she couldn't. All those years of wet beds and snotty tissues, church twice on Sundays and Weetabix. Aftershave and Jesus . . . I mean it's not on is it? . . . I don't blame her one bit . . . and we coped. Dad said I was a solid little trooper and I'd help him to cope with Billy . . . and I did . . . I coped. Yeah, she just packed her bags and left. No goodbyes, no nothing . . . slam . . . gone . . . and that's what I'm going to do . . . I'm going to see my Mum.

MOTHER 'appears' out of congregation. She is glamorously dressed and interacts with imaginary assistants and secretaries.

MOTHER: Nicky . . . Hi . . . Yeah it's me. Look I've got a problem over Friday . . . Yeah that's right . . . can we bring the meeting forward because I'm seeing Martin at 12 . . . yeah . . . if you could fit that in for me it'd be brilliant . . . hold the line will you Nicky . . . thanks . . . Susie they are sensational . . . I really like that one . . . can you get them down to Steve . . . get him to make copies for this afternoon . . . thanks darling . . . Hi Nicky you still there . . . sorry about that . . . no darling I can't do that I've got to be in Glasgow on Friday night . . . flight's at . . . 2.30 . . . So it's got to be earlier that morning, like 10.30? . . . brilliant, I'll bring a couple of my design people over . . . super . . . bye Nicky.

MOTHER 'exits'.

MEG: She's brilliant my Mum. I'm going to be with you soon Mummy . . . when I leave here. Just as soon as I get out of here.

SCENE 3 *Lay me Low – solo voice.*

During the singing the space becomes a park. MEG places three chairs centre together stage. BILLY watches her do it but doesn't help. The three chairs become a park bench. BILLY and MEG sit. MEG hands BILLY a football. TERRI puts on a baseball cap and emerges from the congregation.

TERRI: He doesn't play with his football. He just holds it.
MEG: What?
TERRI: He doesn't play with his football. He just holds it.
MEG: Does he.
TERRI: Yeah. Just sits there holding it . . . is he mental?
MEG: Mind your own business.
TERRI: I was only asking . . . is he though?
MEG: NO.
TERRI: Oh . . . what is he then?
MEG: I said, mind your own business.
TERRI: I only asked 'cos I'm interested . . . He looks mental.
MEG: He's . . . got learning difficulties
TERRI: Same difference.
MEG: No it's not. He's not ill. He's just . . .
TERRI: Thought so. I seen you before, down here. I could see he wasn't normal. I could tell.
MEG: Shouldn't you be at school or something?
TERRI: I don't go to school.
MEG: How old are you?
TERRI: 14.
MEG: Then you should be at school.
TERRI: I told you, I don't go. I haven't been since Christmas. They try to make me but I just bunk off again. They can't make me. School's a waste of time. You don't learn anything.
MEG: Well you won't learn anything if you don't go.
TERRI: What did you learn at school then?
MEG: Look, I don't want to talk about it all right.
TERRI: No, that's all right. We'll talk about something else.

MEG: I don't want to talk about anything. We'd prefer to just sit and watch the ducks.

TERRI: Yeah that's fine by me.

MEG: By ourselves.

TERRI: Are you ashamed of him or something?

MEG: No.

TERRI: Only I just wondered. You seem a bit touchy that's all.

MEG: I'm not touchy.

TERRI: I'd understand if you were.

MEG: I'm not touchy!

TERRI: Right . . . 'cos I talk all the time me.

MEG: I'd noticed.

TERRI: I look out all the time for interesting people and just go up to them and start chatting. You can learn a lot from people. More than you learn at school anyway.

MEG: You shouldn't talk to strangers.

TERRI: You're not a stranger. I've seen you before. I told you. I've been watching you.

MEG: You don't know me. I could be anyone.

TERRI: Yeah you could easily be a maniac couldn't you?

MEG: Don't be stupid.

TERRI: You could be a maniac who sits about in the park with her mental brother waiting to jump on little kids.

MEG: Stop it.

TERRI: Well then . . . Can he talk?

MEG: No. *(Pause)*

TERRI: We had a dog who had learning difficulties. He was mental.

MEG: *(Disbelief)* What?

TERRI: We did. Honest. The vet said he was. You can get mental dogs. Really.

MEG: If you say so.

TERRI: We had to have him put down in the end because the vet said he could never be housetrained or anything.

MEG: What a shame.

TERRI: No we had to really. He could never have lived a normal life. It was the best thing for him.

MEG: *(Angry)* Was it?

TERRI: Oh yeah, because *(realises what she's said)* . . . I didn't mean . . . I wasn't saying . . . I mean it's different for humans.

MEG: Is it?

(Long pause)

TERRI: I've upset you haven't I . . . I'm sorry . . . I didn't mean . . . I'm always saying stupid things . . . I'm sorry . . . I'd better go . . . I'm meeting my mate up the city. I'd better go.

MEG: There's no need to.

TERRI: No?

MEG: I'm not upset.

TERRI: Really?

MEG: Really.

TERRI: Oh . . . right.

MEG: My name's Meg.

TERRI: I'm Terri.

MEG: This is Billy.

TERRI: Hello Billy . . . *(BILLY smiles and takes a tissue from the sleeve of his jumper)* There, he knows his name don't you Billy? What's this?

MEG: He's giving you a tissue. It means he likes you.

TERRI: Yeah? I haven't got anything to give him. He doesn't smoke I suppose?

MEG: No.

TERRI: Yeah well, I've got to go. I'll see you around. See you around Billy. Thanks for the . . . we'll play football next time eh? *(To MEG)* Shall we? Play football next time.

MEG: Maybe. Yeah. OK.

TERRI: Right. See you.

MEG: Yeah.

SCENE 4

DAD: You see the thing is Colin. The thing about Meg, is that she's totally committed.

DAD starts this first speech immediately on MEG's cue 'Yeah' as he and COLIN sweep into the central space carrying a table. MEG moves aside and folds sheets. BILLY remains stock still holding his football. The two outer chairs from the park bench are placed at either end of the table. COLIN and DAD sit and are immediately engrossed in a chess game; the chess set and pieces can be mimed. BILLY leans forward and watches the game with his nose just above the board. Although he doesn't understand the game he watches the pieces move with intensity.

DAD: She's completely committed to Billy. Check.

MEG: This is Colin. He comes round our house on Monday nights to play chess with my Dad. He's a prat. He used to be in my year at school 'cept he stayed on to take about thirty-five A levels. I could have stayed on. I got all my exams. They said I could have gone to university . . . if I'd stayed on. But I didn't. I left . . . and did this.

MEG takes BILLY's football from him, hands him a clean tissue and exits carrying the sheets.

DAD: Oh yes. Extraordinary level of commitment. Don't you think?

COLIN: Yes I had noticed that Mr Curtis.

DAD: Now don't get me wrong Colin. I'm not saying that being committed is a bad thing. Service to others is a wonderful thing. Commitment is what it's all about. You're a committed person yourself Colin.

COLIN: Well I like to think so Mr Curtis.

DAD: Check. But you see the thing about Meg is that she's committed to the exclusion of everything else. That's what worries me Colin. She's got no outside interests, nothing to broaden her horizons. Now in my book, Colin, horizons should be broad.

COLIN: Couldn't agree with you more Mr Curtis. They're always saying that to us at school. They make a point of stressing that . . . point. If you know what I mean.

DAD: I do indeed Colin. Check. Now I've got broad horizons, I've got the church of course. And work. And I don't mind telling you Colin that these are pretty challenging times in the water industry right now and you're no use to anyone with your head in the sand.

COLIN: Right.

DAD: And then there's the chess club. Check. Watch your bishop Colin. And the horticultural society. It's so important to keep the old brain box well oiled. To keep abreast of things. Don't you think so Colin?

COLIN: Yes I do. I was only saying to Mum . . .

DAD: You've got to be receptive to ideas, to possibilities you see. It's no good shutting yourself off from the world.

COLIN: Yes . . . I mean no.

DAD: Okay. Okay we've got our cross to bear in this family. I'd be the first to admit we've got our cross to bear. Billy is not easy . . . he's quite a struggle in fact and there are days when I feel the Lord is really putting my faith to the test. But I cope. One copes. That's all there is to it. But the main thing, Colin. The secret of it is not let it rule your life.

COLIN: Right.

DAD: Keep your mind alive and agile. Develop interests. Get out of the house and keep active.

COLIN: Right.

DAD: But you see Meg doesn't. She doesn't seem able to Colin. It's Billy this and Billy that. That's all there is for her. She can't seem to develop an outlet. That's what she needs, Colin. An outlet. Check.

COLIN: I see what you mean.

DAD: Let me ask you something Colin. Man to man. And I'm not being nosey here.

COLIN: Of course not.

DAD: Have you got a girlfriend . . . at all?

COLIN: No not yet.

DAD: You don't mind me asking?

COLIN: No not really.

DAD: You see Colin, and you're probably ahead of me on this one, Meg's been getting a bit edgy recently. A bit tense really and I think what she needs is an outlet. A bit of a boost. Are you with me?

COLIN: Um . . . no not really.

DAD: Ask her out Colin.

COLIN: What?

DAD: Ask her for a date.

COLIN: But I'm not sure she'd . . .

DAD: She's an attractive girl Colin.

COLIN: Well yes but she's older than me.

DAD: And I'm confident you'd behave appropriately. You wouldn't take advantage of her.

COLIN: Oh no, I wouldn't do that.

DAD: What about next Friday?

COLIN: But maybe she's doing something.

DAD: But this is the point Colin. She doesn't do anything. This is the point I'm making.

COLIN: But she might not want to. She might not like me.

DAD: Colin, listen to me. I think I know Meg pretty well, I think I know what makes old Meg tick. Enough said?

COLIN: Well if you're sure Mr Curtis.

DAD: Good, that's arranged then.

COLIN: I'll ask her then shall I?

DAD: *(Consults his diary)* Oh no hang about, not Friday. I've got a chess club committee meeting. Hang on Colin, Thursday's no good, choir, and Saturday night's the horticultural society AGM and disco. We can't leave Billy see. Now let's see. Monday, Tuesday.

COLIN: Perhaps we'd better leave it.

DAD: Wednesday! It's going to have to be Wednesday.

COLIN: Well . . .

DAD: Yes Wednesday's okay by me. Have a little word with her Colin. It'd be such a boost. You've no idea what a weight off my mind it'd be.

COLIN: Well . . .

DAD: Lovely job. It's all fixed then. Checkmate.

SCENE 5 *Six congregation members transform into bored Year 11 girls. A seventh becomes their teacher. The girls take up position sitting on the table and chairs looking out above the audience. They are looking at an image on a screen. As* MEG *enters and joins the group of girls* BILLY *sits beside her and holds her hand.*

MEG: We had this teacher at school and they all used to laugh at her. Her name was Miss Lovejoy. She used to do this special course called Assertiveness Training for Girls. It was for Year 11 girls only. The boys weren't allowed in it. It was supposed to raise our consciousness and stuff, so we wouldn't spend the rest of our lives doing the ironing or agree to be on page three in the *Sun*. That sort of thing. It was sad really because she really put a lot into it. She really believed what she was saying. But it all fell on stony ground . . . they just laughed at her.
(MEG joins the class)

MISS: So the argument being presented here is that this sort of thing is unacceptable because, Tracey it . . .?

TRACEY: *(Bored and unconvinced)* Degrades women, Miss.

MISS: Because it degrades women and turns us, Debbie into . . .?

DEBBIE: Sex objects, Miss.

MISS: Sex objects. Because it turns us into sex objects.
(Stifled giggles)
And this sort of cultural reinforcement is inevitably going to damage our . . . Mandy?

MANDY: Self-esteem, Miss.

MISS: Exactly. But our bodies are also seen in another, altogether different, cultural context. Or is it actually different I wonder? Mandy, take a look at this photograph. *(The teacher operates a remote for her whiteboard. An image appears on a screen upstage of the group so we are seeing what the girls are seeing. A woman is breastfeeding a baby.)* Right, what do you see?

MANDY: Woman with a baby, Miss.

MISS: And what is the woman doing, Mandy?

MANDY: *(Embarrassed)* Feeding it, Miss.

MISS: Yes Mandy, but how is she feeding it?

MANDY: Miss?

MISS: Well, what is she doing? Is she giving it a doughnut?

MANDY: No Miss.

MISS: Well?

MANDY: She's breastfeeding it.

MISS: Thank you. She is breastfeeding it. One of the oldest and most potent images of womanhood. Mother suckling baby, woman the feeder, nurturer, carer, Madonna and child.

TRACEY: That's not Madonna is it?

MISS: Not *the* Madonna, Tracey. At least not the contemporary one. You see, what you're looking at there is another great cultural and social trap for women. Beware that picture, girls.

DEBBIE: What's wrong with it, Miss? Don't you think breastfeeding is right?

MISS: Of course it's right. Nothing could be more natural, nothing could be more perfect. No, what I challenge are the assumptions that go with that picture. The expectations that accompany it.

MEG: And you could see them starting to glaze over. Assumptions, expectations, they didn't give a toss. She lost them. But not me. She hadn't lost me. It was like she was talking just to me. I understood every word she said.

MISS: What I challenge is the assumption that women are designed by nature to be the carers, the feeders, the nurturers. Our voices, our skins, our rounded shapes all designed by nature to be soft, sympathetic, to give and to care. Designed by nature. Mother nature. So of course we do care. We're brilliant at it, from the cradle to the grave, we do it. We care. A man just recycles the same old image, mummy becomes wife. The breast becomes a Sunday roast and when he's old, she'll be there to tuck a blanket round his legs and push his wheelchair out into the sun on the day he has his final stroke . . . of luck. There's a very odd thing going on out there, girls. The people out there who care, and I'm talking about the ones who get their hands dirty caring, the ones who mop up sick, who wipe bums, who change the dressings on old men's bed sores . . . who are they? . . . They're women, girls, 99 per cent are women. And you know what we have to do about it don't you. We have to say to men 'you can do it too' . . . that's all, 'you can do it too'. Five words. Sounds simple, but making them accept it might be the hardest thing you have to do.

School bell sounds – MISS LOVEJOY and the six girls depart and blend back into the congregation.

SCENE 6 *A lighting change; a darker wash. BILLY comes downstage centre. MEG watches. BILLY is cold. Four girls run on in their coats, scarves and hats. They stop running when they see BILLY.*

ONE: Look, Billy Curtis.

TWO: Oh yeah.

THREE: Where's your sister Billy?

FOUR: Are you all by yourself?
(The four girls freeze)

MEG: I have dreams. Billy dreams. Nightmares. In my dreams he always needs me. I have to get there. I always have to get there in time. *(MEG gently touches BILLY on the cheek and slowly exits)*

ONE: He looks cold, doesn't he?

TWO: Are you cold, Billy?

THREE: He hasn't got a coat.

FOUR: Aaah. Poor, poor little Billy.

ONE: Give him a cuddle. Warm him up.

TWO: Yeah, give him a cuddle.

THREE: You give him a cuddle. I'm not.

FOUR: You want a cuddle, Billy?

ONE: Look, he's smiling. He wants one.

TWO: Go on then.

THREE: You must be joking.

FOUR: I dare you.

ONE: You daren't.

TWO: You're scared of him.

THREE: I'm not.

FOUR: He won't hurt you.

ONE: Chicken.

TWO: Chicken.

THREE: All right . . . All right. *(She gives him a very brief cuddle)*

FOUR: Eugh . . . she did it. She gave him one.

ONE: What's he staring at?

TWO: You looking for the ducks, Billy?

THREE: They're not here. They've flown away.

FOUR: The pond's all frozen over, Billy.

ONE: No . . . Ducks . . . Ducks flown away . . . pissed off.

TWO: *(Pause)* You can walk on that ice, Billy.

THREE: You could skate on that ice if you wanted to.

FOUR: If you had some skates, you could glide right across.

ONE: To the other side.

TWO: Don't you fancy that, Billy?

THREE: Go on, have a go, Billy. I bet your nice shoes would skate really well.

FOUR: He's not that stupid.

ONE: I bet he is.

TWO: He wouldn't.

ONE: Bet he would. Bet I could make him.

THREE: Go on then.

FOUR: Yeah, go on then, make him.

ONE: All right. *(She takes off her glove and throws it on the ice)* Oh look! Look, Billy, my glove's fallen on the ice. *(BILLY stares at the glove alarmed)* Will you fetch my glove, Billy? Please Billy, it's only over there. It's all right it's safe. Go on, Billy. My hands are getting ever so cold.

(BILLY starts to rock. Looks terrified, puts one foot on the ice.)

MEG: *(Scream. MEG sprints on.)* Billy! *(The girls flee. Lighting change.)* I have to get there see . . . Have to . . . I'm responsible.

SCENE 7 *The dream figures disappear as the lights change. Voices sing 'Lay me Low' as TERRI inspects the house. BILLY sits at the table. His eyes follow TERRI.*

TERRI: It's a nice house.

MEG: It's all right.

TERRI: Better than our house. I wouldn't let you see our house. Our house is a dump. What's your dad do?

MEG: He works for the Water Authority.

TERRI: Is that a good job? Does he get loads of money?

MEG: No. He pretends it's a good job but it isn't. It's a crap job. To hear him talk, you'd think he ran the whole water industry but he doesn't.

TERRI: Has he got a secretary?

MEG: No, he's got a van.

TERRI: Oh. Where's your Mum? . . . Are they divorced?

MEG: Sort of. She had to go away. She went away to start her own business.

TERRI: Did she?

MEG: Yeah. She's brilliant actually. She's in fashion . . . and design . . . that sort of thing. She's going to get me a job. And she writes to me . . . she's brilliant, my Mum.

MOTHER reappears and sits at the table. She talks to an invisible assistant. MEG is visibly proud, TERRI is fascinated and impressed.

MUM: Look I want you to tell the Newcastle people that on 40 grand they can get stuffed. We're talking 35 grand or we're not talking at all . . . Well use your charm darling . . . yes . . . I don't want to have to go up there next week without a draft contract in my hand, is that clear?

She coolly stares at the assistant then suddenly returns to the congregation.

TERRI: D'you think she'd get me a job?

MEG: She might do.

TERRI: She might be able to get me a modelling job or something.

MEG: Maybe.

TERRI: Yeah? I fancy that. So where's your Dad now?

MEG: Out. He's always out.

TERRI: Is he?

MEG: Yes.

TERRI: So you have to do everything for Billy then?

MEG: Yeah.

TERRI: What, everything?

MEG: More or less.

TERRI: Do you have to take him to the toilet?

MEG: Sort of.

TERRI: What do you mean sort of?

MEG: Look, you don't want to know all about that.

TERRI: I do. I'm interested . . . do you?

MEG: Well he can usually manage. But he has . . . mishaps.

TERRI: Does he? What, like accidents?

MEG: Yes.

TERRI: In his pants?

MEG: *(Irritated)* Yes.

TERRI: Oh . . . what's it like?

MEG: What's what like?

TERRI: Doing all that for him. Is it really awful?

MEG: What do you think?

TERRI: No, but does it make you feel . . .

MEG: Sick? Does it make me feel sick? No . . . It makes me feel . . . Angry.

TERRI: So what are you going to do?

MEG: Do?

TERRI: What you going to do? You're not going to carry on doing this for the rest of your life are you? . . . Are you?

MEG: No . . . I'm going to get a job. Going to live with my Mum.

TERRI: When?

MEG: Dunno . . . soon.

TERRI: Are you really?

MEG: Yes.

TERRI: You going to leave Billy?

MEG: Yes.

TERRI: What'll happen to him?

MEG: My Dad'll have to cope, won't he? That's what he says to people when they ask how he manages to look after Billy. He says 'it's a struggle but one copes', that's what he says, 'one copes'! But he doesn't. I cope. Well now it's his turn. It's his bloody turn to cope, 'cos I'm going.

TERRI: I bet you don't.

MEG: I bet I do. I've got to. I've got to get out of this. I've got to get away. If I don't do it now I'll be here forever. *(Pause)* You think it's terrible don't you? You think I'm selfish, go on say it.

TERRI: I think . . . yeah . . . you've got to go.

MEG: You're not just saying that?

TERRI: No I'm not. You've got to go. I mean it. You can't keep on doing this for the rest of your life. It's not your fault he's like this. You didn't ask for this job. You're going to still be taking him to the park, to watch the ducks when he's sixty? Are you going to spend the rest of your life with a spare pair of pants in your pocket? Are you really going to do that?

MEG: Someone's got to.

TERRI: But it doesn't have to be you. I wouldn't do it. Even if he was my brother, I wouldn't do it. It's too much. It's not fair. He's not your kid.

MEG: I know . . . I know.

TERRI: Then go.

MEG: I'm going.

TERRI: Go tonight. Go now.

MEG: I can't go now.

TERRI: Yes you can. I'll sit with him till your Dad gets back. He'll be all right. Go and pack your bags. Go on. Do it.

MEG: I can't . . . not now.

TERRI: Told you so. Told you, you wouldn't.

MEG: I will.

TERRI: When?

MEG: Soon. When the time's right. I've got to be ready. Very soon. Maybe tomorrow. I'll know when the moment's right. You don't believe me, do you? You don't think I can do it? Do you?

TERRI: No.

(TERRI exits)

MEG: You wait. When the time's right. You'll see. When the time's right, you just watch me go.

MEG joins BILLY at the table. Out of her jeans pocket she takes a pair of boys underpants. BILLY sees the pants and stares at them intently for a few seconds as if he's expecting something to happen with them and then without warning . . .

SCENE 8 . . . *COLIN enters. MEG hastily grabs the pants and hastily puts them back in her pocket. She is tetchy with COLIN from the outset.*

COLIN: Hello Meg.

MEG: You didn't knock.

COLIN: Um. Door was open. Sorry . . .

MEG: You're supposed to knock. What d'you want? It's not your night for chess, is it?

COLIN: Well, no. No, it's not actually.

MEG: He's not in anyway.

COLIN: Isn't he . . . oh . . . that's a pity.

MEG: I'll tell him you called round.

COLIN: Right . . . Actually Meg . . . I was wondering if . . .

MEG: Yes?

COLIN: I thought you might like . . .

MEG: Like what?

COLIN: Pardon.

MEG: You thought I might like what?

COLIN: I thought you might like to go out.

MEG: Oh, that's really nice of you Colin.

COLIN: Is it?

MEG: Yeah. It's very thoughtful.

COLIN: Oh . . . good.

MEG: It's the first time anyone's ever offered.

COLIN: Is it?

MEG: Yes.

COLIN: I can't believe that.

MEG: It is. You're the first, Colin.

COLIN: Am I?

MEG: Yeah. You're the first person who's ever come round and said, 'I thought you might like to go out, Meg,' and offered to look after Billy. It's very kind of you.

COLIN: What?

MEG: It's not that I particularly want to go out or anything, but it'd be nice if people offered to come round and sit with Billy.

COLIN: Oh . . . no.

MEG: I think people are scared of him. They think he'd be difficult or something.

COLIN: No, actually . . .

MEG: You'd have thought somebody would've offered. Somebody from the church maybe. Somebody might have considered the possibility that I might just occasionally fancy a night off.

COLIN: Well, no, the thing is Meg . . .

MEG: 'Cos he never does. It never crosses Dad's mind. He packs his social calendar full of events, activities, meetings, anything. Anything to get out of the house. He believes in broad horizons see. But he never offers to sit with Billy.

COLIN: No . . . the thing is, Meg, this isn't quite what I meant.

MEG: No?

COLIN: Although obviously I would be happy to look after Billy any time you wanted . . . to go out. But the thing is that . . . um. What I meant was . . . I thought you might like to go out . . . with me.

MEG: With you?

COLIN: Yes.

MEG: What for?

COLIN: Um . . . well, we could go and see a film . . . or something, on Wednesday. Are you doing anything on Wednesday?

MEG: Let me get this straight, Colin. Are you asking me out?

COLIN: Um . . . well yes, I am really. Yes.

MEG: *(Suspicious)* Why?

COLIN: What?

MEG: Why are you asking me out?

COLIN: I don't know. I just thought.

MEG: Did he put you up to this?

COLIN: Who?

MEG: Dad. Is this his idea?

COLIN: No.

MEG: Colin. Did he tell you to ask me out?

COLIN: No . . . well, yes. He sort of suggested it.

MEG: Right, that's it.

COLIN: He was thinking of you Meg.

MEG: He's asked for it now.

COLIN: He said you needed a boost.

MEG: He said what?

COLIN: He said you were getting a bit tense and you needed a boost. He said he'd be available to look after Billy . . .

MEG: On Wednesday?

COLIN: Yes.

MEG: Bastard.

COLIN: No. He was thinking of you Meg. He was thinking of your horizons.

MEG: This is it. This is the last straw. My horizons . . .

COLIN: He didn't mean any harm.

MEG: Shut up, Colin . . .

COLIN: *(Pause)* So it's . . . not on for Wednesday then . . .
(MEG looks at him)

COLIN: No, I suppose not. *(He looks at his watch and swiftly exits)*

SCENE 9 *DAD appears. MEG is furious. BILLY remains at the table. He reacts to the angry tones of voice and is distressed when MEG raises her voice to DAD.*

MEG: How could you do that!

DAD: Meg, I really don't see what all the fuss is about.

MEG: How could you!
DAD: He's a nice lad, Meg.
MEG: He's still at school!
DAD: I don't see what that's got to do with it.
MEG: You don't understand, do you?
DAD: No, to be perfectly frank I don't actually.
MEG: Do you think so little of me? Do you think I'm such a pathetic, shrivelled-up, hopeless little person that I need you to do that for me?
DAD: I thought you'd be pleased. I thought you needed . . .
MEG: A boost wasn't it? You thought I needed a boost.
DAD: Well you do, Meg. You haven't been your old self for some time.
MEG: And you thought that little prat would supply me with a boost?
DAD: Meg, I won't have you talk about Colin in that tone.
MEG: You thought that a night out with Colin would solve all my problems did you? You thought I'd come home refreshed and renewed after a night out with Colin.
DAD: Meg, for goodness sake.
MEG: You thought I'd come home and wash another load of Billy's dirty sheets with a song in my heart just because I'd spent the evening with bloody Colin?
(Pause)
DAD: I see. So that's what all this is about is it? Yes I thought so. I knew it.
MEG: You knew what?
DAD: I've seen it coming, Meg.
MEG: Seen what?
DAD: I've seen it all before, Meg.
MEG: What're you talking about?
DAD: You're very like your mother in many ways.
MEG: I don't know what you mean.
DAD: Don't play the innocent with me, girl. You can't fool me. I know exactly what you're thinking. Go on. Say it. Say it to my face. Say it to Billy. Or are you going to do what she did . . . slink off in the middle of the night without even saying goodbye? Go on, Meg, tell him or haven't you got the guts either?
(Pause)
No . . . I didn't think so. You disappoint me, Meg. I thought you'd be stronger than her.
MEG: She was strong.
DAD: She was nothing.
MEG: She did it 'cos she had to. She had no choice. It was her only chance. She was strong.
DAD: SHE WAS NOTHING . . . She is nothing.
MEG: No! You're jealous. You're only jealous 'cos she's made something of herself.

DAD: Oh yes . . . oh yes she's really made something of herself all right.

MEG: She has. She's told me all about it. I've got letters.

DAD: What letters?

MEG: She sends me letters.

DAD: No she doesn't.

MEG: I've got letters.

DAD: Well, where are they? Where are these letters . . . Come on, show me the letters. Where do you keep them?

MEG: Don't.

DAD: Where are they? . . . Come on, Meg. Where are they?

MEG: Dad, please.

DAD: There aren't any there. She hasn't sent you any, has she? You've made them up. I've heard you tell Billy about them. 'I've had another letter from Mum today, Billy. She's doing ever so well.'

MEG: Stop it.

DAD: 'She's going to a meeting in Glasgow this week, Billy.' I've heard you, Meg . . . There aren't any letters . . . are there?

MEG: No.

DAD: No.

MEG: But she has made it. I know it. I can feel it. She's out there somewhere and she's made it really big. I know that because . . . she must have done. 'Cos she got away from here.

DAD: She was full of dreams, Meg. Full of dreams. Just like you. She never quite seemed to be able to . . . pin things down. She never quite got to grips with the situation. When Billy was little . . . very little, she gave him a plastic saxophone for Christmas. And he loved it. He used to play with it all the time. Do you remember it?

MEG: Sort of.

DAD: Horrible noise it was. Eventually it got all bunged up with dribble or something and it wouldn't work anymore. She used to say, 'Look at him on his saxophone. He'll be playing in a band next.' And when there was somebody playing the saxophone on telly she'd say, 'Look that'll be Billy one day.' I mean, she knew what he was like. We knew right from the beginning what he was like but she couldn't ever accept it. She could never quite pin it down. Always full of dreams. 'When I get my shop. When I open my first boutique,' she'd say. 'When we move to Cornwall,' she'd say. 'When you get your promotion,' she'd say . . . full of dreams. It never happened. None of it. It was all wishful thinking. Just like Billy's saxophone.

MEG: Maybe it did happen for her. Maybe she did make it.

DAD: Meg you're too old now for all that nonsense. You can't carry on believing all that. Not at your age.

MEG: It could have happened. It happens to some people.

DAD: All right I'll tell you. I'll tell you what she does. Oh it's a big business all right. Just about the biggest there is.

MOTHER appears wearing a department store uniform.

MOTHER: No Madam I don't think we've got a large in stock. I'll just check for you . . . Sonia, do we have this in a large? . . . she's just checking . . . yes, they're pure wool. Excuse me . . . No you want lingerie, madam . . . Turn left at the serve-yourself-sock-counter and straight on past woolly hats . . . Right, thanks Sonia. Sorry madam, apparently we've only got medium in the beige. I could order you a large . . . You'll take this? . . . Lovely. That'll be £39.99. Do you want cash back with that at all? *(MOTHER freezes for a moment. MEG stares at her as she returns to the congregation.)*

DAD: I'm sorry. You had to know. I'm sorry.

MEG: It's all right.

DAD: You need a holiday, Meg. That's what you need.

MEG: Yes.

DAD: I tell you what we'll do, Meg. We'll pop down to Devon eh? I've got a spot of holiday coming up and what we'll do is we'll motor down through Wiltshire, show Billy Stonehenge and then make straight for . . .

MEG: Exeter.

DAD: Yeah . . . yeah that's what we'll do eh? Lovely old job . . . Right . . . Well I think I'll turn in actually . . . You all right?

MEG: Yes.

DAD: Right . . . Night, Billy . . .

MEG: Dad?

DAD: What.

MEG: I do love Billy.

DAD: Course you do, course you do . . . *(stops as he remembers)* Listen, He that loveth not his brother whom he hath seen, how can he love God whom he hath not seen, 1 John 27. Worth remembering that . . . eh, Meg?

MEG: Yes . . . thank you.

DAD exits, leaving MEG and BILLY alone on stage.

Congregation leaves benches and assemble tightly upstage. They stare intently at MEG. A church organ softly plays 'Lay me Low' as MEG stands centre stage staring ahead as she hears the following voices . . .

MUM: Look you can tell the Newcastle people that on 40 grand they can get stuffed.

TERRI: Is he mental?
MRS C: Are you going to sing this morning Billy?
TERRI: He looks mental.
TEACHER: Designed by nature to be soft, sympathetic, to give and to care.
MRS B: A truly remarkable girl.
TEACHER: Designed by nature. Mother nature.
GIRL: You could skate on ice like that, Billy.
TERRI: What's it like. Is it really awful?
DAD: And the beaches, Meg. You wait till you see the beaches.
DEBBIE: Sex objects.
DAD: I think I know what makes old Meg tick.
TERRI: Are you going to spend the rest of your life with a spare pair of pants in your pocket?
DAD: Say it to my face. Say it to Billy.
COLIN: He said you needed a boost.
DAD: Or are you going to do what she did.
MUM: Lovely, that'll be £39.99.
DAD: Slink off in the middle of the night . . .
MUM: Do you want cash back with that at all?
DAD: . . . without even saying goodbye.

TERRI comes out of the crowd. She is carrying a letter, a suitcase and an overcoat. She helps MEG put on the coat then hands her the case and the letter. She takes hold of MEG's hand and whispers . . .

TERRI: Go tonight, Meg. Go now.

The congregation return to their benches leaving BILLY alone sitting at the table. He stares at MEG.

Song, 'Lay Me Low'.

SCENE 10 *MEG carefully puts the letter on the table.*

MEG: Well this is it then, Billy. I'm going now. Going to get a train . . . or maybe a bus. I've got some money. I'll be all right. I'll write you a . . . I'll get in touch. Don't worry. He'll look after you. He'll cope. He'll be down in a minute for his cocoa and he'll see you and he'll . . . put you to bed. He'll manage. It'll be great just the two of you. It'll be . . . Billy, you've got to understand. I can't do this any more. I can keep on . . . If I stay I'll end up hating you and I . . . don't want to hate you.
(BILLY gives her his tissue)

No, Billy! I'm not doing it any more. I won't do it. You're so stupid. Why are you so stupid? Don't look at me. Don't look at me you stupid, stupid . . .
(She makes to leave but stops in her tracks and goes back. BILLY is crying.)
I'm sorry, Billy. I didn't mean that. It's all right . . . it's all right don't cry. It's all right. He'll come down in a minute. He'll look after you . . . all right? Right.

MEG leaves. BILLY is now alone. He goes to the exit through which MEG has left and stares after her puzzled. He slowly returns to the table and looks at the letter. Then he waits patiently for something to happen. We need to feel the weight of MEG's absence. Suddenly DAD enters wearing dressing gown etc.

DAD: Just make myself a warm drink, Meg . . . You still up, Billy? *(Pause)* She in the other room is she? Meg? . . . Meg? *(Sees letter)* What's this? . . . What's this? Oh I see *(Sits down)* . . . I see . . . I thought she'd . . . I thought she was . . . Never mind, Billy eh? . . . We'll cope . . . We always cope don't we . . . I'll take you up. Put you to bed . . . Not to worry . . . She'll probably be back in the morning. Yeah, you mark my words. She'll be back . . . She'll be . . . *(He becomes more and more distraught till he is shouting)* You want to go to the toilet, Billy? . . . eh? You normally go to the toilet before you go to bed? Do you . . . What normally happens? . . . Billy? . . . What happens now?
(MEG is standing in the doorway)
Meg? You came back . . . You came back, Meg. Let me take your coat. Look Billy it's Meg. She's come back, I told you didn't I. Well take your coat off, Meg. That's it. I'll make us a warm drink shall I? I'll make us all one. Now come on, Meg. You come and sit down. That's it. Lovely job . . . Meg I'm not angry . . . I understand *(She glares at him)* I know you don't think I do but I do . . . understand . . . See this letter? Well I haven't even read it and I tell you what I'm going to do Meg. I'm not going to read it . . . I'm going to give it back to you and forget I've ever seen it . . . go on take it back . . . that's my girl . . . there . . . that's right . . . now you dispose of it in your own good time . . . and let me make this absolutely clear, Meg. I'm never going to refer to this incident again. In my book this is a closed chapter . . . You did what you did but I'm not going to hold it against you . . . See? Finished. That's the end of it . . . Right? . . . Yeah . . . Look, Meg . . . Look what I've got. I meant it to be a surprise but now is as good a time as any. Look. It's the Michelin guide. Campsites in Devon and Cornwall. It's the new one. Only just out. It's got over 300 sites in it . . . Got

it on Amazon . . . I've pencilled in a few likely looking ones . . . eh? . . . What d'you say?

MEG: I think I'll take Billy up now.

DAD: Right . . . right. Get some sleep. Sunday tomorrow. Big day . . . We'll talk about it in the morning.

(MEG gets up and goes to BILLY)

DAD: Meg, before you go up. Shall we? . . . Come on Meg. It'll make you feel better. It'll make us all feel better . . . *(MEG nods tired)* Lovely job.

DAD starts the prayer. As he does so the congregation come out of the benches and fill up the space looking at the audience and joining in the prayer. Two voices sing 'Lay Me Low' to run alongside the prayer which gets louder and louder as more and more voices join in.

Our father
Which Art in Heaven
Hallowed be thy Name
Thy Kingdom come
Thy will be done
On Earth as it is in Heaven
Give us this day our daily bread
And forgive us our trespasses
As we forgive those that trespass against us
Lead us not into temptation
And deliver us from evil
For thine is the Kingdom
The power
And the Glory . . . . *(silence)*

MEG: For ever and ever. Amen.

(Black)

Chapter 8

Peer perspectives

Buckethead

Alun Bliss wrote *Buckethead* while a teacher at Springwood High School in King's Lynn. The play was first performed in July 2008 and made available to any teachers interested through the drama_uk e-group. It is published here for the first time.

The author explains his reason for writing the play thus:

> Having taught for nearly 20 years, it shames me to admit that it is only recently that I have begun to understand the world of the child on the autistic spectrum.

Having undertaken some background reading and considered some of the children he had or was still teaching, he became particularly focused on Asperger's syndrome.

> What interested me was how the people who come into contact with the Asperger's child manage to cope. How do teachers learn to communicate differently with the Asperger's child? Indeed, to what extent should they be expected to? How do the peer group come to accept that s/he is different? How does a mother deal with 'difficult' behaviour every day?

While Bliss modestly proclaims that *Buckethead* 'does not necessarily give me the answers, but it has begun to pose some of the right questions for my students and is proving an interesting learning tool', the play does suggest some helpful answers without preaching or lecturing.

The piece opens with a slideshow of famous people who are known or presumed to have been on the autistic spectrum: Mozart, Howard Hughes, Sir Isaac Newton, J. R. R. Tolkein, Andy Warhol, Henry Ford, Jane Austen. Indeed, Michael Fitzgerald (2003) has ventured that Lewis Carrol and W. B. Yeats would also be on a list of famous artists that may be regarded as having displayed characteristics of autism. The important point being made here is that, while it may be true that children on the autistic spectrum might well, like Raymond Babbitt in *Rain Man*, have particular skills in mathematics, others can focus on other areas sometimes with astonishing results: 'Until recently, the focus has been on the link between autism and logical ability, such as enhanced mathematical skill. Creative ability, meanwhile, has been considered beyond the reach of those with autism' (Jackson 2011).

The slideshow switches to pictures of jazz icons Jelly Roll Morton, Bessie Smith and Ma Rainey who then appear as narrators and commentators through the play, the protagonist of which is fascinated by jazz music and its exponents (both Sidney Bechet and Bix Beiderbecke were, we learn, most likely to have been on the autistic spectrum).

Like Sheila and Brian in *A Day in the Death of Joe Egg*, Buckethead's parents are tasked with telling the audience a little about his birth and early years. Flashbacks are used to show some significant scenes, such as his entry into nursery school (illustrating his inability to play with other children) and a family holiday during which he discovers a fascination for pebbles. We are never told his real name, which effectively estranges the character from the audience and so aligns its members with the other characters in the play who find him odd. Bliss bravely allows the other characters to openly state the difficulty that they have dealing with Buckethead. For example, a speech by his father illustrates the struggle that many people have with children both with Asperger's and wider-ranging disabilities, and deserves some sympathy for its honesty and sense of bewilderment:

> He's not what I call disabled. Well, he is – but not what I call it. I mean he's all there. He wasn't born defective. You know what I mean? I suppose he is defective – a bit . . . And it is a sort of disabled. Just not what you might call a physicality . . . He has got a disability. We know he has. But he's maybe got more of an a-bility. Maybe his disability is his being able. He's on a spectrum. The doctor says to think of it as a result of him being focused. Like he focuses too much . . . P'raps he's just bloody odd. He is bloody odd – always has been.

It's not so easy though to afford such sympathy to the character of the grandmother, who expresses the not uncommonly held view that Buckethead's problems stem from him being spoiled and all he needs is a good smack. While she is constructed as a sharp-tongued malevolent whose world exists only in terms of black and white, even more scathing criticism is reserved for Buckethead's form teacher who cannot be bothered to read a comprehensive document on inclusion produced by the school's SENCO on the grounds that, 'I've never read anything with 46 pages in it', and voices on stage what has doubtless been voiced in staffrooms across the country: 'Don't know why we don't just call them "naughty" any more.' The teacher duly goes off to encounter his new pupil and comically makes an ass of himself by working his way through a catalogue of things that are simply inappropriate when dealing with children with Asperger's by, for example, using ellipsis, sarcasm and idiom, and interpreting the boy's confused responses to these as being insolent. As a result of this encounter, the boy removes himself to the girl's lavatory and puts a bucket on his head. Another teacher proceeds to give an object lesson in how not to deal with such a situation, while the voice of humanity and reason comes from a student, Belinda, who remembers him from playgroup: 'Just leave him, Miss. He didn't know this was for the girls – he's new. He just wanted a quiet place – 'cos he's had a tough day. People have been giving him a hard (time).'

In an earlier scene, it is Belinda who probably sums up the key message of the play for all those teachers and pupils who ever come across such children: 'Leave him. He's all right when you get to know him. He's not stupid. He's a bit odd, that's all.'

Children can be cruel

It is often said that 'children can be cruel'. Without constantly seeking to address this, however, the likelihood is that discriminatory, prejudicial and indeed abusive behaviours will continue into adulthood. Quarmby reports that a 1999 Mencap survey of 500 children with learning difficulties found that 80 per cent had been bullied and 60 per cent physically hurt. Disabled children are twice as likely to be abused as non-disabled, and nearly three quarters had been taunted in public. In 2006, a National Autistic Society survey (*B is for Bullying*), which had 1,400 responses, found that 40 per cent had been bullied at school. In almost half of these cases, the school had taken no action (Quarmby 2011: 146).

Some might suggest that everyone is the butt of humour at some time or another, and that we must all toughen up and learn to live with it. Indeed, in *Wait Until Dark*, Frederick Knott's 1966 thriller, the blind protagonist is advised by her husband to call their bespectacled 12-year-old neighbour 'four eyes' on account that, 'That's what the kids at school are calling her and she can't take it, so they'll go on till she can.' Colin Barnes, however, posits that:

> being mocked publicly is only acceptable if the negative images which ensue can be offset against positive ones, or if those being ridiculed are able to defend themselves should they choose to. At present there are virtually no positive images of disabled people in the media, and disabled people do not have the resources or a legal framework within which to fight this type of discrimination.
>
> (Barnes 1992: 14)

From my own experience and the experiences reported to me by the trainee teachers with whom I work, Bliss is certainly touching on a raw nerve in his exposure of the amount of ignorance that exists in schools regarding the autistic spectrum and how to manage behaviours associated with it. However, as Darren

Jackson, principal of Beechwood College, a specialist residential college of further education for students with an Autistic Spectrum Disorder or Asperger's syndrome, points out, autism is now the second most common developmental disability in the world after intellectual disability, and is 'observable in at least one in 200 children today, compared with one in 2,500 four decades ago' (Jackson 2011: 25). On this basis alone, there would seem to be an imperative to discuss more openly in schools what autism, along with other disabilities, involves in order to dispel ignorance and move towards a more equitable society. The question is: To what extent might the dramatic literature commonly available to young people contribute towards such a quest?

One of the most commonly studied plays in secondary schools in the UK is Dennis Potter's *Blue Remembered Hills* (1979), which, until the introduction of a new specification in 2010, had long been a set text on the AQA GCSE Drama course. It was an unusual choice of play for such an examination, partly because it was written for television (it was first screened by the BBC as part of their Play for Today season in 1979) and also because Potter intended the child characters to be performed by adults.

The play is set in the Forest of Dean in 1943 and follows the actions of a group of 7-year-olds through a day. Not far into the play, Peter, who is depicted as a bully, and the cleverer Willie spot a squirrel that they chase and corner up a tree. They are joined by two other boys who help them to force the squirrel down the tree, after which they trap it and kill it. Meanwhile, a boy known to them all as Donald Duck is in a barn playing Mummies and Daddies (and later Doctors and Nurses) with two girls who tease him. Donald Duck is clearly a vulnerable child who, it is inferred, is abused by his mother. After later being taunted and persecuted by all of the other children, Donald Duck goes back to the barn on his own to play by himself. The play ends in tragedy, though, when he sets fire to the barn and finds himself trapped inside. *Blue Remembered Hills* shows that childhood can be a fearful place, where emotions are deeply felt and social pressures enormous, especially from other children. It explores the themes of cruelty, social exclusion and status as the children struggle to establish themselves with their peers; failure to do so leads to misery and loneliness. The pressure to conform and to belong causes the children to behave carelessly and even with cruelty to one another, especially to the most vulnerable, and reinforces the notion that, from a vulnerable person's point of view, any kind of friendship is better than no friendship at all. Sadly, frequent cases of what has become known as 'mate crime' illustrate that the consequences of vulnerable people not being taught how to recognise the difference between genuine friendship and exploitation may be horrific.

Potter's decision to use adults to play the parts of the children did not come from a desire for novelty or humour. He did not want to complicate the audience's reactions with any sentiment or sympathy they might feel to the sight of real children playing. He also felt that real child actors would subtly censor their actions as children naturally do when under adult scrutiny. By using adults, the audience would be able to see and experience the actions and emotions directly. Nonetheless, *Blue Remembered Hills* is regularly performed by young actors in schools and youth theatres. This again raises the issue of why plays that feature disabled characters are performed in schools, what the outcomes of such performances might be, and what ethical issues may be involved. For example, National Drama's magazine 'Drama: one forum many voices' (Spring 2008, 15.1) carried the advice that Howard Brenton's 1969 play *Gum and Goo* was ideal for use in school due to its cast size, minimal set, and challenging balance between lighter moments and underlying savagery.

The main character of this play, Mary, appears to have an inner life built around violently skewed images of childhood. It is not stated explicitly what medical condition, if any, Mary has, though reviews of the play unquestioningly interpret her behaviour as a manifestation of, variously, autism or epilepsy with touches of Tourette's syndrome thrown in for good measure. At one point, Mary adopts a 'cutting, official doctorish voice' and states that: 'In the extreme condition, the child's senses are totally dislocated. Fire is cold, cold burns. Words screech. Animate objects are stone. The child wakes on another planet, converses with beings not conceived of by the natural world.'

There is an innocence to much of what we see of Mary. On the other hand, pulling her mother's hair, kneeing her father in the groin, and calling a policeman a 'FUCKING COPPER' when he tries to stop her going off with an old man to 'play', suggests a severe behavioural disorder. At the end of the play, a game of cowboys and Indians turns into an excuse for two boys to bully and abuse Mary. She ends up still and silent at the bottom of a dark hole while others search for her with torches. While this final image may be intended as a metaphor for Mary's condition, the overall tone of the play is one of nightmare and menace. The audience are not clearly positioned towards Mary other than to experience her world as being strange and savage. There are overtones of *Lord of the Flies* without the reasoning and *A Clockwork Orange* without the moral comment. Viewed like this, the expediency of the decision to stage it in school due to its cast size, minimal set, and opportunities for young actors to strut their stuff seems short sighted and perhaps rather unsympathetic.

Accentuating the positive

Disability is a highly sensitive issue. Playwrights, teachers and commentators, this author included, are understandably wary of the responses their work might induce from any one of numerous lobbies, each of which will have its own political, personal, moral and ethical standpoint. Thus, no matter how well intentioned an attempt to create a positive dramatic portrayal of disability is, the likelihood is that it will still be problematic. A case in point here would be Roy Kift's *Stronger than Superman* (1980). The play was first performed by Grips Theater, Berlin, one of the foremost children's theatre companies in the world, in response to the United Nations designating 1981 as the Year of the Disabled.

In his introduction to the published text, Kift expresses his reaction to the term disabled – 'ugh! Horrible word!' – and recalls that:

> When . . . the director of the West Berlin Grips Theater first suggested to me the idea of a children's play on the theme of the handicapped, I was horrified. For a start, I thought the subject too gruesome for a children's audience.

Such an attitude doesn't seem a particularly encouraging embarkation point for a play designed to raise awareness and understanding of disability. Rather, it seems uncomfortably reminiscent of what became known in the last century as 'the Ugly Laws', the most commonly cited of which is the 1911 Chicago Municipal Code, sec. 36034 which declared that:

> No person who is diseased, maimed, mutilated or in any way deformed so as to be an unsightly or disgusting object or improper person to be allowed in or on the public ways or other public places in this city, or shall therein or thereon expose himself to public view, under a penalty of not less than one dollar nor more than fifty dollars for each offense.
>
> (Quarmby 2011: 60)

This ordinance was not in fact repealed until 1974.

Reporting on her classroom experience of exploring inclusion and diversity as part of the Personal, Social and Health Education (PSHE) curriculum, Liz Owen (see Chapter 6) noted that the class believed that 95 per cent of disabled people used a wheelchair. Kift's play could be seen as reinforcing this narrow view. It tells the story of Chris, who has spina bifida, and his sister Paula who move to a new district and make friends with Kevin. The play imparts a fair amount of information in a quite didactic way by stating, for example, that there is a difference between people with spina bifida and 'spastics', and that not all disabled people (though the play consistently uses the term handicapped) are 'mentally deficient'. Some dubious comedy is made of how it is sometimes impossible to tell who is disabled. For example, when the play opens, Paula enters in a wheelchair but she is just playing in it. Later, Kevin is in the wheelchair when Mr Barraclough from social services visits. The scene is used to make fun of Mr Barraclough's attitude and patronising manner towards Kevin, who he thinks is Chris. Similarly, Mr Wright is mocked when he tells Kevin off for being in the chair not knowing that he has broken his leg. Generally the adults are shown up to be irrational and patronising. They assume that, because Chris is in a wheelchair, he must also have a learning impairment and should be sent to a special residential school. When it transpires that Kevin can go to a mainstream school in his wheelchair having broken his leg, Mr Wright (a wheelchair-using adult) promises to go and see the headmistress with Chris to claim his rightful place there.

Perhaps when it was first produced *Stronger than Superman* would have been regarded as a brave if not quite revolutionary attempt to address the issue of disability with young people. Indeed, German newspaper *Der Abend* proclaimed that: 'Rarely has a play for children and about children combined so much meaning with so much pleasure . . . fresh, cheeky, quite the opposite of po-faced, this enlightening, optimistic play is a direct hit.'

Publishers Amber Lane Press report that the play has been translated into 21 languages and performed all over the world. Nonetheless, to a contemporary British audience, its language might well seem cringe-makingly incorrect, while its own dramatic devices seem implausible and patronising. For example, Mr Wright is described as a lively man in his late fifties, yet Chris has to explain the difference between spina bifida and spastic to him. The play echoes the sentiment that, 'We are all, in some ways, disabled' (Lewis 1995: 3). Such a view may seem to some to be an egalitarian, liberal humanist perspective, which celebrates difference while recognising homogeneity and so serves as 'a deterrent to condemning the disabled as abnormal and treating the minor imperfections of us all as faults to be denied or disguised' (ibid.). However, simply regarding everyone as disabled in some way fits into neither the medical or social model of disability: it is clearly not true that everyone has a medical impairment, and neither is it the case that all impairments result in a substantial and long-term adverse effect on a person's 'ability to carry out normal day-to-day activities' (Disability Discrimination Act 1995). Thus, to draw an analogy between 'minor imperfections' and impairments that have a substantial effect on everyday living seems naive and offensive:

Kevin: Do all handicapped people have bags?
Chris: *(amused)* No.
Paula: *(pleased because he asked directly)* Not all of them.
Chris: Spina bifida people like me –
Paula: A lot of *them* do –
Chris: But spastics and others probably don't at all.
Kevin: I thought they was all the same.
Chris: What! There's about a hundred
Paula: Thousand –
Chris: Million –
Paula: Billion –
Chris: Trillion –
Paula: Different sorts of handicap.
Chris: About as many different sorts as there are people.

Embracing the notion that we are all disabled in some respect or other, Kift writes,

> Faced with a wheelchair person, it is we, the so-called healthy people, who gape in blinkered embarrassment, or turn away in dumb awkwardness,

> frightened by this living challenge to our world of fitness, beauty and perfection. A 'natural' feeling of sorrow arises in our hearts, but sorrow never helped anyone.

which perhaps goes some way towards explaining why he chose to end *Stronger than Superman* with a song that unintentionally out-parodies Monty Python's *Always Look on the Bright Side of Life*:

> Many of us may look funny
> A few of us may look quite sad
> But if you'd only get to know us
> You'll find it ain't so bad.
> Some of us have floppy muscles,
> Some of us have jerky arms,
> But if you'd take the time to know us
> You'll find there ain't no harm.

Accessing the student voice

In *Stronger than Superman*, the author assumes the voices of his young characters having, he claims, to have spent 'many hours in the company of handicapped children and their parents' (www.roy-kift.com, accessed 3 August 2011). Richard Cameron took a different approach to create *Strugglers*, which won the Sunday Times Playwriting Awards at the 1988 National Student Drama Festival. A drama teacher at the time, Cameron took his Year 10 and Year 11 students to a special school for a week, and came away with the overriding impression 'that it was full of happy, helpful people'. The question for Cameron's students was: What happened to their counterparts when they left the special school? Rather than focus on that, Cameron chose to examine the transition point.

The play is episodic. A number of short scenes are structured to give insight into the lives of the different members of the special school class, their interpersonal relationships, home life and potential future by way of a series of monologues addressed to a careers officer. The careers interviews are warming and moving by halves:

Lyndsay: I'm not bothered what kind of job I do. I could work anywhere where you meet people and you can have a bit of a laugh. I wouldn't mind a factory. I don't want a lot of money because it makes you snobby, just enough to buy some clothes and go to dances with my mates. I know I couldn't do some jobs because you need brains and Mrs Clark told me I wouldn't be able to do some jobs because I'm too clumsy. I sometimes can't hold things proper. Nursing I can't do because she said I wouldn't be able to give injections. *(Pause)* I'd like to be a famous pop singer. Like Madonna.

The catalyst for the action is something that happens to one of the girls, Wendy: 'She had another apple-epic fit only she had it in the kitchen and knocked a pan of boiling water and a boiled egg on top of her.' The students' response to this is to organise a number of sponsored events in order to buy Wendy and her mum a microwave oven that will be safer to use.

The main characters are Hannah, '16, hearing and speech difficulties. Shy, loving, sensitive', and Bernard, '16, likes sport, has to be busy. Physically mature'. Hannah's careers interview is a good example of how Cameron authentically captures the teenage voice:

Hannah: I don't really want a job with people because of not hearing and speaking properly. I would get embarrassed and customers might get annoyed if they couldn't understand what I was saying and I couldn't hear them properly. I'm too slow. *(Reading)* My work experience – I worked at Kwiksave from 7th to 14th December, last year. Personal manager Mr Kitchin. *(Looks up)* I was stacking things on shelves. One day I helped put the prices on the crisps and one day I was on collecting the trolleys up from the car park but I wasn't very good at that because I could only push a few at a time. *(Pause)* Yes, Miss, I enjoyed working there. They were friendly to me and patient.

The relationship between Hannah and Bernard provides a deal of dramatic tension for the audience and allows Cameron to draw his characters as rounded, sympathetic humans who demand our interest and attention. For example, Bernard tries hard, perhaps too hard, to encourage Hannah to say more when they go in search of sponsorship money but Hannah finds this excruciatingly difficult:

Hannah: Hello. I'm Hannah O'Brian and I go to St Peter's special school. *(Again)* I'm Hannah O'Brian. *(Again)* I'm Hannah O'Brian. *(She looks to Bernard for help)*

We're doing some sponsored events to raise money for our school and for a microwave. *(Again, as carefully as she can)* Microwave oven. This girl has epileptic fits. *(Again)* Epileptic fits. *(In agony, again)* Epileptic fits!

(She turns and runs off, crying)

When Hannah tells her friend why she is upset, she proclaims, 'He can't love me if he can do that.' We do not know who to feel sorry for most – shy Hannah with her speech impediment, or Bernard who was trying to help her get over it. As it turns out, Bernard meets a young unmarried mother while gathering sponsorship. The Young Woman exhibits behaviour that suggests that she too may have special educational needs, and perhaps represents a sobering vision of what life in the future may hold for the young characters at the centre of the play. Bernard runs off with the Young Woman, taking a good deal of the collected sponsor money with him. The event serves to show that young people with learning disabilities experience the same urges and desires as anyone else and act to satisfy these; in so doing, they may make the same kinds of mistakes as anyone else. Bernard returns at the end of the play and, while most of the class initially reject him, Hannah eventually accepts his apology.

Just as Bernard's adventure suggests that he has reached an age where school will no longer be able to give him all he needs, so, for two of the other characters, their vulnerability at this moment of their life is suggested. The dancer, Victor, for example, is enticed by an older man, no doubt leaving the audience wanting to call out to warn him:

Victor: This man says he might be able to get me fifteen pounds! . . . He might be able to get me some money later on if I go now . . . Just for a walk . . . I've seen him before. I don't know his name. He stops and talks to me sometimes. Fifteen quid! I told him what we'd be doing and he thought it was great and he said he'd like to help us. I think he's just a bit lonely and he wants to give me money so I'll be his friend.

Victor later swears that his own father gave him the money, saying that, although he did go for a walk with the man, 'he started to make me feel scared so I left him'. Lyndsay similarly finds herself the subject of predation. Unable to sing in a pub as she was promised, unknown males try to get her out of the toilet in which she has locked herself:

Voice 1: We're not going home yet. We're off for a drive. Come on, we're off to celebrate our success.
Voice 2: *(Quiet)* Few drinks. Back of the van. You can be my groupie, if you like. Come on. We'll make sure you get home.

Exactly what happens to Lyndsay, if anything, is left ambiguous, and thus leaves the audience feeling uncomfortable and somehow responsible for not being in a position to call out when such incidents occur in the real world. In fact, Cameron uses a number of neat theatrical tricks to ensure that the audience becomes increasingly implicit in the unfolding lives of the characters. For one thing, their teacher is never present on the stage. Rather, when the characters address her, they address the audience. Other than Darrell and Linda, brother and sister to two of the characters and aged just 18, and the Young Woman who is between 17 and 19, no adults actually appear on the stage, making the fictitious world the domain of the special school classmates. Nonetheless, references are made to adults that sometimes suggest that, while the young people are still naive and generally happy, their existence does have an impact on the lives of others who care for them in ways they may not always notice or understand:

Victor: I used to go their house . . . Her mum was really nice, like she was always pleased to see us. I remember playing Cluedo and her mum was sat watching us and she started crying.
Billy: What for?
Victor: I don't know. I pretended not to notice.

At the end of the play, the young characters join hands and hold up a sign saying 'Goodbye Miss and Good Luck':

Lyndsay: Miss, we're going to walk backwards all the way out of the school till we get to the school gates so we don't turn our backs on the school.

And off they go, walking back upstage neatly inverting the play's final message, for while the banner wishes the audience, in the position of Miss, 'Good luck', that same audience knows that it is them that will need good luck in a world that is not as full of happy, helpful people as most special schools.

Inclusion through drama

Following an engaging telephone conversation with Alun Bliss, I asked him to send me some notes on his experiences of including children with special educational needs in his drama work. What he sent me was rather better than a few notes. Other than changing the names of those mentioned and making a few tiny edits for the sake of clarity, what follows are his words:

> One of the first pupils I had met who was obviously on the autistic spectrum was Alyssa. We were auditioning for the school production *Tom Sawyer.* Alyssa smiled serenely and drifted through the workshop-style audition showing no real ability when it came to following instructions, creating character or even understanding the situations and scenarios proposed. As I had decided to involve all of the pupils who wanted to get involved, I offered her a part in the chorus. In order to support her and ensure health and safety risks were minimalised during both rehearsal and performances, I assigned mentors to her. Staff involved in the production met to discuss her individual needs in the early stage of the work and continued to monitor closely how she was coping. On stage, her mentors were characters such as older sisters or aunts or, in some scenes, other students who were simply asked to look out for her. Alyssa's fellow cast members took their responsibility seriously and were incredibly understanding and patient. Alyssa still talks fondly of her experiences with the theatre group.
>
> Some years later a young student auditioned for another annual production, *The Golden Masque of Agamemnon*. She had been born with severe physical disabilities. She had very small legs but was adept at getting about on crutches. In contrast to Alyssa she was socially and cognitively

switched on and revealed a fine understanding of text and character during the auditions. I decided to completely ignore her disability and she joined a cast of around seventy all of whom multi-roled. Her commitment was complete and her enthusiasm was infectious. She scurried around on a pair of crutches that she wrapped in black cloth and gaffer tape. My only real concern was including her in the risk assessments for the production.

Theatres, especially during the latter stages of rehearsals are clearly very dangerous indeed. School halls that are transformed into theatres for two weeks a year are even more dangerous. Sets can be unstable, lighting cables and wiring need judicious taping and before the actors are confident with the walkways and the stage itself, they can be plunged into darkness and lose their sense of place. For *Agamemnon*, we had a huge cast of nearly 100 young actors. They all wore masks whilst crawling over several levels of scaffolding and rostra, often in very dim light, with smoke and low fogger effects throughout. It was clear that an actor with limited mobility needed special consideration. We placed her at the front of the chorus whenever possible and always gave her 'escape' routes. Her needs were always thought through when we rehearsed exiting the acting space and she took priority.

The key to the risk assessment is actually just taking time to write in some thoughts about special consideration. Actors on the autistic spectrum may not be as aware of the inherent dangers involved with performances. They are less likely to deal with sudden change in a calm manner – so the most important element once the risk has been identified is to rehearse some scenarios so that all of the performers and technical crew are prepared. A simple example of this is to walk through an evacuation of the stage under emergency lighting. We used to fuse our rather weak theatre lighting system on a regular basis so walking through an evacuation was a routine and useful exercise for cast, crew and FOH team.

The real inspiration for *Buckethead* came from teaching John and then his brother Dan. Both had Asperger's Syndrome. Teaching John in a GCSE group forced me to confront the condition and try to find out more about it. He was not at the severe end of the scale but still found communication with his peers awkward at times. He engaged with the topics and the ideas in a way that was always slightly different to his peers but gradually they accepted and warmed to him. He found role play challenging and his characters were always the same. Similarly, he found it virtually impossible to make imaginative leaps into fictional contexts and irony could easily be completely lost on him. In response, my teaching had to become much more precise and ordered. I had to ensure that I explained why we were attempting each exercise and make sure that he didn't get left behind. On reflection, I would say that these experiences of integrating pupils with a variety of individual and sometimes complex needs into the mainstream classroom have helped make my teaching sharper and more effective.

In other words, I would say that all of the pupils have benefitted as a result of these efforts to be inclusive.

John's brother Dan was extremely good at drawing, and would create very accurate representations of the work we had done in class in minutes. If we sketched out our use of space or ideas for scenery he was able to create drawings that revealed a fine understanding of how the scene could be blocked. It was through this skill that I was able to discuss the drama. Once the language of drama had been introduced in this way, that is, through his drawings, we went from strength to strength. Dan went on to do A level Drama and Theatre Studies and thoroughly enjoyed it. He threw himself into performance with real energy and enthusiasm, following direction well and trying to incorporate new ideas into his work. I cast him as Duncan in a production of *Macbeth*. Dan can present himself as being rather distant, aloof and detached from what is going on around him. This was absolutely right for the character of Duncan though I felt that this was the result of his Asperger's rather than his acting. My concern was that he was not really learning from the experience of taking part. I noted that he knew his lines by heart in time for the first rehearsal and that he also knew the complete text for all of the scenes he appeared in. He found it difficult to cope with the inevitable cuts that I introduced and became quite irritated and stressed when stage directions changed or were altered.

These two students certainly made me think hard about the way I was teaching drama. I think both got something valuable from being involved, but I'm not totally convinced that students on the autistic spectrum can always engage with their peers well enough to do well in our subject. If a student finds communication difficult, then communicating ideas through drama and exploring ideas within a group will also be difficult. Performing will be challenging. How can a student with Asperger's, for example, understand the human condition with a fine degree of subtlety? It is, after all, their inability to do so that defines their condition.

Buckethead is, in some ways, a response to the difficulties that I faced as a teacher trying to engage with students on the autistic spectrum. I was also interested in how families cope. How do parents deal with day-to-day issues and how might their siblings respond? Alyssa is now a young woman in her twenties. She came to see *Buckethead* with her parents. She was still smiling serenely and seemed still to be drifting through life without really engaging with it. Her parents, however, sat through a play that brought their difficulties to life. The characters they watched on stage were grappling with the disability that they continued to face daily. They came over to speak to me after the performance and I could see that they had both been crying. If the play has an educational quality perhaps that rests as much in recognising the difficulty the condition poses for others as much as for the person who has it.

After the play was first performed, a member of the audience wrote to me. He wondered whether a character on the autistic spectrum could really be brought to life on stage. If theatre relies upon characters communicating with each other and with the audience, how can a character 'incapable of communication' be at its centre? As an audience, we perhaps cannot empathise with Buckethead as a character for the very reasons that others find him difficult to empathise with in the play. But if the central character does not communicate with us, perhaps his music, his poetry and his 'magical world' might do.

Play script

Buckethead

Alun Bliss

The play is an ensemble piece with music. All of the songs can be performed as pieces of choral speech. The cast act as Chorus and can play more than one part. Snatches of music play throughout – Bechet, Beiderbecke, etc. where possible. The original production used a slideshow projection throughout, including photographs of the cast and some key words about Asperger's.

SCENE 1 *A bedroom, BUCKET conducts the music as slideshow begins and the cast enter. JELLY, MA and SHOWGIRL act as a CHORUS and remain onstage throughout.*

A slideshow of famous people thought to have been on the autistic spectrum: Mozart, Howard Hughes, Isaac Newton, J. R. R. Tolkien, Andy Warhol, Jane Austen, Mr Bean, Beethoven, Alexander Graham Bell, Thomas Edison, Henry Ford, Alfred Hitchcock, Socrates, Leonardo da Vinci, Charles Darwin, Marie Curie . . .

JELLY: What's my name? What's my part? Get that light on my face.

SHOWGIRL: Do you need a name? Do you have to have one? Just be the quiet, nameless entertainer that plays, sings and goes home alone each night.

JELLY: 'I'm Mr No-name – but why I can't explain . . .' I don't want no-body thinking I'm somebody I'm not – I got a reputation, girl.

SHOWGIRL: We all knows your reputation. You's always gonna be a nobody . . . jus' like us all . . . nobodies. You're the Storyteller – so tell the story.

JELLY: The Storyteller! I don't get no real character to play! 'Mr No-name, but why I can't explain . . .' I don't get to jive with nobody? What about humour? My wit? What about rapport with my audience?

MA: Only if we let you – which we won't. 'Wit' . . . why wit? What's with yo' wit?

SHOWGIRL: Tha' sounds like him talkin'. Tha' sounds like him.

JELLY: What's he doing over there? What you doin', boy?

MA: Don't you complicate yourself. He's shy – not schizophrenic.
SHOWGIRL: What?
JELLY: Now who's jivin'?

A jazz dance. JELLY, MA and SHOWGIRL with BUCKET. This is his imaginary world.

SCENE 2 *JELLY etc. move into shadows.*

MOTHER: What's going on? You're making a lot of noise. Why are you in the dark?
BUCKET: Turn the hurting-light off! Turn it off. Light bulb off. Bulb off! Really bright, hurting bulb light off off.
MOTHER: Sorry – I forgot, sorry.
BUCKET: Dazzled. Head will hurt. Dazzled. Head will hurt with hurting-light-bulb.
MOTHER: I said I'm sorry. I didn't expect you to be in the dark. What was that noise?
BUCKET: It will hurt for ten minutes – or even longer now.
(BUCKET puts blanket over his head. Pause. MOTHER waits.)
BUCKET: Mozart was an aspie. Aspie-Mozart-probably. I don't know about Bechet. I don't know about him.
MOTHER: Ummmm?
BUCKET: And Einstein . . . probably. Definitely autistic person, probably. Def-def-aut.
MOTHER: I don't like the word 'aspie'.
BUCKET: Bechet had difficulty making friends. He did. It's because it sounds like asp – a poisonous snake. Dr Spock has Asperger's too.
MOTHER: Dr Spock is an alien.
BUCKET: An alien half-breed Vulcan – with Asperger's. Vulcan – Asperger-breed. Alien. Cleopatra was killed by an asp. She was.
MOTHER: He is also not real and has false ears.
BUCKET: The Geek site says he's real – most of them haven't heard of Bechet. I'm starting a new thread about him.
MOTHER: A what?
BUCKET: When you start a new topic for discussion and interaction it's called a thread. On a website it is. I'm going to start one on Bechet and Beiderbecke. On the Geek site. And Lisa Simpson – she's one and she plays the saxophone. She plays one. The thread is about musical aspies. Musical.
MOTHER: 'Geek' is another word I don't like. Finish your words properly – and your sentences.
BUCKET: Perhaps I should have a thread just for saxophonists like Lisa and Sid. Then another for Bix? He played the cornet. He played a cornet.

MOTHER: You can't be on first name terms with them. You haven't met them. I don't like you being on the Internet this late at night either. Is that what you were doing when I came up? You can't include the Simpsons, they don't even have proper hands. I didn't know she was on the spectrum.

BUCKET: She's not real. I'm researching my condition.

MOTHER: 'Condition'?

BUCKET: The autistic spectrum. I might write a musical play about it. Write a musical play. I want to know more about it. I don't think I'm going to be an Einstein or a Mozart – or a Bechet. Wouldn't want to be a Simpson.

SISTER enters – woken from her sleep.

SISTER: No – just an annoying brother who wakes everyone up. You woke me up again! *(Under her breath)* Geek!

MOTHER: What are you doing? Back to bed this instance!

BUCKET: 'Geek' is a made-up word that doesn't mean anything – 'geek' is.

SISTER: Can't sleep with all the noise can I?

MOTHER: Don't call him names.

BUCKET: Don't come in my room either – sister free zone. Zone-sans-sis.

SISTER: What? In case I catch something?

MOTHER: That's enough.

BUCKET: You can't catch Asperger's. It's not a disease. It's not like a cold . . . or chicken pox. You did catch chicken pox.

SISTER: You're a disease . . . and you woke me up.

MOTHER: He is not ill – how many times must I tell you?

SCENE 3 *A DOCTOR enters – this could be played by JELLY.*

DOCTOR: No, no, no . . . he's not ill . . . just different. Special. You have a special child.

FATHER: We knew he was different – that's why we came. We knew he was special, didn't we, mother?

MOTHER: I'm not your mother.

FATHER: No.

DOCTOR: I suggest you tell him. Entirely up to you, of course. Have a good think about it. At some point he'll need to be told – but just when is best is up to you.

FATHER: We'll chew it over. Won't we? Me and his mother . . . we'll chew.

MOTHER: What did you call it again?

DOCTOR: 'Asperger's syndrome'. Funny little chap isn't he? Intelligent lad. You can be proud of him. Does he always have a blanket on his head?

FATHER: We are . . .
MOTHER: Proud.
FATHER: We're his parents.
DOCTOR: 'Asperger's' . . . after Hans Asperger.

SCENE 4 *BUCKET's room.*

JELLY: Now I got you. You're being sneaky. Now I see what you're saying. Get in tune with your audience, boy. Go back a few years to the beginning. Get back to the source, man. Show them where you're coming from . . . we'll help.

MA: How can you 'see' what he's sayin'? Who's telling the story? Him or us?

JELLY:
This is where it all begins
This is where you see the things
That make you feel he's crazy

This is how you analyse
This is how you empathize
You hear the lies
You know he's really crazy.

So just relax
Enjoy the show
Just question what you think you really know

MA:
This is where we make a start
A plea from the heart
This is where he plays the part
That makes you feel he's crazy

SHOWGIRL:
This is how you face the facts
This is where you watch the acts
You see what he lacks
You know he's crazy

JELLY:
So just relax
Enjoy the show
Just question what you think you really know

And if he makes you think a little harder
And if you understand a little more
Then he will laugh inside and hold his head up
While you question what it was you really saw
While you question what is was you really saw

FATHER walks into light downstage. Pause.

JELLY: 'Madness is hereditary. We get it from our children.' Who said that? Did I just say that?

FATHER: He's not what I called disabled. Well, he is – but not what I call disabled. I mean he's all there. He wasn't born defective. You know what I mean? I suppose he is defective – a bit. And it is sort of disabled. Just not what you might call a physicality. Lots of people have got it – more than you'd think. He's all there – nothing missing. He's my lad after all.

He has got a disability. We know he has. But he's maybe got more of an a-bility. Maybe his disability is being able. He's on a spectrum. The Doctor says to think of it as a result of him being focussed. Like he focuses too much. I can't focus hardly at all. Used to say that on my school reports: 'He lacks focus'. P'raps he's just bright – clever, you know. P'raps he's just bloody odd. He is bloody odd – always has been.

SCENE 5 *Cast become the audience inside a cinema.*

FATHER: Can you stop fidgeting?

MOTHER: Brian?

FATHER: What now?

MOTHER: Brian . . .?

FATHER: You don't need to go again do you? What have you been drinking? You shouldn't have had that bottle of pop with the chips should you? This is what happens with all that fizz. E-numbers. You've been up and down to the loo five times already!

MOTHER: It's not E-numbers . . . something's happening!

FATHER: We've not been here five minutes. Well – if you have to. Try not to step on the big woman with the hat again. She looked fit to mesmerise us last time. How can she wear a hat like that in the flicks?

MOTHER: No . . . it's . . .

FATHER: . . . and get us some sweets or something from the cubicle, will you?

MOTHER: It's me waters . . . ooch.

FATHER: Not popcorn . . . it gets stuck in me teeth . . . Waters? It can't be.

MOTHER: I think it must be. Ooh, I think it is.

FATHER: Is it? It can't be. It's nearly a month too soon!

MOTHER: It definitely is . . . ooh.

FATHER: You can't have a baby in the Odeon. It's not hygienic. It can't be here . . . what will that lady think?

The birth. Chorus act as cinema-goers then doctors and nurses.

FATHER: We've not bought a pram yet!

MOTHER: Brian!

FATHER: Breathe deeply . . . breathe deeply . . . or is it not deeply. Try not to breathe too much! Does it hurt? Don't breathe!

Excuse us! Pregnant lady coming through. We've not painted his bedroom. Or her bedroom. We don't even know if it is a her. Evacuate, evacuate! We only told your mother last week. I don't think she took it too well, do you? Your mother . . . emergency . . . pregnant wife here . . . can I have some help please? Hello, nursery . . . she's passing water. It's ever so early – we weren't due for . . . I think she's feeling faint. Are you feeling faint? The baby is at least three weeks pre-meditated!

SCENE 6 *FATHER talking to a friend in a pub (JELLY).*

FATHER: It was a miracle. Birth is a miracle, you know. Miraculous. She's fine. They're fine. Resting, you know. I didn't want to be in the way. Thought I'd slip out for a quick pint . . . let them sleep . . . just for a bit.

MOTHER moves to centre where BUCKET is curled up asleep.

MOTHER: But he didn't sleep. Not much. He always seemed restless. His eyes were always wide and watching. As if he wanted to sleep – but was too afraid to close his eyes. He slept in my arms, but panicked when he woke up on his own.

And it's already hard
Being mother, being young
I'm so alone

And it's already hard
On the outside looking down
He's on his own

With doctors and midwives
With cleaners and nurses
With family and friends
And staring eyes
With everyone

A grown up fear
Though he's so small
He's so heavy and I'm not strong
The walls are cold now
They threaten me
It's all too clean

Old now
Responsible – he's mine to keep

I'm scared now, feeling lost now
Feeling weak, cannot speak
He's mine to love

He's here too soon
I'm not prepared
He's small, he's thin
And I'm so scared . . .

I need to get some rest. I haven't slept for three nights. I keep watching his little body. It's like when he was in the incubator. I don't want to sleep in case I wake up and he's gone.

GRANDMOTHER moves into light and looks suspiciously over the sleeping BUCKET.

G'MOTHER: Where's Brian? Where's his father?
MOTHER: Working – doing some overtime so we can get the things he needs.
G'MOTHER: The pub's a funny place to save money. Odd place to do overtime.
MOTHER: His little arm goes ever so tense if you touch him.
G'MOTHER: Leave him be. There's too much fussing over babies these days. He wasn't due to be born 'til Tuesday week – scraggy little thing.
MOTHER: Do you think he's hungry? Does he need changing?
G'MOTHER: Babies soon let you know when they want something. I don't know how the nurses manage with all of the screaming. Mind you, I could always tell you above the rest. You were a screamer. And I wasn't kept in for two weeks.
MOTHER: But how can I tell when he needs something? He never makes a sound . . .
G'MOTHER: There's something wrong with a baby that never cries.

SCENE 7 *Doctors arrive to examine BUCKET.*

DOCTOR: I'm no expert, but I can tell you that there is nothing physically wrong with him. He is a good size for a premature baby . . . his vocal chords do work.
DOCTOR 2: It wasn't until quite recently that we started to test for Asperger's at all.
DOCTOR: Was he bottle-fed?
DOCTOR 2: Hans Asperger was a forgotten man to a certain extent. He identified the traits as far back as 1944.
FATHER: But he wasn't born until 2000 . . .

DOCTOR 2: Studied a whole collection of patients. Many of them were rather shy – not great at conversation . . .

JELLY: Time out? Who's jivin' now?

SHOWGIRL: 1981 – Lorna Wing revisited Asperger's work. She was examining neonatal issues.

JELLY: I'm confused – you got doctors, births . . . people singing.

MA: Problems with birth.

DOCTOR 1: Impaired cognitive development leading to complicated communication malfunctions . . .

JELLY: That definitely sounds like him. Get back to your acting parts. I'm storytelling here. Now he's a toddler . . . toddling in his playgroup. If you find it difficult to spot him, he's got a towel on his head.

SHOWGIRL: Why does he do that?

MOTHER: It helps to block out all of the bright lights and loud noises and all of the other things that distract and upset him.

SCENE 8 *A playgroup. Cast become children and carers.*

JELLY:
Three little pigs were sitting in a sty
Three little pigs turned and caught my eye
Hope I die
Hope I die
Hope I die

MA:
Little Jack Horner was always sitting down
Is Little Jack Horner wearing a frown?
Bring on the clown
Bring on the clown

SHOWGIRL:
The clown's all sad – he looks like Dad
Clowns are happy – but this one's sad
Bad, bad, bad

ALL:
Sticks and stones gonna break your bones
Words are gonna bother you
Sit in the corner
Swing on the swing
What else is there to do?
What else is there to do?

SISTER:
Oranges and lemons
Nectarines and melons
Spit out the pips
It makes you feel sick
When can you go?

Says the big bell of bow
When I say so
She always says no
Here comes a chopper
To light you to bed
Here comes a candle to chop off your head

ALL: Oranges and lemons
Clementimes and melons
What is your name?
That's such a shame
Here comes a melon to make you feel sick
Here comes a toddler to give you a kick!

CARER: Come and meet some of the other little boys and girls. Look – let's take the little blanket from your eyes, shall we? That's better, isn't it? You're still hiding from me, aren't you? Peek-a-boo. Shall I get Belinda to play with you? She's new too. OK – I'll let you keep the little blanket. Look, Belinda, I've found you someone to play with. He's very shy . . . would you like to play with him?

BELINDA: He's got a blanket on his head!

DOCTOR 2: He's not shy . . . just has 'complicated communication malfunctions . . .'

MA: Sssssh.

BELINDA: I've got some squishy stuff you can squish if you want to.

It's not nellow any more. When it came here it was nellow but it got dirty in the sandpit. It got dirty in the sand pit it did. The boy with the greeny nellow stuff coming out of his nose threw it in the sand pit. You can squish it through your fingers and make a pooing noise . . . listen.

MOTHER: Is he all right today?

CARER: Hello – sit down and watch for a while. We've introduced him to the new girl. She's very open . . . quite loud.

(BELINDA makes pooing noise)

She's very loud. We're hoping that she might get through to him. We're hoping. She came with some gunky stuff in a tin.

MOTHER: 'Gunky' stuff?

SISTER: Can we have some Clunky stuff?

CARER: He's not allergic to anything is he? Skin reactions or anything?

MOTHER: He doesn't like touching things usually. Only soft things.

SISTER: What's that girl doing? Is that his girlfriend?

BELINDA: Look – you can squirt it on the floor and make it blob. It sounds like poo – but it doesn't look like poo. Poo isn't nellow. Dog's poo can be nellow if the dog is poorly.

MOTHER: They're making a mess.

CARER: Don't worry, Mum, I think Glunky stuff comes off clothes and things. I'm sure it does.

MOTHER: I'm not your 'Mum'.

CARER: No. Ahhh . . . look, she's being lovely to him.

BELINDA: Do you want my lorry? It's a goo lorry. It carries the squishy stuff. You can put the squishy stuff in the back of it. 'Cos it's squishy.

CARER: Well . . . is he looking at her? Interacting?

MOTHER: He's taken the toy.

CARER: It's a start – accepting the toy. He's accepted her friendship . . . accepted the lorry.

MOTHER: He's just taken the toy. Taken the lorry. He's spinning the wheel. He likes things that spin.

SISTER: Mummy, can we go?

BELINDA: You're supposed to drive it. It's a lorry and it's a goo lorry to take the goo from the goo factory to the sand pit. When the goo gets to the sand pit we nake it into nashed potatoes we do. But they're not the sort of nashed potatoes you can eat 'cos they're nellow and they look like poo.

ALL: Mummy!
He won't play with me
Mummy!
He just can't see
He's always in the corner on his own
Sister free zone

DOCTOR 1: Does the child lack an understanding of how to play with others?

ALL: Mummy!
What's wrong with him?
Mummy!
He likes thing that spin
He never ever speaks
This lasts for weeks and weeks and weeks

DOCTOR 2: When free to play with other children, such as school lunchtime, does the child avoid social contact with them?

ALL: Mummy!
He won't play with us
Mummy!
He makes such a fuss
He takes up all your precious time
Spoilt child crime

Cast create spiralling playground world.

SCENE 9 *Outside, playing.*

FATHER: Don't look at me like that. I didn't do anything, honest.
MOTHER: Has he hurt himself? What have you done to him?
FATHER: I was getting him to run.
MOTHER: Why? He hates running. He can't run. He doesn't like it.
FATHER: Well . . . he's not very quick. Won't be much of a footballer. But you've got to keep him fit. He can't be hurt, he's not crying.
G'MOTHER: Didn't cry when he stepped on a nail last year and it went through his shoe.
MOTHER: A little cut – nothing much. Just a scratch.
FATHER: He fell over his own feet. He hasn't got good co-ordinates, that's all.
G'MOTHER: 'Coordination'. Clumsy, like his father.
JELLY: So – aged about three, the family began to think that he wasn't much like other children. His first memory was when he was about four – at the beach.
SHOWGIRL: A beach? We have to create a beach?

Cast create beach scene.

MOTHER: What do you mean . . . you don't know where he is?
FATHER: Well, I thought he was with you!
G'MOTHER: What's happened?
MOTHER: He's gone!
FATHER: I thought he was here . . . where did you go?
MOTHER: Ice creams – we went to get . . .
G'MOTHER: What's happened now?
SISTER: Can I have one? Can I have a strawberry one?
MOTHER: Oh, be quiet!
FATHER: What should we do? Get a . . .
SISTER: Can I have a strawberry ice cream?
FATHER: P'raps we should try to get some help?
G'MOTHER: I'll look down the beach – he's only four for goodness sake, he can't have gone far . . .
MOTHER: Brian! Call the police, the coast guard . . . anyone . . . do something!
SISTER: With chocolate crumbles . . .
MOTHER: Will you be quiet! Brian!
FATHER: He hasn't run off – he can't run.
G'MOTHER: Fan out and search. And you *(to FATHER)* find someone in uniform!!

BUCKET counts pebbles.

MA: I'm a little pebble sitting on the beach
I'm a little pebble I'm here within your reach
If you see me shining
Won't you take me home with you?
Round and white, sleek and blue
Lying on the sand, just waiting for you
Pick me up and polish me please
I'm begging you to.

SHOWGIRL: He's a little boy sitting on the beach
Mum and Dad are calling just within his reach
If you see him smiling
Won't you take him home with you?
Small and pale, sad and blue
Sitting on the sand just waiting for you
Pick him up and talk to him please
I'm begging you to.

BUCKET: But I wasn't really lost. I was there all the time. I was over there near the tall grasses. All the time. I had found some pebble stones. Peb-sand-stone search it was. I had put them into an order of size. I had put them into a long line and then two long lines. I wasn't worried, frightened, lost or anything . . . some of them are white and have little bits of blue and they glitter in the sun . . .

G'MOTHER: We searched for two bloody hours!

FATHER: We weren't looking in the right place, were we?

BUCKET: . . . lots of the really nice ones are buried just under the sand . . . you scoop . . .

MOTHER: I thought the police were understanding.

FATHER: They thought we were mad . . .

MOTHER: They were ever so patient . . .

FATHER: Honestly, they thought we were mad.

G'MOTHER: *(Looking at FATHER)* Half the family are mad . . .

BUCKET: I think they may be precious stones because they glitter.

G'MOTHER: Especially the male members!

BUCKET: Glitter-stone-shine-peb-glitter.

G'MOTHER: How can you lose a four year old?!

FATHER: It's easily done. Who'd have guessed he'd be doing a pebble pattern? All of the other kids are making sandcastles and paddling and doing normal juvenilia activities . . .

G'MOTHER: I never lost any of my children . . . never! What are you going to do with all these stones?

MOTHER: He has found some pretty ones . . .

BUCKET: The line starts with the big ones and then the little ones.

G'MOTHER: Well?

FATHER: They're his pebbles.

G'MOTHER: We must have been shouting his name right next to him. Loudly, in my case. What was the point? Doesn't he respond to his name?

FATHER: He does know his name, mother.

G'MOTHER: Mercifully, I am not your mother!

FATHER: No.

G'MOTHER: My dog responds to his name when called. He responds. 'Wolfy', I call. 'Wolfy' . . . and he responds. He comes straight away. He's been trained, you see.

FATHER: I can't call out dogs' names, can I?

MOTHER: Let's go home and have a cup of tea.

FATHER: Can I?

G'MOTHER: I'll need a brandy – a large one.

BUCKET: Grandma? Is 'Wolfy' a dog or a wolf?

G'MOTHER: Shut up, child.

SCENE 10 *BUCKET's room.*

JELLY: Despite what Grandmother might think, Asperger's is not caused by poor parenting – or abuse. If it were, there'd be many more autistic children in the world . . .

MA: 'Children on the autistic spectrum' . . . It could be caused by a virus . . .

SHOWGIRL: Doctors always say that, don't they?

MA: Or there is tentative evidence to suggest something neuro-psychological . . . Dysfunctional frontal lobes . . .

JELLY: Whoa there . . . I don't understand . . . and this my story . . . well . . . his. Hey, am I him? Are we all him?

MA: Recap time . . . When you were little you didn't speak much?

JELLY: Or cry?

SHOWGIRL: Even when you got hurt?

JELLY: And you didn't play well. Spent time on your own . . . all on your own! Your sister didn't play with you . . . didn't understand you. You had a squint and you put a blanket on your head to hide from people . . .

MA: No sarcasm . . . no teasing!

JELLY: And you liked collecting pebbles . . .? Putting dates on them . . .

SHOWGIRL: Still does – does it with CDs now – has all of Beiderbecke's recordin's with the Goldkette Orchestra . . .

MA: He was probably one – Beiderbecke. He had a savant ability – could play jus' about any tune by ear. Like Mozart – a prodigy. He never really worked out how to read music all that well.

JELLY: 'Savant' – what's that? French?

MA: 'Not taught' – like you can do things without being taught how to do it.

SHOWGIRL: Like the man who sees things once and paints them – flies over London and paints really detailed pictures. He has a form of autism – he's on the spectrum.

MA: Like Spock or Einstein – brilliant scientists or painters or musicians . . .

SHOWGIRL: Mathematicians like that film with what's his name . . .

JELLY: And that mad woman who talks to cows . . .

BUCKET: She doesn't talk to cows. Temple Grandin. She designs cattle chutes because she understands how cattle react to them. That's not talking to them. Lot's of autistic people like animals . . . I like dogs. Dogs.

Cast create primary school scene.

MA: 'Does the child lack subtlety of expression . . .?'

BUCKET: No!! No no no. Won't go. Don't want sky and trees and space.

BELINDA: He pushed me and pulled my hair and scribbled on my book. He doesn't want to play properlee!

JELLY: Did you have tantrums?

MOTHER: You've got to understand me
Now it's time to go school
Yes, please try to understand me
You are going to have to go to school
You'll have fun, you'll love it
'Cos I know you're not a fool.

MA: 'An apparent lack of emotion'??

G'MOTHER: You better understand, girl
We just don't know what to do
You'd better understand, girl
We just don't know what to do
Teacher's all confused, girl – she hasn't got a clue.

TEACHER: Aren't you enjoying playtime? Don't you want to join in with the other boys and girls? Hide and seek and football and hopscotch and stuck in the mud . . .

BUCKET: Trees and sky and blue . . . birds. Do birds get dizzy when they fly?

TEACHER: Birds?

SHOWGIRL: We don't know what's wrong, miss
We just think he's really weird
We don't know what's wrong, miss
We just think he's really weird
He was looking for a pencil – but now he's disappeared

TEACHER: Where has he gone? He's not walked off again has he?
BELINDA: No, Miss.
TEACHER: Well . . . where is he?
BELINDA: You told him to go to the cupboard and put the pens away, Miss.
TEACHER: . . . and?
BELINDA: That's what he did, Miss.
TEACHER: That was nearly five minutes ago.
BELINDA: But you didn't tell him to come out. We think he's still there, Miss.
JELLY: You have to tell him or he gets confused, Miss.
MA: 'Is he unsettled by changes to routine?'
TEACHER: Oh no. Oh my goodness, are you all right? Poor little boy. I'm sorry. Are you all right now?

ALL: I don't know what's wrong, girl
This is getting out of hand
I don't know what's wrong, boy
This is getting out of hand
Better take him to a Doctor – that can help you understand
Better take him to a Doctor – that can help you understand

SCENE 11 *FATHER is chatting in the pub. BUCKET is centre stage from where he moves into other scenes.*

FATHER: He don't really like me touching him.
JELLY: He's got taste – I wouldn't want you touching me.
FATHER: He fell over and cut his knee – not a sound. Then I went to carry him indoors – and he just went odd. It wasn't like carrying a little boy. It's like he deliberately went all limp. He can be ever so heavy when he feels like it.
SHOWGIRL: Perhaps he's nervy of you – scared.
JELLY: You're not fit – get some exercise. Do some body-building.
FATHER: He doesn't like the dark much. He's scared of the dark.
SHOWGIRL: Nothing odd there – so am I. I hate the dark and spiders. . ..
FATHER: I bet you haven't got two thousand three hundred and forty two pebbles in your room. In date order. They have to be in the right order too – or he knows.
MA: A little order in his life. Something he can feel in control of . . .
JELLY: Checking the pebbles – a control thing . . .
FATHER: He hates it when we have to change things . . .
MOTHER: He hates change.
JELLY: Our hero, now aged seven is about to undergo a major change – he's going into town for a haircut!!

BUCKET'S house.

MOTHER: But do we have to go today?
BUCKET: Not going!
G'MOTHER: For goodness sake, can't you two get a grip?
MOTHER: He hates it. It's strange for him.
BUCKET: Definitely not going to Hair-Lady-Place. Haircut-lady-place hurts hurts.
G'MOTHER: You're too soft with him.
BUCKET: Hurts Hurts.
FATHER: He's going. He's started to disappear inside his hair as it is.
MOTHER: But you know he hates the hairdresser's – he likes it over his eyes.
FATHER: Well, Mother, we're not going . . .
MOTHER: I am not your bloody mother!
FATHER: We're not going to the hairdresser's! We're going to the barbers . . . he's going with me.
BUCKET: Can't definitely go to 'Hair-Lady-Place' . . . can't go there!
FATHER: We're not going to 'Hair-Lady-Place'. You are coming with me.
G'MOTHER: For once – perhaps for the only time in his life, sunshine-boy here is right. You are being manipulated by a 7-year-old demon. He's a little beggar!
MOTHER: No – he dislikes the sound and the touch and everything . . . I know he does . . . It's the hair!
G'MOTHER: Yesterday you turned up to see me an hour late because he wouldn't wear his raincoat.
MOTHER: He can't stand the plasticy smell.
FATHER: He looks like a girl with all that hair.
G'MOTHER: 'The hair' – what do you expect at a hairdresser's?
MOTHER: Can't we leave it until next week – he'll be more prepared?
FATHER: We're not going to the hairdresser's!!
MOTHER: He genuinely hates that coat.
G'MOTHER: You are spoiling him.
FATHER: He's got to have his hair cut!
G'MOTHER: He's being awkward – smack him and put him in the car!
MOTHER: You are not smacking my son!

A barber's shop.

ALL: Don't you touch me – it's shockin'!
Razors slice my back – shockin'!
Rope twists round my neck – shockin'!
Snip, snip, snip – shockin'!

MA: Sharp-edged knife – shiny floor
Bang head on the plastic door

SHOWGIRL: Switch-back blade – badger's coat
Is he going to cut my throat?
Shockin'!

JELLY: Watch the mirror – plastic cape
He is smiling – my eyes gape
Shockin'!

BUCKET: And the thing I hate the most
Is the scissorsound snip and the touch of hair on my skin

ALL: And the thing he hates the most
Is the scissorsound snip and the touch of hair on his skin
He likes his head to rock/I like my head to rock
He likes his/I like my like, I like
He likes his head to rock/I like my head to rock
He likes his/I like my like, I like
Just rockin', just rockin'

JELLY: Coffee cup
Pickled combs
Conversations – voices drone
Snip, snip, snip:

ALL: Shockin'
Cut your ears off
Burn your neck
Can your scream get out?
Cut your ears off
Burn your neck
No one hears you shout!
It's shockin'!
Don't you touch me . . .
It's shockin'
Razors slice my back – shockin'
Rope twists round my neck – shockin!
Snip – snip – snip
Shockin'!!

JELLY: Snip – snip – snip.
SHOWGIRL: Hating the touch of hair on his skin.

SCENE 12 *The supermarket – BUCKET's nightmare.*

JELLY: Supercharging noises – aged eight. He don't like nothing. The trolleys sliding across the floor; the tannoys; the rush of people slamming veg and meat and bread – tins and packages into cages

. . . and the smells overpowering. Deli counter spices, pickles, cheeses, little chicken shapes rolling over themselves in a roasting window . . . and the chill of the freezers . . . and staring eyes of pudgy people picking at the produce. Picking and poking at plastic wrap . . . fat fingers licking thumb and finger, squeeze and poke . . .

ALL: Red label soup?
Never heard of it!
We've marg – don't know about butter
Don't you ever check?
I've found it
It's green label – thought you wanted red
It is red
I didn't like it last time we had it – it's chunky I like
Why don't you do something with him?
Stop pulling the trolley
I'm not touching the trolley
How many loaves?
I hate people pulling when I'm pushing – I can push
I fancy a pie tonight
What's the matter with you?
Push the thing yourself, then
You have to make a fuss, don't you?
Is he lost?
Got his hands over his ears?
I've two tins – I've already got two tins . . .
That's expensive!
They don't look ripe!
That's enough – I shan't tell you again
Stop shouting
Don't make a scene
I've warned you once . . . haven't I?
Should we report him? What do you think?
There's the man!
Poor little thing
Stop it

BUCKET: It's oclophobia – a fear of crowds. Oclophobia.
JELLY: But it's the noise you don't like.
BUCKET: The eyes stab, stab, stab.
JELLY: And the hair on your skin . . . Snip, snip, snip.

The DOCTORs enter.

DOCTOR 1: It wasn't until quite recently that we started to test for Asperger's at all. Hans Asperger was a forgotten man to a certain extent. He identified the traits that your son has way back in 1944.

FATHER: But he wasn't born until . . .

DOCTOR 2: Studied a whole collection of patients. Many of them were rather shy, not great at conversation and had unusual hobbies . . . many were rather clumsy too.

The cast become a series of doctors examining BUCKET – the scene is rather nightmarish. If music is used, it should be reminiscent of Gilbert and Sullivan.

ALL:

We need to look him over
This will take some time
We need to analyse him
Make sure that he's fine

We need to understand the signs
We must investigate
We need to pigeonhole and file
We can't leave it too late

Has he always looked this way?
Has he always squinted?
Does he always look away?
Those glasses should be tinted.

We need to look him over
This will take some time
We need to analyse him
Make sure that he's fine

Can you tell us what he eats?
Does he take his greens?
Does he move his bowels each day?
Is he keeping clean?

SCENE 13

DOCTOR 2: Does he have special interests?
What sort of books does he read?

MOTHER: Factual, mainly factual books.

DOCTOR 1: A good memory for facts, has he?

FATHER: Like a little encyclopaedia, he is.

DOCTOR 1: Communication?

FATHER: Ummm?

DOCTOR 2: How advanced is he? Does he talk well – an unusual tone of voice? Does he talk in a peculiar manner? Old for his years, perhaps?

FATHER: He's a bit pedantic at times.

MOTHER: Pedantic?

DOCTOR 2: It's not an illness. It's a difference. Like an ability. He's wired up differently.

MOTHER: Some things he's not much good at. Polite conversation – small talk – reading body language.

FATHER: He can't run very well.

BUCKET: I focus – hyper focus. I really do focus upon things. If a fire alarm was going off I might not hear it, but I can listen to all of Louis Armstrong's Hot five recordings and follow the scores without a break. Hyper focus. Maybe Mozart had it.

JELLY: Not much good for walking across a road – walk – don't walk – walk – don't walk . . .

DOCTOR 1: I suggest you tell him. Entirely up to you, of course. Have a good think about it. At some point he'll need to be told – but just when is best will be up to you.

FATHER: We'll chew it over. Won't we?

MOTHER: What did you call it again?

DOCTOR 2: 'Asperger's Syndrome'.

JELLY: Now we got a Geek Test!! Let's get down to what makes him different!

MA: Three areas that he struggles with – the triad of impairments.

FATHER: Triad – like Chinese . . . ?

MA: Impaired –

SHOWGIRL: Remember, he's just different.

JELLY: 'Communication' – the first impairment!

G'MOTHER: Well, his father isn't exactly bookish. What she saw in him I'll never know. That's why the poor child doesn't speak. And when he does, does he really make any sense? Does he? Mind you, does his father?

SHOWGIRL: But he's not stupid is he?

G'MOTHER: I can assure you that his father is a few pork pies short of the full picnic.

SHOWGIRL: And the little one?

G'MOTHER: Didn't speak for years and hardly cried. He hardly speaks now. He never looks at you when he speaks and spends hours in the dark in his room. Is that normal for a young boy? Depends upon your idea of stupid, I suppose.

MOTHER: He lives in a world of his own for much of the time. He can communicate with us. I think it hurts him to sometimes. It's as if he's sensitive. No one taught him to read, you know, he just could. Picked up a book and started reading.

DOCTOR 2: 'Hyperlexia' – the ability to read without being taught. Ummm . . . 'hyperlexia'.

JELLY: The second impairment – 'Social Interaction'
How is your lad settling in at school, then?

FATHER: Oh – better than ever I was. Gets good marks in nearly everything. 'Cept PE – he can't run very well. Oh, he's doing well.

SHOWGIRL: Who's he friendly with?

FATHER: I don't know. He doesn't mention friends much.

JELLY: Has he learnt to play yet? With other children I mean. Does he still have all of those stones in his room?

FATHER: He's interactive. He really is. He's interactive.

MOTHER: He is happiest on his own. He hates crowds and takes a while . . . a long while before he trusts people.

JELLY: The third impairment – 'Imagination'.

MOTHER: Oh no, he's really imaginative. He loves music, he writes, he writes plays and music.

MA: What does he write about?

FATHER: He writes about music, jazz and stuff, doesn't he?

MOTHER: Musicians and things. And geology, he likes that – nearly always has stones in his pockets.

JELLY: Is he just a little obsessed? Blinkered?

FATHER: He likes Sidney Bechet – and Beiderbecke.

MOTHER: Bix Beiderbecke – he played jazz.

DOCTOR 2: Ah . . . like Louis Armstrong – I've heard of him. He played the trumpet.

MOTHER: He played the cornet at first. He likes the early stuff.

DOCTOR 1: Jokes? Sarcasm? Does he understand them? Can he think outside the box?

FATHER: He can be a bit literal at times . . .

MOTHER: He can get scared by things people say . . . he takes them to heart.

JELLY: Did you hear what I said?
I'm speaking to you
Here is a candle
Chop off your head

ALL: It speaks for itself
Don't you know?
Speaks for itself
He's counting chickens, counting chickens
Counting chickens

BUCKET: I didn't know he had chickens.

G'MOTHER: Here is a candle
Chop off your head

Did you hear . . . I said?
He's got his mother's eyes
Can you see his mother's eyes?

BUCKET: I haven't got her eyes . . . they're my eyes, mummy, my eyes!

MA/S'GIRL: His mother's eyes
Her eyes, her mother's eyes
It speaks for itself
It speaks for itself
It's raining cats and dogs
It's raining spots

BUCKET: I can't see them . . . can't see the dogs.

JELLY: That's OK,
There's more than one way
To skin a cat
Skin a cat

BUCKET: No, horrid, horrid, not skin a cat

ALL: Here is a candle, a candle, a candle
Chop off you head, your head
Did you hear what I said?
When you put your hand on your heart
Hope to die
Hope to die
Cut off your nose
To spite your face
To spite your face

Kiss the girls and make them cry
Make them cry them cry
Pigs might fly, might fly
Pie in the sky – hope to die.

JELLY: And the diagnosis??
DOCTOR: A High Functioning Autism – he is HFA.
MA: But he now needs a PMA.
SHOWGIRL: A 'Positive Mental Attitude' – for high school.

SCENE 14 *BUCKET's room. Preparing for school.*

SISTER: You won't get lost, it's not that big when you get used to it. They will get someone to show you around – and you get a map anyway . . . and a diary.

BUCKET: I have already got a diary. I've got my diary. It's a blue one. Blue-diary.

MOTHER: You must know someone else who is going.

BUCKET: I don't think I do know other people who are going. I know some of the other pupils who will be in my class as I met them, I met them already. Am I allowed to wear my coat in the classroom?

SISTER: No. They won't let you wear a hat either. No hoods, hats or towels, cloths or blankets!

MOTHER: Nothing on your head at all. Big school – high school – is different to special school.

BUCKET: Can I wear my coat outside if it gets cold?

SISTER: Yeah . . . duh!

MOTHER: Stop it . . . I want you to help him, remember. Now, how do you show teachers that you are listening to them?

BUCKET: You look at them.

MOTHER: And nod at them every now and again.

SISTER: Even in Bloaty's lessons.

BUCKET: Who's Bloaty?

MOTHER: And don't stare out of the windows.

SISTER: Mr Broat. He's huge and he keeps burping. He's really windy. *(Imitating)* 'Windows are not for staring out of!'

BUCKET: Why are they made of glass then? I think they would be made out of another, possibly cheaper material if they were not for looking out of.

MOTHER: And you must not look bored. If you are interested – look interested.

SISTER: You'll be bored in some lessons.

MOTHER: But look as if you are listening.

SISTER: And don't just talk about the things you are interested in. No one wants to know about Bix Beiderbecke, believe me. It's when you talk about things you like without letting others talk about what they like that things go pear-shaped.

BUCKET: What does?

MOTHER: It doesn't, it's just a turn of phrase.

SISTER: 'Pear-shaped' means going wrong, going funny.

BUCKET: They have new PCs and Macs and interactive whiteboards and pupils can use the Internet at break time and they have ICT club on Thursdays at 3.45 p.m. Music is on Wednesday at 2.25 p.m. and you can go to the Learning Resource Centre. But I don't play an instrument, I don't play an instrument.

SISTER: 'Library' – no one calls it the Learning Resource Centre. All of the geeks hang out there at break and lunch. You can go there.

MOTHER: Important bits. You put your hand up to answer a question.

SISTER: But don't always put your hand up. It's not cool. Even if you know it, even if you know the answer. You don't have to.

BUCKET: Can I put my hand up sometimes?

MOTHER: Of course.

SISTER: Loads of people never put their hands up. I don't. It doesn't mean that you don't know the answer. Karen 'Snogger' Sharpe always knows the answer and she just sits there like she's sunbathing.

MOTHER: I don't want you to appear rude – that seems rude.

BUCKET: Is her name 'Snogger'?

SISTER: Some people always know and they don't put their hand up. And then they say they don't do any work and they really do loads. It's not cool to admit to doing work.

MOTHER: But sometimes it is – don't worry. Don't worry about what others do and say.

BUCKET: I don't think I know anyone else who is going. I don't think so. I have got my diary. I've got my diary.

SISTER: We've just told you about that!

SCENE 15 *The big school!*

JELLY: Roll up, roll up . . . the greatest feat of skill and endurance . . . I am proud to present . . . 'The Boy who went to School'!

SHOWGIRL: Should we just walk away? Leave him to figure out how to survive in there?

MA: Would you want to be left alone?

JELLY: One day, you just gonna have to be on you own, boy.

BUCKET: One of my friends on the website said that writing about being an aspie might help the others to know what it is like.

MA: We're listening.

SHOWGIRL: So you get to know how others see you too?

JELLY: We know how we see you!

MA: No teasing.

BUCKET: You are in my story so I know what you think.

JELLY: I'm lost, boy.

SHOWGIRL: You're excited about going to school, huh?

JELLY does a final check of BUCKET's uniform and they walk to school. The cast create the school.

BUCKET: When I started the new school it was very different to the little school I was used to. My teachers were all new to me and I didn't know who they were.

MRS A: Ah . . . you must be new. What's your name? Don't tell me . . . let me have a little look at my list. Ah, yes. You look smashing.

How are you, today? What a lovely tie. You are going to be fine. Don't worry.

BUCKET: Every time she sees me now, she asks me the same question. I don't like her touching my tie.

TEACHER 1: Have you read this?

TEACHER 2: Nope.

TEACHER 1: I'm not surprised. There are 46 pages. I can't read it all.

TEACHER 2: What is it?

TEACHER 1: Something from Dreary Do-good.

TEACHER 2: Who?

TEACHER 1: Special Needs woman . . . what's her socks?

TEACHER 2: The new one? Waffled on at briefing. She's supposed to be good.

TEACHER 1: That's her.

BUCKET: I'm going to my new classroom today and I have a new Form Tutor. I know where the Main Hall is for assembly, but we don't have an assembly today . . .

TEACHER 1: I've never read anything with 46 pages in it!

TEACHER 2: Philistine, you must have. How many sugars?

TEACHER 1: Sports book at Christmas maybe. No . . . just leave it black and strong, thanks.

TEACHER 2: Have we all got one?

TEACHER 1: No – I've got a new kid coming. Transfer from down the road. Mother was worried he'd be bullied.

TEACHER 2: Let's have a look . . . 'The Student with Asperger's Syndrome at Secondary School'. A syndrome, hey?

BUCKET: I like looking at the walls. In my old school, the walls were blank and clear and empty. The pictures and the information were on the ceiling so we didn't get distracted.

TEACHER 2: Never heard of it. Must be bad news. Is his name Wayne?

BUCKET: I walked round the school with Mum. It was at night so I found out where to go. I have Registration and Geography and Science and Music and Lunch . . .

TEACHER 1: Don't know why we don't just call them 'naughty' any more.

TEACHER 2: What's his file say?

TEACHER 1: They haven't sent it yet. Mum thinks he'll be picked on.

TEACHER 2: Might be something physical then. Best skim read it.

TEACHER 1: I haven't got time. I'll read it in class. Well, here we go. Which rooms are getting the new carpets?

BUCKET: I have got all of my pens in my bag and I've got all of my books. I've got them in alphabetical order. I'm organised and I know what I am having for lunch. I'm not having cheese in case it makes me funny . . .

JELLY: You're not worried then?

BUCKET: I was worried, but not now.

MA and SHOWGIRL sing 'Backwater Blues' softly behind next section.

MOTHER: Who were you talking to just now?

BUCKET: People sang the blues when they were sad – and some people think that the black people in New Orleans played it because they were the saddest. They understood the blues. Bechet was a Creole. Perhaps he thought he was different from black people. You don't have to be black to understand the blues.

MOTHER: *(Gently removes blanket)* Do you have to be sad?

BUCKET: Some blues are happy.

MOTHER: What's this one?

BUCKET: 'Backwater Blues' – originally by Bessie Smith. There was a flood in 1927. The Great Mississippi Flood – 1927.

SCENE 16 *School.*

TEACHER 1: 'Typically, by secondary age, a student with Asperger's will want to interact with peers and make friends . . .'

BUCKET: I'm new.

TEACHER 1: '. . . but is not skilful in managing social relationships.'

BUCKET: I have a bag like that. I keep my pens in the front pocket because the zip in my pencil case sometimes doesn't work properly.

BELINDA: What yer telling me for?

TEACHER 1: 'The whole school inclusion policy . . .'
(Bucket is standing too close)

BELINDA: You fancy me or something?

BULLY: You done his 'Summer task'?

BELINDA: Hiya. Nah. Have you?

BULLY: Didn't know what it was. Anyway, the dog ate it and my little brother wee'd on it. And the printer's broke. And my Mum and Dad had a row – a big one. And I've lost my memory stick.

BUCKET: We haven't got a dog. I have a new memory stick with me. A new one.

BULLY: We ain't got a dog neither, durh-brain.

BUCKET: My sister comes to this school.

BELINDA: Anyway, he won't ask for it. Won't want the marking.

BULLY: Is he new? You new are yer? Borrow that coat off your Dad, did yer?

TEACHER 1: '. . . find a venue for small group skills training' . . . what sort of bloody training is he going to need?

BELINDA: You went to my playgroup didn't you? He went to KiddieCare. I remember you. You used to have a little patch in your glasses. You always sat outside on the swing. Never played with no one. Didn't you end up going to . . .

BULLY: You're right – proper weirdo. Where'd he go to?

BELINDA: You used to sort of squint – it's gone now.

BUCKET: I used to have a strabismus – which is a problem with the eye, which is why I had to have a small patch in the spectacles.

BULLY: Ooooh . . . 'in the spectacles'. A spectacular little patch in the spectacles!

TEACHER 1: 'Common anxiety triggers may include . . . crowded places, such as the corridor or when pupils are lining up.' Well that'll be easy to avoid in a school!

BUCKET: I don't have the patches any more . . .

TEACHER 1: Right, in you go. Welcome back. *(They all go in)*
'Yes, hi, Sir, and how were your holidays?' 'Very good thank you . . . lovely weather, etc., etc.'

BULLY: We've got a new kid. He used to have something in his eye – a stig or something . . .

TEACHER 1: Really? Who might that be? I would never have guessed . . .

BELINDA: The tables and chairs have gone!

BULLY: We ain't got no chairs to sit on!

TEACHER 1: OK – settle down, just sit down anywhere.

BUCKET: Sir, shall we just sit on the floor?

BELINDA: I ain't sitting on the floor – it's minging. You can't make us sit on the floor!

BULLY: Why ain't there no chairs?

TEACHER 1: No one told me. Oh . . . they're fitting carpets this morning. Sit down, Belinda.

BELINDA: The floor ain't been cleaned. I don't want to. Can I stand?

TEACHER 1: Do as you're told. Sit. Right, books . . . and diaries. Someone get the register, please.

BELINDA: Bell'll go soon. Getting messed up for two minutes registration time. We shouldn't have to sit on the floor!

TEACHER 1: Well, you do have to sit on the floor. Don't start this term like the last one.

BELINDA: I ain't done nothing!

TEACHER 1: Don't push it.

BELINDA: I hate this place.

TEACHER 1: Well, there's plenty of space down the road. See how you like it there.

BULLY: Is that where the new kid came from? We get loads of kids from there now. All mingers.

TEACHER 1: What was that? Belinda – last warning – or you'll spend lunch with me. Sit down.

BULLY: He must fancy you.

BELINDA: The bell's about to go, Sir. There ain't nowhere to sit.

TEACHER 1: OK – keep the noise down . . . what did you say?

BULLY: Nothing.
TEACHER 1: Who needs their diary signing?
BELINDA: Are you gonna sit in all this mess?
BULLY: Sit on the new kid's coat.
TEACHER 1: Has it been signed?
BELINDA: Yeah . . . but . . .
TEACHER 1: Not you. *(To BUCKET)* Are you listening?
(No answer)
TEACHER 1: Calling Earth . . . come in, please. Are you listening to me?
BUCKET: Of course I am.
TEACHER 1: Well? Cat got your tongue?
(Cast act as a Chorus and echo the teacher's words as this builds)
CHORUS: 'Cat got your tongue?'
BUCKET: Well what, Sir?
TEACHER 1: Diary?
BUCKET: Would you like it?
TEACHER 1: Are you trying to be clever? I told you to get your diary and homework out.
BUCKET: *(On 'clever')* Yes, I am.
TEACHER 1: You what? Hang on for a second, what did you say?
BUCKET: I beg your pardon?
CHORUS: 'Hang on for a second.' 'Hang, hang, hang!'
TEACHER 1: I know you're new here, but don't get off on the wrong foot, sunshine.
CHORUS: 'Sunshine'.
TEACHER 1: I didn't give you homework, but you've got a diary and I told you to get it out.
BUCKET: You said 'books' and I think 'diary'. I didn't know that you wanted me to get them out. You didn't say get them out.
TEACHER 1: Sit up when I'm talking to you!
CHORUS: 'Sit up, up, up ,up!'
(BUCKET is confused and does not know what to do so, hesitantly, stands up)
TEACHER 1: I didn't ask you to stand. My God, you'd better pull your socks up . . .
CHORUS: 'Pull your socks up . . .'
TEACHER 1: . . . if you want to survive five minutes in this school. Don't you dare look at your socks! I thought you were supposed to be bright! I'll have your guts for garters if you play me up. What's that?
BUCKET: Ummmm?
CHORUS: 'Guts, guts, play me up. Guts for garters.'
BELINDA: The bell definitely is about to go now, Sir! So what's the point?
TEACHER 1: In your hand . . . what is it?
BUCKET: An amethyst . . . it's for . . .

TEACHER 1: A stone? You've picked up a stone?

BELINDA: Can we go now?

TEACHER 1: What were you going to do with that? Put it on the table. Now!
(BUCKET does so – but it hurts him)

TEACHER 1: Right, you two. Great start!! You need some manners. I want to see both of you at the start of lunch. Don't be late.

CHORUS: Get to a corner
Cling to a wall
Hide in the shadows
Make yourself small
Even if they see you
They will not know you're there
Pretend you haven't noticed
Even when they stare
And run to the corners when the bell goes

BULLY: You must be a weirdo
Or maybe just a freak
You looking for trouble? Geek!

BELINDA: I try to be assertive
Don't want to answer back
But the floor is really muddy

Don't want to sit in cack.

TEACHER 1: Pull your socks up
Hang on a second
Diary – books
I'll have your guts for garters

CHORUS: Get to a corner
Cling to a wall
Hide in the shadows
Make yourself small
Even if they see you
They will not know you're there
Pretend you haven't noticed
Even when they stare
And run to the corners when the bell goes.
(BULLY picks up pamphlet)

BULLY: Wha's he got? Asparagras syndrome? Did you come from the spazza's school?

BUCKET: You shouldn't have that, it belongs to the teacher.

BULLY: It belongs to me now. Finders keepers, Nerdy. Is that what they call you? Nerdy?

BUCKET: I don't know what a 'nerd' is . . .

BULLY: 'Special interest – geology'. Oooh – an ology. Are you a little boffin then?

BUCKET: I have to go to see the Form Tutor. I have to go see him at lunch.

BULLY: Oh yes. Been a naughty little boffin, haven't you. Answered him back and you were ever so cheeky!

BUCKET: I have to see him at the start of lunch – at the start of lunch time. He didn't tell me where to go, though. He didn't tell me where to go.

BULLY: Where'd you reckon? Mars? Nerd!

(BUCKET left alone)

JELLY: So it's not been the best of starts at the new school. Our little hero is struggling to find his way – he's struggling to understand . . . he's struggling to make friends.

SHOWGIRL: I don't think the teacher understands.

MA: That teacher didn't make no effort to understand.

JELLY: Well – what happens next? A lunch time detention?

SHOWGIRL: What about that horrible kid?

JELLY: We need a twist to the story, boy.

MA: And we got the girl from play school standing there.

SHOWGIRL: He don't know where he knows her from . . .

JELLY: Hey! He's not worried about the detention – that doesn't make any sense to him. But how is he going to talk to the girl? How does he do that? He's got hormones now!!

JELLY: If you think that life is really hard, boy
Just you wait until you are in your teens
If you think that walking is a bind, boy
I tell you kissing's just as tough as anything!

MA: Do you think that algebra is daunting?
Do you find geography a chore?
Well, just imagine you have got a date boy
And you've walked her home and stood outside her door!

ALL: What do you do?
What do you say?
Can you hold her hand?
Is it OK?
Nothing is as hard as the first time
This is just the start of nightmare day:

BULLY: Weirdo. What's he look like. Not even cold and he's wearing a coat.

BELINDA: Leave him. He's all right when you get to know him.
BULLY: Don't even look at us when he speaks . . .
BELINDA: A bit odd, that's all.
BULLY: What you got for lunch? Asparagras?
BELINDA: Leave him – it's his first day . . .

JELLY: Are you getting too close already?
Does she think you need to walk away?
Are your hands and teeth and clothes all clean, boy?
Have you used enough underarm spray?

MA: How do you begin a conversation?
Is it cool to talk about your stuff?
Will she softly smile at you and wink, boy?
Or will she slap your face and treat you rough?

ALL: What do you do?
What do you say?
Can you sit down there?
Is it OK?
Nothing is as hard as the first time
This is just as bad as it can be.

BELINDA: I remember him at nursery. Used to throw some right wobblies – then go and sit on the swing. Just sit on the swing.

ALL: What do you do?
What do you say?
Can you touch her hand?
Is it OK?
Nothing's as hard as the first time
This is just as bad as it can be.

JELLY: You don't know what she's thinking
Girls are not the same
It's dangerous – it's scary
It's the wicked witch's game!

SCENE 17 *MOTHER and FATHER are voices at the side, rather than in the scene.*

MRS A: Unbelievable! What on earth were you thinking of? What have you done?
TEACHER 1: I don't know what you're talking about – I've asked him to come because he was being cheeky. I didn't ask him – I told him.

JELLY: Just ignore them
Get them out of your mind
Leave them to shout and cry.

SHOWGIRL: Because we know what's inside
We know how you feel
We know how you feel
Try to be real.

MRS A: I can almost guarantee that he was not being cheeky. He will find it very difficult to be cheeky – or even know when someone else is being cheeky. Have you read the booklet I gave you?

TEACHER 1: I haven't had chance to read it all . . . I've had a good skim through.

MRS A: Then you will know that young people on the autistic spectrum do find it difficult to cope with new situations. Sticking him in detention on his first day hardly seems fair. Shouting at him might even be cruel. Idiotically cruel.

TEACHER 1: I didn't shout . . . he refused to look at me.

MOTHER: Eye contact is difficult for him – he feels you are looking inside him. It hurts him.

MA: And when you find a place to be
Look around and you will see
You can run
You can walk

TEACHER 1: The room was in a mess, there are no chairs or tables – nothing to sit on. Belinda kicked off.

FATHER: He's odd – gets upset by change – finds it difficult to cope with.

MRS A: He needed reassurance. I hope you at least gave him very clear instructions.

TEACHER 1: Look, everyone else knew exactly what I meant.

JELLY: When they shout and bawl at you
When the walls seem thin
If the bell cuts through you
Remember what's within . . .

ALL: Because we know what's inside you
We know how you feel
Try to be real
Try to be real.

MRS A: They are used to you and have learnt to mind read – he can't. He thinks literally. You ask him to get on his bike and pedal faster, he'll look for a bike. Or did you say, 'Shake a leg'? 'Put your skates on?' What did you actually say? 'Pull yourself together?' 'Roll your sleeves up?' Well – something like that he will take literally. I hope to goodness you weren't sarcastic. He has only just arrived here – his first day in a normal school.

TEACHER 1: I'll apologise to him. I'll read the booklet tonight.

MOTHER: When he was little, he was terrified of the dentist, the barber and hand dryers. Noises can hurt him. He failed to do a school test when he was eight because the clock was too loud. For him, it really was.

TEACHER 1: I thought he was bright, intelligent? How's he going to cope here?

FATHER: He is a bit of a sensitive lad.

MRS A: If and when you get to know him, you'll find him a very intelligent boy. He writes music and has his own website. He researches famous musicians. But he won't make progress if he is bullied by staff – especially his own Form Tutor!

TEACHER 1: That's not fair . . . I didn't . . . we do have some bullying issues, I know.

MOTHER: Please try to understand him.

FATHER: He can be odd – very odd at times.

MRS A: He will be victimised because he is different. He will be teased, bullied. Pupils will call him 'nerd' and 'freak' and 'boffin' and 'four-eyes', etc., etc. It has already happened. Where is he now? He will be totally lost and upset, very stressed and very confused. He will not cope with this. Especially not on his first day. He is probably hiding somewhere.

TEACHER 1: He wouldn't do himself any harm, would he? He's not a self-harmer is he?

MRS A: I just don't know. This could confuse and upset him. I haven't had much chance to get to know him. Probably not – but he could do anything. He will want to get away from the stress you have caused him!

ALL: And you know the score
Let's open the door
If you try
You can walk
You can run

SCENE 18 *Music under BUCKET's speech.*

BUCKET: It's sometimes called Dixieland. Dixieland. Americans call it that – white Americans. White ones. Jazz black folk music and plantation songs, minstrel songs, work songs. African music. Work and celebration music, rituals and dancing. Birth and death and marriage. Drum, foot stamp, trumpet calls – rhythm carrying the spirits away.

New Orleans. Black slave dance in Congo Square. Creoles, Hispanics and European traders and music and mazurkas, schottisches and quadrilles. Dancing at dusk.

Fighting, kick-back music. Hollering. Shouting. Sitting on a swing.

Rhythms getting mixed up. Strong beat. Mixed up. Clapping and shouting. Attack and beating drums, off-beats. Holler, call and response. Shouting back. Dream music – play it with your eyes shut – move to another world.

Kick-back something new and out on the edge. Clubs, speakeasies, smoky, dives, gin-house, brothel, honky tonk, rough, shady, violent – gamblers and pool sharks and a piano in the corner.

When I get picked on, when I get upset . . . this is the world I think about. This is the world I go to in my head.

SCENE 19 *BUCKET stands centrally with a bucket on his head. Gradually, all the cast will gather around him.*

PUPIL: Oi, Miss. There's a boy in the girls' toilet with a bucket on his head . . .

MRS A: What have you done?

TEACHER 1: What?

PUPIL: Honestly, Sir, in the girls' loo with a bucket on his head! Oi, get out, minger! He's got a bucket on his head!

BELINDA: Don't touch him.

BULLY: Buckethead!

TEACHER 2: Now then, what on earth is going on?

BULLY: New boy, Miss – a weirdo. He's gone into the girls' bog and put a bucket on his head.

BELINDA: Leave him – all of you be quiet.

TEACHER 2: I beg your pardon? Now then, young man, I want you out of there straight away. This instant, do you hear?

BELINDA: Don't shout at him, Miss.

BULLY: He's not listening – Bucketbrain!

TEACHER 2: Did you hear? And I think it would be helpful if you could all stand back and make less noise.

BELINDA: Don't shout, Miss. He's not listening to you. Stop shouting at him!

TEACHER 2: I can see that's not listening. This is outrageous. I'll handle this. Now, young man, I don't know what you think you're playing at, but . . .

BELINDA: No, Miss. Get off him, honestly. Just leave him, Miss. He doesn't know this was for the girls – he's new. He just wanted a quiet place – he's had a tough day – people have been . . .

TEACHER 2: How dare you interfere? How dare you touch a teacher in that way? You can go to the Head's Office straight away. I'll deal with you later.

BELINDA: No, Miss. I ain't moving. Get Mrs A . . .

TEACHER 2: Don't you dare say 'No' to me! Mrs who?

BELINDA: The new teacher . . . she knows about him. He's got something, Miss. I can't remember what it is, but he's no trouble.

BULLY: Yeah – he's only been here a day and got put in detto!

TEACHER 2: That's enough! I hardly need advice about trouble-making from you two.

BELINDA: Honest, Miss, I just heard her talking about him . . . he's got . . .

BULLY: A bucket on his head and he's standing in the girls' bog!

BELINDA: Just leave him a minute or two, Miss.

TEACHER 2: I cannot leave a boy standing in the girls' toilet with a bucket on his head. Especially the girls' toilet!

BELINDA: But he doesn't mind.

TEACHER 2: Well I most certainly do!

BELINDA: He's just gone to a quiet place. A place with no distractions. His imaginary place. His magical place. He used to go to the swing, Miss.

TEACHER 2: Well, he'd better magic himself out.

MRS A: In a moment – all of you!! Give him a little space.

BELINDA: That's what I told them, Miss.

TEACHER 2: I beg your pardon??

MRS A: Move back a little – and keep the noise down.

Whole Cast gathered around – MRS A creates space. JELLY etc. come forward.

JELLY: If she stands beside you, is that good, boy?
Does it mean she really understands?
Can it be the start of something big, boy?
Do you think you'll end up holding hands?

ALL: What do you do?
What do you say?
Can you sit down there?
Is it OK?
Nothing is as hard as the first time
This is just as bad as it can be.

MA: How do you begin a conversation?
Is it cool to talk about your stuff?
Will she softly smile at you and wink, boy?
Or will she slap your face and treat you rough?

ALL: What do you do?
What do you say?
Can you sit down there?
Is it OK?

Nothing is as hard as the first time
This is just as bad as it can be.

During song, Belinda quietly and unromantically helps him to remove the bucket and takes him by the hand.

BUCKET: I was just finishing off the musical play in my head, in my head.
BELINDA: What is it about? We'd like to hear it. What's it called?
BUCKET: It's about someone with a bucket on his head.

ALL: How do you begin a conversation?
Is it cool to talk about your stuff?
Will she softly smile at you and wink, boy?
Or will she slap your face and treat you rough?

What do you do?
What do you say?
Can you sit down there?
Is it OK?
Nothing is as hard as the first time
This is just as bad as it can be.

The End

Chapter 9

From the horse's mouth

A girl called Lauren

When Lauren was 15 years old, she joined a new school for her last year of compulsory education. The school she joined was a special school that catered for students aged 2 to 19 years with a wide range of learning needs. In addition to pupils with severe, moderate, and profound and multiple learning difficulties, the school had a specialist resource for pupils with autism. Most of her schoolmates were from White British backgrounds. Boys outnumbered girls in the school and the proportion of pupils entitled to a free school meal was slightly above the national average.

Lauren's class consisted of 12 students aged between 14 and 16. Some were in their last year but others still had one more year to do before starting work or college. All of them had learning difficulties deemed as moderate, but severe enough to mean that it was unlikely that they would manage in a mainstream school. Two of the students were autistic. Two were quite seriously epileptic. Others had speech defects and emotional and behavioural difficulties. Some experienced the effects of social deprivation.

When Lauren first joined the class, her classmates were not sure what to say to her or how to get to know her. Their teacher encouraged them to think about what they would like and need if they were in Lauren's situation. As a result, they soon began to help her integrate into the school and local life by advising her what she should wear and how to 'speak cool'. They even took her to a local nightclub, though on one occasion this rather backfired and she became the victim of some bullying by other youths in the town.

It transpired that Lauren's mother and grandmother were both dead and she lived with her father and grandfather. While her grandfather was kind and loving, her father was abusive and frequently hit her. When her grandfather suddenly died, Lauren ran back to a care home that she had spent some time in after her mother's death rather than live alone with her father. Given further support from her classmates, though, Lauren managed to get through her final year at school. She started going out with a boy called Bob who lived next door to her. Bob told his friends that he had liked Lauren ever since she came to his tenth birthday party!

The most extraordinary thing about Lauren was that she didn't actually exist. The rest of her class did, though, and it was them who created her in a drama project I led that ran over 11 sessions of one hour forty minutes each. The culmination of the project involved spending a whole day of filming Lauren's story after parental and student consent was obtained. For the duration of the project, I was assisted in the classroom by a full-time teaching assistant and a part-time learning support assistant.

Drama in the special school

A number of challenges need to be overcome in order to make effective use of drama in the setting of a special school. It is often the case that pupils are unused to it being taught as a subject in its own right or used as a method for delivering other aspects of the curriculum; as Melanie Peter (2009: 9) notes, 'drama as a learning medium is still under-used in specialist settings'. Teaching staff in special schools often invest a lot of time and energy in producing plays and performances that parents and carers may enjoy. Such presentations are testaments to and celebrations of the caring, social ethos of the school, but while they may be a showcase for what the school can achieve, there is often less evidence of how much input the children themselves have in them or what they learn from their involvement. Such manifestations of drama raise questions regarding the purpose of such activities and lead to a re-assessment of the expectations on teacher workloads. Many teachers specialising in the education of children with special educational needs often lack training in the use of drama as a method of teaching. So, while some may sense the potential of drama as a learning medium, not so many possess the knowledge and skills required to realise that potential. The amount of research that explores the use of drama as an educational tool with students who have special educational needs is limited (Jindal-Snape and Vettraino 2007), and this constitutes a further hindrance for teachers who wish to increase their competence in this area.

Another challenge lies in the fact that many children with learning difficulties palpably lack confidence in their own creative and communicative abilities (Whitehurst 2007). This aspect of their life is present for them every day at home and at school, yet there are often too few opportunities for them to gain confidence by discovering what they are good at and building on that. Certainly, the current education system in England is dominated by the requirement for children to achieve set levels in key subjects such as English, mathematics and science. Such a regime tends to exacerbate problems of low confidence levels by emphasising the need for children to do things they are not very good at while limiting the time and space available to explore other potential avenues of achievement. Peter (2009) points out that it is often assumed that children with learning disabilities are unable to work interactively with a narrative form rather than being simply the passive audience for stories told by the teacher. Similarly, it can be the case that adults, in trying to be supportive, too often speak and act for children when they see them to be struggling, and thus deny them the right to take charge of their own words and actions (Kempe 2005: 157–60). In a society in which the medical model of disability continues to dominate, 'activities which encourage personal autonomy and independence are not on the list of priorities' (Jennings 1981: 40). In contrast, by embracing the social model, drama can provide a context in which narrative ability can be learned and students realise their own creativity and capacity to communicate their ideas. It was with these challenges in mind that the 'Lauren' project set out to explore further what contribution drama could make to the education of young people with learning difficulties, and so provide an example for other teachers to use and build upon.

There's nothing special about it!

I have argued elsewhere (Kempe 1991, 1992, 2005) that drama for children with special educational needs need be no different, essentially, to any of the drama work undertaken with any other group of young people. In fact, the inspiration for the 'Lauren' project derived, in part, from a research project involving teenage girls undertaken in mainstream schools in Australia and London. The project was grounded in the belief that narrative-based drama methods offered: 'an enactive space to explore their lives through the art form of drama whilst providing opportunities to travel through and play with the workings of culture, gender and identity' (Hatton 2003: 139).

One of the values of drama in education is that it affords students the opportunity to learn from the experience of casting themselves in different parts, and experiencing what it is like to be cast in a role by others. Hatton had undertaken her study of the importance of drama as a medium through which adolescent girls could explore their own developing identities on the grounds that both drama in education and mainstream theatre has historically marginalised women, and especially young women. In her opinion:

> Girls are rarely invited to share their knowledge and resources in the broader curriculum of secondary education. What is more concerning is that even when teachers aim for inclusive practice, girls' worlds and stories can remain hidden and untapped in the drama classroom.
>
> (Hatton 2003: 142)

If the voices of adolescent girls in mainstream education too often remain hidden and untapped, is this even more true for teenagers with learning disabilities? The 'Lauren' project set out to uncover and use the voices of the students involved by offering them the chance to create a fictitious character who they could play themselves or who they could cast in any role they chose. The primary aim was to create a drama that would reflect their perceptions of what young people sharing similar circumstances as themselves needed to know, understand and be able to do and so reveal something of their hopes and expectations for the future as well as their fears and concerns. The pre-text for the drama was captured in a question:

> If a new student joined this group, in this school, in this area, what would they need to know? What would their hopes and fears be? What would you be able to tell them that neither their parents nor their teachers could?

Although drama is currently a strand of the National Curriculum for English, the reality is that many children with special educational needs are taught little about drama as a subject in its own right or experience it as a learning medium. This was certainly true of the students in the 'Lauren' project. They had all been involved in some performances, for example Christmas celebrations and light-hearted 'reviews' (including a short, bizarre, cross-dressed interpretation of *The Sound of Music* as a part of a multi-cultural festival!). Some had a little experience of drama clubs outside of school, but only one girl, who transferred to the class from another school in the third week of the project, had experienced drama as a part of the taught curriculum. On this basis, a second aim of the project was to introduce the students to a range of dramatic techniques that might be used to develop Lauren's story. Students were thus introduced to still images, improvisation, narration, choral speech, masks, puppets, ritual and writing in role. Teaching strategies also included using teacher in role, role on the wall and conscience alley.

Being in Key Stage 4, there was an expectation that the work should contribute to the Entry Level Certificate qualification in English. The third aim of the project therefore addressed the following specific aspects of the syllabus:

> - Reading: The student will experience a play in performance which may be live or recorded and read material from/about the play. S/he will participate in discussions and will be encouraged to respond individually to the play.
> - Writing: The student will experience a play in performance which may be live or recorded. S/he will participate in discussion and will respond in writing to the play.
> - Speaking and Listening: The student will participate in a range of speaking and listening activities related to drama.
>
> (AQA 2009)

Each session was planned so as to incorporate new drama experiences and move the story along. In truth, the term 'planned' is being used rather loosely here! Other than being pretty sure how I would start the session, I only ever had a sketchy idea of how it might develop and what we would cover, not least because I never knew exactly:

- how many students would be present;
- how much disruption there would be in the session because of students being taken out of the class for one reason or another;
- how they would respond to the initial stimulus for the lesson; and
- what they might offer up that would be worth pursuing.

As each session progressed, I made notes on how the drama was being developed and sometimes asked one of the teaching assistants to write down things the students said while I listened and interacted with them. The work included some writing in role and also collaborative writing where ideas were recorded and edited on the whiteboard. Towards the end of the project, all of the students' written pieces and much of the spontaneous speech recorded in the session notes were edited into a loose film script. Involving the students in the writing of the script provided an opportunity to teach them some subject-specific terminology. The script, which is appended to this chapter, provided a guide as to how we might re-tell Lauren's story rather than representing a polished piece of dramatic literature. A number of scenes were improvised in the film, the students drawing on their memory of how they had first been created in the classroom. Two film and television students from the University of Reading were recruited, and a day was spent making a film about Lauren using the school and its surroundings as a location.

The project in practice

Having introduced the idea that a new student would be joining the class in the first session, we set about deciding a few basic details of who the person was and how they might feel. This led to some lively and amusing dialogue between the girls, which was recorded in note form and later edited into a script. Verbal contributions from most of the pupils tended to be quite limited in the early sessions. Nonetheless, all of their ideas were accepted and used in the developing drama. As a result of careful questioning and structured tasks, the fictional character of Lauren developed rapidly. For example, it was suggested to the class that Lauren felt uncertain what to wear in order to fit in. The students were invited to give her an item of clothing. This involved them taking turns to walk towards an empty chair, address it as if Lauren were sitting on it and mime giving her an item of clothing. I modelled the activity for them first. One of the girls offered Lauren a denim cap, another a black velvet scarf. Before the following session, I found an actual denim cap and black velvet scarf; thereafter, Lauren was always signified by placing these on the same chair at the start of each drama session. On the first occasion I placed the cap and scarf, one girl said, 'Good morning, Lauren'. From this arose an enjoyable and humorous routine way of starting each session, which involved me ritually placing the objects on the chair and the whole class saying, 'Good morning, Lauren'. The fact that Lauren was never seen in the flesh but was only signified by two items of clothing meant that she could be played by any member of the group, boy or girl, when the need arose. Learning to accept Lauren as an idea rather than a physical presence ultimately led to one boy suggesting that the film we eventually made was shot largely from her point of view. This was an imaginative suggestion and created a new challenge, in that the teenagers had to respond to the camera as if it were Lauren. The nature of drama as a pedagogy makes it flexible and responsive to situations. Its unpredictability can sometimes seem intimidating to teachers with little experience of it, but if this flexibility is embraced, it can lead to the creation of a teaching situation that has little scope for failure for students and therefore represents a 'safe environment' in which to practice important social skills (Attwood 2006). The paradox of using drama in education is that the safest lesson is often the one in which the teacher takes the most risks!

It quickly became clear, both through the way the class were constructing Lauren and their own actual responses to the drama exercises, that confidence and self-esteem was an impediment for many of the students. Even exploring how they might say 'hello' to Lauren and make her feel welcome was initially a challenge. The first reaction of some was to say, 'I can't do it. I don't know what to say.' Was this really because they did not have the vocabulary? Or perhaps it was a defence mechanism they were well practised in using to simply avoid feeling exposed and tested. A number of devices were employed to try to tackle this. For example, the teacher-in-role strategy proved an effective way of modelling what they might say to Lauren and how they might respond to her. Paddy Masefield notes that 'People who have learning disabilities may lack an extensive physical voice but still possess sensitive powers of communication . . . above all, a conspiracy prevails that they should not be allowed to speak for themselves when decisions are being taken about them' (Masefield 2006: 76). In this project, I encouraged the group to focus on facial expressions and body language to represent emotions, thus taking away the reliance on speaking. When the class explored how Lauren might be feeling on entering a new situation, words and physical expression worked symbiotically: if someone suggested a word to describe how Lauren might be feeling, I asked if anyone could show us what she might look like if she was feeling that emotion. Conversely, if someone adopted an expression or position in space, I asked what words might be used to describe that.

In one session, the class improvised what happened when they invited Lauren to join them at a local nightclub. Following the improvisation, the students were asked to imagine what Lauren might have written in her diary about the event. In a subsequent session, one pupil suggested that Lauren went back to the nightclub on her own, only to discover that her school friends were not there. Instead, she encountered a group of local youths who mocked the way she was dressed. The students were invited to suggest what the youths could have said to Lauren to upset and intimidate her. They circled the chair that signified Lauren and took turns at taunting her. A ritualised sequence evolved in which the pupils, wearing blank white masks, stomped around and pointed at the scarf and cap that signified Lauren in time to a piece of vibrant music suggestive of children taunting (*Powaqqatsi* by Philip Glass). The energy and repetition involved in this simple piece of choreography was something that the class particularly enjoyed. The scene in which Lauren confronted her classmates and asked why they had not turned up as they said they would, however, was played out with a genuine sense of betrayal on Lauren's part and sincere remorse from the classmates who, I estimated, knew very well what it was like to be on the receiving end of nastiness when there was no one to stand by them.

An especially productive session developed from an idea for which I am indebted to Peter O'Connor (2008). In role as a classmate of Lauren's called Bob, I told the class how, just before the start of school that day, I had taken her mobile phone to tease her. Rather than joining in with the jibe, though, she had run off in tears. On looking at the phone, Bob had discovered a distressing message on it, which he shared with the class: 'I don't care what they say. I'm not going back 2nite. If u r my friend pls don't tell. L.'

One girl spontaneously volunteered that she thought the message was meant for her. Others in the class asked her: Why? What did she know? What was going on? A story emerged: Lauren's mother and grandmother were dead, and she lived with her abusive father and kindly grandfather. Sadly, her grandfather had died the previous weekend and Lauren was frightened of living alone with her father. Another girl suggested that she had probably gone back to a care home where she had spent some time. We visited the home and were told by the warden there (another girl in role) that she would often visit the graveyard to speak with her dead mother and grandmother. Sometimes, she said, Lauren would leave letters on their graves. Such rich ideas are, of course, a gift for the drama teacher but also sound evidence of drama's capacity to release young people's creativity and sensitivity.

Still images were employed to explore and capture aspects of Lauren's family life further by imagining that she possessed a personal photograph album that she had taken with her to the care home. The introduction of Bob as a character opened up the possibility of giving Lauren a love life. Given that the class had found simply saying 'hello' to Lauren difficult enough, I was wary of asking them to use role play or improvisation to dramatise such a relationship. Drawing on McLintock's work with withdrawn children (McLintock 1984), I wondered if using puppets might help to remove them from the immediacy and potential embarrassment of a romantic encounter. The idea worked, and we had a lively and laughter-filled session learning how to operate two specially bought puppets, experimenting how Bob might ask Lauren out for a date, and what their first kiss might have looked like!

Arts philosopher and educator Malcolm Ross (1984) has argued his case for the centrality of the aesthetic experience in our lives when he says that to be 'aestheticised' is to be turned towards life. In the 'Lauren' project, opportunities were sought to help the students consider how life experience could be understood not just in words, movement and gesture, but also through colours, textures and objects. In turn, this led to an exploration of metaphor. For example, a whole-class exercise considering Lauren's personality resulted in a piece of collaboratively written choral speech. Two of the girls in the class were considered to have autistic spectrum disorder. It was particularly interesting to note that these two girls suggested what I thought were the most powerful ideas in this sequence:

> If Lauren could be an object, she would be a glass window; then she'd be able to see just who was talking about her.
>
> If Lauren could be an animal, she would be a crab. She could give her father a pinch. It might hurt a bit, but he needs to wake up.

What was once the received wisdom that people with autism are unable to communicate or interact, have no imagination and lack creativity is, fortunately, rapidly proving to be a popular and disabling myth. The suggestion that Lauren could be a crab illustrated that the girl not only possessed a sound grasp of metaphor, but a strong visual and kinaesthetic imagination when she complemented her comment by using her hands as claws and pulling a determined yet hurt looking face.

Trying

Hatton (2003: 147) commented that, in her experience, teachers too often impose material for drama on students without questioning the validity of the fiction or interrogating whose views were being privileged in the action. As a result, classroom dramas, either directly or indirectly, often tend to 'reinforce the dominant or meta-narratives of our society'. She goes on to note, though, that teachers have the possibility of travelling alongside their students as they make their journeys in drama: 'We can guide their selection of route and help their understandings of the landscape to emerge. We help to pack the personal backpack they take on their drama journeys and the journeys of their lives' (ibid.: 153).

This belief seemed to me to be reflected in the 'Lauren' project. The last session before we went on to film Lauren's story incorporated a plenary on what we had done, and what the project had meant to them. By jotting their comments on the whiteboard, I realised that we had the material for a piece of choral speech. Their final remarks about adults summed up how they were dealing with a disabling society:

Sometimes they argue
Sometimes they swear

They're not always helpful
Or kind.

Perhaps they try to behave
And that's what we do –
Try.

In conclusion, working on the story of Lauren with this group of teenagers, who faced many challenges in their lives, reinforced for me the belief that drama is a radical and positive educational force, particularly when 'working with students and groups who continue to be disadvantaged or marginalised in schools and societies' (Hatton 2007: 198). The impact of the project was further illustrated when, three months after the project ended, I visited the class to say goodbye to those who were leaving the school. I had prepared fifteen questions that I wanted to ask to ascertain how much they remembered about the project. The questions ranged in detail from:

> What was the name of the girl we invented in our drama?

to others that were rather more testing such as:

> Who stole Lauren's phone and discovered the text message?
>
> What did Lauren take with her to the care home for Christmas?

The class's usual teacher was impressed with the level of recall. Eleven students were present for the session, meaning that a total of 165 answers were possible: 76 per cent of these were correct. Lauren had made an impression on these students, just as they had made an impression on me. Drama, disability and education had synchronised in a most satisfying way.

Lauren

1 Our new classmate

Tintagel classroom. Students at work behind desks. Emma, the TA, calls their attention and gets them to come and sit in the circle inside the square of desks.

Individual class members take turns to say the following:

Andy said we could have a new classmate. We could choose who they would be.
So we chose Lauren.
She was fourteen and lived in Thatcham.
We thought having a new girl would be good because

girls are more helpful,
girls are happier,
we could share her make up,
girls are kind,
and girls are good at gardening!

Of course not everyone agreed.
Boys are best, they said,
because I'm a boy
and we haven't got many in our class.
And I'm single, and some new talent would be good!

2 Lauren's arrival

The journey into school from Lauren' P.O.V.: We see the school sign. As she goes through the gate, she looks behind. Her father is leaning out of the car window. He shouts at her and tells her to 'get on with it'. She turns back towards the school. Her granddad appears and tells her she'll be all right. At the steps to the entrance, Lauren must go through a crowd of students. They stop talking as she approaches and stare at her. Once through the doors, she is greeted by the receptionist, who telephones the class teacher. As she waits, she looks around the reception area. Karen, the class teacher, comes and collects her. Karen takes her through the school, pointing things out and talking to her all the time. They arrive at the classroom.

3 Hello Lauren

In this sequence, the class make a series of still images to illustrate Lauren's emotions with the following voice-overs (V.O.s):

When Lauren came to our class
she was
frightened,
nervous,
shy,
and shakey.
She was
quiet
and lonely.
She wanted to make friends,
but she found herself speechless.
Even so,
she was happy to be here

Extreme close up (C.U.) of a girl's smile.

4 *Lauren's diary*

C.U. of handwriting in an exercise book. V.O.:

Dear diary,

When I first came to this school I was scared and worried because I didn't have any friends to play with until someone came down to see if I was ok. I made some friends there called Tom and Faye. I was frightened on my first day at school when I was meeting new people but I was happy after one week. I knew everyone and I went to Liquid with my mates. This is the best school I have ever been to.

Lauren's P.O.V.: Two students asking if she is OK and then inviting her to the nightclub, Liquid.

C.U. of handwriting in an exercise book. V.O.:

Dear diary,

I was frightened when I first went into Liquid but then I felt happy. It was a good night on Monday. I felt a bit scared until one of my friends called me over to come and dance and have something to drink of coke and I felt a bit better. When I saw my friends from school there and I was happy. All the people were dancing and they had a disco and a dance floor and a DJ person and the people were having a good time.

The nightclub: dancing, music, some flashing lights, etc.

C.U. of handwriting in an exercise book. V.O.:

I made some friends and I enjoyed being at Liquid and I had a good time in there as well. But when I went back to school in the morning I was a bit worried and petrified about what people would say. Then I met a friend. She was called Katie and we went outside to play and had lunch. I had fun.

Lauren's P.O.V.: Katie takes her around the playground pointing things out. They sit on a bench. Katie shows Lauren what she has in her lunchbox ('Banana yoghurt. Low fat – the healthy option') and asks what Lauren has in hers.

C.U. of handwriting in an exercise book. V.O.:

My mates from the class are cool. At first my classmates did not say a lot but when it was break time they spoke to me. A boy named Ashley came up to me and spoke to me. I was happy. I like going to school. My new class is the best. I think they are good and very funny. They are so cool they are the best friends I can ever have. I will go back to Liquid when it is on next with my classmates.

Lauren's P.O.V.: Ashley saying hello and holding out his hand to shake hers.

5 Liquid

Lauren's P.O.V. of exercise book being written into. V.O.:

Dear diary

Well, as you know, I have started at The Castle School. I am in Tintagel class. People seem nice there but it is hard to join in because I don't know what to say or do.

Last week I went to Liquid with some of the class. It was good but I was a bit scared.

I wish I knew what to wear and how to look cool like them.
What music should I listen to?
What TV should I watch?
What sort of things should I say to make me cool like them?
I wish they could help me.

The class mill around and talk to the camera as if it were Lauren:

We got Lauren dressed up ready to go to Liquid.
We told her what to wear.
Then we taught her how to speak cool:
Yo Bro!
All right blud?
Cool.
Innit?

Etc.

But when she got to Liquid
We weren't there.
Things weren't that great for her that night.
Some nasty guys started stomping around her and chanting.

Lauren's P.O.V.: A group of youths start to dance round her. The dance becomes more like a ritual. The youths don blank white masks. They circle her, stomping to the rhythm of the music and start prodding her.

Aaaagh! Look at you!
What are you wearing? We ought to take those clothes off and burn them.
Oh my God! Look at the state of you.
You look good – but not as good as me!
You look like a pink lollypop.
You great pink umpalumpa.
Umpa Lumpa Umpa Lumpa.

Umpa Lumpa turns into a chant. She runs out.

Lauren asked us why we didn't show up.
It was just a mistake.
We got the day mixed up.

I'm sorry Lauren.
I'm sorry too. Sorry Lauren.

6 *The tell-tale text*

One day a boy called Bob asked us what he should do.
He'd nicked Lauren's phone and found a message . . .

Extreme C.U. of mobile phone:

I don't care what they say. I'm not going back 2nite. If u r my friend pls don't tell. L.

But Lauren was nowhere to be found.
Jade said:
I beat Lauren up this morning.
Faye said:
I think that message was probably meant for me.
We asked:
Do you know something the rest of us don't?
We decided that Faye should tell Emma.
So Faye hung around at break.

Faye tells Emma, the TA, that Lauren's grandfather has recently died and that he was the only one who really looked after Lauren because her dad drank too much and sometimes hit her.

We wondered how Jade felt now about beating Lauren up!

C.U. of Jade's looking ashamed!

Emma asked the other teachers what they thought she should do. And a group went off to search for her.

The staffroom: Emma shares the news about Lauren and asks their advice.

Meanwhile, we discovered that she'd run back to a care home where she'd stayed before. We talked to the lady there.

Mary, the warden of the home, tells the classmates that sometimes Lauren used to go to the cemetery to sit by the graves of her mum and gran. Sometimes she used to leave letters for them there. Mary suggests they go and look in the churchyard themselves.

7 The cemetery

Lauren's P.O.V.: Walk through graveyards to grave. A number of letters already lie there. She picks them up one by one.

V.O.s with suitable music:

To mum and nan,

I love you and miss you. I am upset about granddad. I am going to live at the care home because they care about me and I don't have to be with my dad. I think dad will go to prison. I am happy about that. He won't beat me anymore.

Lauren

To mum and nan,

I miss you so much and can you help me please as my dad has been beating me up and I go to a care home and the staff have been looking after me. My granddad has died and I am scared of my dad. I want him to go to prison and I can go to the care home. I say a prayer to you both and I light a candle every day and night. I go to school still and I have a great time at school and the care home.

Dear mum and nan,

It's the worst day of my life. I've been to my granddad's funeral. I don't want to be near my dad because he killed him! I got upset and angry and he hit me on the face. I miss him so much.

From Lauren

P.S. Mum, Nan, I miss you.

Dear mum and nanny,

I love you. I need to tell you that dad is hitting me.

From Lauren

To mum and nan,

I miss you very much. I wish you were here and I need you a lot. I have gone to the care home because dad has beaten me up again. Granddad has gone to heaven and I got no one to care for me. I have gone in the care home. I think they need my help there. So I went to help them and now they have given me a room. When I go back to school I hope that they will be kind to me and my teachers will too. My dad does not exist to me anymore. My life has been upside down so much now I have no family left.

8 Lauren's Christmas

Lauren went back to the care home for Christmas.
She didn't want to be with her dad.
But she had some nice memories
And took a photo album with her.
There were pictures of . . .

Still images of the following:

Mum, nan and me all bought grandad a tie. He didn't want to upset anyone so he wore them all!

Dad tried to make us laugh by putting on a Santa disguise but it was a bit crap really.

Nan got us all up dead early to see the pile of presents she had made. We were tired but amazed.

Nan loved the Santa hat I gave her.

After lunch nan and grandad fell asleep in front of the telly – as usual!

A rare picture of mum and dad cuddling (even though he was a bit drunk).

All of us together – me, mum, dad, nan and granddad all together. Not all my memories are bad!

9 *If Lauren could only be*

The class are sitting around a table piled with bits of fabric and other stuff.

Sometimes Lauren wondered how different her life might be.

What if she wasn't Lauren at all?

What if she was something else?

If Lauren was a colour s he would now be black. Bad things have happened to her and everything seems dark.

If Lauren could be an object she would be a glass window then she'd be able to see just who was talking about her.

If Lauren could be an animal she would be a crab. She could give her father a pinch. It might hurt a bit, but he needs to wake up.

If Lauren could be an ornament then she would be a knife, sharp and bold and able to protect herself.

If Lauren could be a piece of jewellery then she would be a locket with pictures of her mum, nan and granddad locked inside its heart.

If Lauren could be a colour she'd surely choose to be white because it's so bright and clear, or violet because it smells so sweet, or red because it's alive and warm, or maybe yellow for sunshine and happiness.

If Lauren could only be . . .

10 *Lauren and Bob*

Bob is played by a puppet. He speaks directly to camera:

The thing is, I really fancy Lauren. I've fancied her ever since she came to my birthday party when I was ten. It's not easy living next door to a girl you fancy especially when you don't know what to say to her.

I asked my mate Craig what he thought I should do.

Bob's friend Craig, played by a real student, gives him some advice on how to ask Lauren out.

Bob and Lauren: both are puppets. Bob nervously ask Lauren out. She agrees. They snog!

11 Lauren's last day

We'd been counting the days until we could leave – HURRAH!
. . . though some of us had another year to do – BOO!
We knew that Lauren was going to leave.
She had her ups and downs since joining our class
But things were looking OK for her now . . .
Her dad had been to rehab and was much better now.
Lauren was living with him and they were getting on all right.
She was going out with Bob
And they looked really happy together.
But we didn't know what she was going to do next.
We thought we could ask her though when she came to the prom . . .

Music. Dancing in background. Lauren's P.O.V. as classmates ask her . . .

So, have you got a job Lauren?
Are you going to college?
What are you going to do there?
Are you and Bob going to get married?
Are you going to stay at home or get your own place?
Will you miss us, Lauren?

Then suddenly it was the last day.
Lauren, we've got something for you to remind you of us.
Here it is . . .

Group photo of class. V.O.: chorus of 'Goodbye Lauren . . . good luck', etc.

Lauren's P.O.V. walking back down the drive. She turns round to see the class waving from the front steps and shouting 'Good Luck'.

12 Us and them

Lauren's story made us think about ourselves.
What we wanted.
Things we could do
And things we couldn't.
Things people expected of us.

Teachers expect us to
Be good
Behave
Be helpful
Be kind

Work hard
Have respect.
Parents expect us to
Listen to them
Tidy up
Not to swear
Not answer back
Let them know where we are.
Which isn't always fair because adults don't always
Listen to us
Show us respect
Tell us where they are going –
Or what time they'll be home!

Sometimes they argue
Sometimes they swear
They're not always helpful
Or kind.

Perhaps they try to behave
And that's what we do –
Try.

Plays referred to and date of first performance

4.48 Psychosis	Sarah Kane	2000
A Day in the Death of Joe Egg	Peter Nichols	1967
Adult Child Dead Child	Clare Dowie	1987
Arcadia	Tom Stoppard	1993
Ballerina	Arne Skouen	1984
Blasted	Sarah Kane	1995
The Blind	Maurice Maeterlinck	1890
The Blind Boy	James Kenney	1807
The Blind Wife	John Wilkins	1850
Blue/Orange	Joe Penhall	2000
Blue Remembered Hills	Dennis Potter	1979
Brimstone and Treacle	Dennis Potter	1977
The Brylcreem Boys	Peter Durrant	1979
Buckethead	Alun Bliss	2008
The Caretaker	Harold Pinter	1960
Children of a Lesser God	Mark Medoff	1980
Cooking With Elvis	Lee Hall	1998
The Cripple of Inishmaan	Martin McDonagh	1996
Deaf and Dumb	Thomas Holcroft	1801
Death of a Salesman	Arthur Miller	1948
The Dumb Man of Manchester	B. F. Rainer	1837

The Effect of Gamma Rays on Man-in-the Moon Marigolds	Paul Zindel	1970
Effie's Burning	Valerie Windsor	1987
The Elephant Man	Bernard Pomerance	1979
Equus	Peter Shaffer	1973
Every Good Boy Deserves Favour	Tom Stoppard	1977
Find Me	Olwen Wymark	1977
Fireworks	Valerie Jack	2010
The First to Go	Nabil Shaban	1996
Flight Path	David Watson	2007
Flowers for Algernon	Bert Coules	1991
For Ever and Ever	Rob John	1991
Ghosts	Henrik Ibsen	1881
The Glass Menagerie	Tennessee Williams	1944
The Golden Masque of Agamemnon	John Wiles	1978
Graham: the World's Fastest Blind Man	Mark Wheeller	2001
Gum and Goo	Howard Brenton	1969
Hamlet, Prince of Denmark	William Shakespeare	1600
Hard to Swallow	Mark Wheeller	2000
Head/Case	Ron Hutchinson	2004
Home	David Storey	1970
Keeping Tom Nice	Lucy Gannon	1988
King Lear	William Shakespeare	1605
Lives Worth Living	Lawrence Evans and Jane Nash	1983
Macbeth	William Shakespeare	c.1603
The Madness of George III	Alan Bennett	1991
Mary Barnes	David Edgar	1978
Mother Courage and Her Children	Bertolt Brecht	1939

The Mute Girl of the Forest	René Charles Guilbert de Pixérécourt	1828
The Miracle Worker	William Gibson	1957
Nobody Here But Us Chickens	Peter Barnes	1989
Not About Heroes	Stephen MacDonald	1986
Oedipus Rex	Sophocles	429 BCE
Of Mice and Men	John Steinbeck	1937
Off Centre	Haresh Sharma	1993
peeling	Kaite O'Reilly	2002
Peter Pan	J. M. Barrie	1904
The Pillowman	Martin McDonagh	2003
Richard III	William Shakespeare	1592
Rosencrantz and Guildenstern are Dead	Tom Stoppard	1966
Shut Up	Andrew Payne	2006
The Skriker	Caryl Churchill	1994
Sparkleshark	Philip Ridley	1997
Spoonface Steinberg	Lee Hall	1997
Stronger Than Superman	Roy Kift	1980
Strugglers	Richard Cameron	1988
A Tale of Mystery	Thomas Holcroft	1802
Those Legs	Noel Clarke	2011
Tom Thumb	Henry Fielding	1730
Tribes	Nina Raine	2010
Wait Until Dark	Frederick Knott	1966
Whose Life is it Anyway?	Brian Clark	1972
Woyzeck	Georg Büchner	1837

References

Abberley, P. (1987) 'The concept of oppression and the development of a social theory of disability', *Disability, Handicap and Society*, 2(1): 5–19.

Abbs, P. (1994) *The Educational Imperative*, London: The Falmer Press.

Aftah, K. (2011) 'My problem was having compassion for a monster', *The Independent*, Arts & Books, 5 August, p. 10.

Ainscow, M. and Booth, T. (eds) (1998) *From Them to Us: International Study of Inclusion in Education*, London: Routledge.

Alexander, J. (2011) 'On the ability to metaphorize: talking trees and singing tigers in the English classroom', *Changing English*, 18(3): 265–75.

Assessment and Qualifications Alliance (AQA) (2009) Entry Level Certificate, English 4970 Specification, Guildford.

Aristotle (1974) *The Politics*, London: Penguin.

Attwood, T. (2006) *The Complete Guide to Asperger's Syndrome*, London: Jessica Kingsley Publishers.

Barnard, H. C. (1947) *A History of English Education from 1760*, London: University of London Press.

Barnes, C. (1992) *Disabling Imagery and the Media: An Exploration of the Principles For Media Representations of Disabled People*, The British Council of Organisations of Disabled People, Halifax: Ryburn Publishing.

Barnes, P. (1993) *Barnes Plays Two*, London: Methuen.

BBC (2011) 'Undercover Care: The Abuse Exposed', *Panorama*, 31 May.

Beasley, K., Morrison, C. and Quicke, J. (1990) *Challenging Prejudice Through Education: The Story of a Mental Handicap Awareness Curriculum Project*, London: The Falmer Press.

Biklen, D. and Bogdan, R. (1977) 'Media portrayals of disabled people: a study in stereotypes', *Interracial Books for Children Bulletin*, 8.6 & 7.

Bolton, G. (1990) 'Four aims in teaching drama', *London Drama*, July.

Burton, B. (1988) *Living Drama*, Melbourne: Longman Cheshire.

Chandler, D. (2001) 'Semiotics for beginners', available at www.aber.ac.uk/media/Documents/S4B/sem07.html (accessed 7 October 2011).

Cole, A. (1993) 'Scratching the surface of intolerance', *The Guardian*, 25 August.

Connor, D. J. and Ferri, B. A. (2007) 'The conflict within: resistance to inclusion and other paradoxes in special education', *Disability and Society*, 22(1): 63–77.

Conroy, C. (2010) 'Disability: creative tensions between drama, theatre and disability arts', *Research in Drama Education: The Journal of Applied Theatre and Performance*, 14(1): 1–14.

Cooper, S. (2005) '*Whose Life is it anyway?* activities', Heinemann GCSE English Literature for GCSE resource sheets, available at www.pearsonschoolsandfecolleges.co.uk/Secondary/Drama/14-16/HeinemannPlaysFor14-16+/Resources/Whose LifeisitAnyway(OCRGCSEsettext)/WhoseLifeAnyway_OCR.pdf (accessed 13 October 2011).

Cumberbatch, G. and Negrine, R. (1992) *Images of Disability on Television*, London: Routledge.

Dacre, K. and Bulmer, A. (2009) 'Interview: Into the Scene and its impact on inclusive performance training', *Research in Drama Education – The Journal of Applied Theatre and Performance*, 14(1): 133–9.

Department for Education (2008) *The National Curriculum*.

Esslin, M. (1987) *The Field of Drama*, London: Methuen.

Esslin, M. (2000) *Pinter the Playwright*, London: Methuen.

Evans, R. J. (2005) *The Third Reich in Power*, London: Allen Lane.

Fitzgerald, M. (2003) *Autism and Creativity*, London: Routledge.

Goodwyn, A. (2011) 'The impact of the Framework for English', in A. Goodwyn and C. Fuller (eds), *The Great Literacy Debate*, pp. 117–35, London: Routledge.

Harper, D. (2001–12) 'Online etymology dictionary', available at www.etymonline.com/index.php?allowed_in_frame=0&search=character&searchmode=none (accessed 4 August 2011).

Hartnett, A. (2000) 'Escaping the "evil avenger" and the "supercrip": images of disability in popular television', *The Irish Communications Review*, 8: 21–9.

Hatton, C. (2003) 'Backyards and borderlands: some reflections on researching the travels of adolescent girls doing drama', *Research in Drama Education*, 8(2): 139–56.

Hatton, C. (2007) 'Can I get a witness? Mapping learning in and beyond the drama classroom', *Journal of Artistic and Creative Education*, 1(1): 171–204.

Hatton, N. (2009) 'The labelling effect: drama, mental health and learning disability', *Research in Drama Education: The Journal of Applied Theatre and Performance*, 14(1): 91–5.

Hennessy, J. and McNamara, P. (2011) 'Packaging poetry? Pupils' perspectives of their learning experience within the post-primary poetry classroom', *English in Education*, 45(3): 206–23.

Hodkinson, A. and Vickerman, P. (2009) *Key Issues in Special Educational Needs and Inclusion*, London: Sage Publications.

Holmes, M. (2001) 'Performing affliction: physical disabilities in Victorian melodrama', *Contemporary Theatre Review*, 11(3): 5–24.

Horitz, T. (2001) 'Beyond the barriers: developing disability theatre for schools', *Drama Research: The Research Journal of National Drama*, 2: 71–84.

Iyer, A. (2007) 'Depiction of intellectual disability in fiction', *Advances in Psychiatric Treatment*, 13: 127–133.

Jackson, D. (2011) 'Time to challenge the Rain Man stereotypes – the autistic mind can be spectacularly creative', *TES*, 27 May, p. 25.

Jennings, S. (1981) 'Dramatherapy with Multi-handicap', in G. Lord (ed), *The Arts and Disabilities*, Macdonald, pp. 38–46.

Jernigan, K. (1974) 'Blindness: is literature against us?', Presidential address, Annual Convention of the National Federation of the Blind, Chicago, 3 July.

Jindal-Snape, D. and Vettraino, E. (2007) 'Drama techniques for the enhancement of social-emotional development in people with special needs: review of research', *International Journal of Special Education*, 22(1): 107–17.

Johnson, M. (2006) *Disability Awareness – Do it right! Your All-in-one How-to Guide*, Louisville, The Advocado Press.

Kawakami, K., Dovidio, J., Moll, J., Hermsen, S. and Russin, A. (2000) 'Just say no (to stereotyping): effects of training in the negation of stereotypic associations on stereotype activation', *Journal of Personality and Social Psychology*, 78(5): 871–88.

Kempe, A. (1991) 'Learning both ways', *British Journal of Special Education*, 18: 137–9.

Kempe, A. (1992) 'Enthusiastic beginners', *Drama: One Forum Many Voices*, 1: 13–16.

Kempe, A. (2005) *Drama, Education and Special Needs*, Athens: Patakis.

Kennedy, D. (2009) *The Spectator and the Spectacle*, Cambridge: Cambridge University Press.

Kyle, C. and Davies, K. (1991) 'Attitudes of mainstream children towards mental retardation', *British Journal of Special Educational Needs*, 18(3): 103–6.

Leicester, M. (2007) *Special Stories for Disability Awareness; Stories and Activities for Teachers, Parents and Professionals*, London: Jessica Kingsley Publishers.

Lewis, A. (1995) *Children's Understanding of Disability*, London: Routledge.

Lockett, M. (2010) 'Close reading: a synergistic approach to the (post) modern divide', *Changing English*, 17(4): 399–409.

Lodge, D. (1989) *Nice Work*, Harmondsworth: Penguin.

Lougher, S. (2011) 'Kevin Spacey has great fun with Richard III in a triumphant production', available at www.metro.co.uk/lifestyle/868026-kevin-spacey-has-great-fun-with-richard-iii-in-a-triumphant-production#ixzz1QqnoE100 (accessed 13 October 2011).

Machon, J. (2011) *(Syn)aesthetics: Redefining Visceral Performance*, Basingstoke: Palgrave Macmillan.

Martin, R. (2010) 'Theatre trip: Fireworks', available at www.mpw.co.uk/lon/londonnews-dec-2010.pdf (accessed 14 October 2011).

Masefield, P. (2006) *Strength: Broadsides from Disability on the Arts*, Stoke-on-Trent: Trentham Books.

McLintock, A. (1984) *Drama for Mentally Handicapped Children*, London: Souvenir Press.

Nightingale, P. (2011) 'Now you see me, now you don't: from reader to student and back again in A level English Literature', *English in Education*, 45(2): 146–60.

O'Connor, P. (2008) 'I'm not telling', *Keeping Ourselves Safe*, Wellington, New Zealand: NZ Police, Education Service.

Office of Public Sector Information (OPSI) (2005) *Disability Discrimination Act*, London: OPSI.

O'Reilly, K. (2009) 'Practitioner statement: a playwright reflects on alternative dramaturgies', *RiDE: The Journal of Applied Theatre and Performance*, 14(1): 31–5.

Peter, M. (2009) 'Drama: narrative pedagogy and socially challenged children', *British Journal of Special Education*, 36(1): 9–17.

Power, D. (2007) 'Disability in the news', *Comunicacion e Cidadania*, 7: 251–62.

Quarmby, K. (2011) *Scapegoat: Why We Are Failing Disabled People*, London: Portobello Books.

Rampley, H. (2010) 'Fireworks at #61 The Etcetera', available at http://londontheatreproject.wordpress.com/2010/11/04/fireworks-at-61-the-etcetera/ (accessed 14 October 2011).

Reid, L. A. (2004) *Meaning in the Arts*, London: Routledge.

Rideout, N. (2009) *Theatre and Ethics*, London: Palgrave Macmillan.

Roper, L. (2003) 'Disability in media', available at www.miusa.org/idd/resources/files/mediaresources/disabmedia/view (accessed 9 October 2011).

Ross, M. (1984) *The Aesthetic Impulse*, Oxford: Pergamon Press.

Rubin, E. and Watson, E. (1987) 'Disability bias in children's literature', *The Lion and the Unicorn*, 11(1): 60–7.

Rushby-Smith, T. (2009) 'Hey! I want you to put me in the picture', *The Times*, 30 September, 'Times 2', pp. 8–9.

Sandahl, C. (1999) 'Ahhhh Freak Out! Metaphors of disability and femaleness in performance', *Theatre Topics*, 9(1): 11–30.

Saunders, K. (2000) *Happy Ever Afters: A Storybook Guide to Teaching Children About Disability*, Stoke-on-Trent: Trentham Books.

Schechner, R. (2006) *Performance Studies: An Introduction*, London: Routledge.

Shieble, M. (2010) 'Reading between the lines of reader response: constructing "the other" though the aesthetic stance', *Changing English*, 17(4): 375–84.

Snyder, S. and Mitchell, D. (2001) *Narrative Prothesis: Disabilities and the Dependence of Discourse*, Ann Arbor, MI: University of Michigan Press.

Softely, R. (2008) 'Nabil Shaban: The First to Go', available at www.disabilityartsonline.org/the_first_to_go_review (accessed 30 April 2012).

Speakman, R. (1989) 'Introduction and notes', in B. Clark, *Whose Life is it Anyway?*, Oxford: Heinemann.

Spencer, C. (2005) 'Theatre review', available at www.telegraph.co.uk/culture/3635748/First-night-Cattralls-touching-teasing-triumph.html (accessed 14 October 2011).

Tansley, A. E. and Gulliford, R. (1960) *The Education of Slow Learning Children*, London: Routledge & Kegan Paul.

Taylor, P. (2005) 'Theatre review', available at www.independent.co.uk/arts-entertainment/theatre-dance/reviews/whose-life-is-it-anyway-comedy-theatre-london-488409.html (accessed 11 October 2011).

Taylor, S. (2011) 'The pragmatist reader: reading as a meaning-making transaction in the English classroom', *Changing English*, 18(2): 151–60.

Wald, C. (2007) *Hysteria, Trauma and Melancholia: Performative Maladies in Contemporary Anglophone Drama*, Basingstoke: Palgrave Macmillan.

Walter, H. (2000) *Other People's Shoes – Thoughts on Acting*, London: Penguin.

Warner, L. (2011) '"Disabled" characters in plays', *Changing English*, 18(4): 371–82.

White, P. (2008) 'Lost in the woods', *The Guardian*, Tuesday 5 February.

Whitehurst, T. (2007) 'Liberating silent voices: perspectives of children with profound & complex learning needs on inclusion', *British Journal of Learning Disabilities*, 35(1): 55–61.

Wymark, O. (1983) *Plays by Women*, Vol. 2, London: Methuen.

Yandell, J. (2008) 'Mind the gap: investigating test literacy and classroom literacy', *English in Education*, 42(1): 70–87.

Index